VISCOUNT
COMET & CONCORDE

Stewart Wilson

Original illustrations
by
Juanita Franzi and Dennis Newton

INTRODUCTION

Welcome to the third book in our *Legends of the Air, Series* this one departing from the military themes of the first two and instead dealing with three pioneering airliners of the postwar era: the Vickers Viscount, de Havilland Comet and BAC/Aerospatiale Concorde.

Each broke new ground, each suffered various trials and tribulations at some stage of their careers and each achieved operational success, although in the case of the Comet, this was some considerable time in coming.

The world's first production turboprop airliner, the Viscount remains Britain's most successful commercial transport aircraft (excluding general aviation types), with 444 built and service with some 200 operators over the years. At first rejected by its first and primary customer – British European Airways – the Viscount soon proved to offer an irresistible combination of operating economics, speed and passenger appeal and formed the main equipment of many major airlines in the 1950s and 1960s until jets began to take over.

Even after that, second hand Viscounts found a ready market with smaller operators after having established new standards for the industry. The Viscount was responsible for allowing the British aircraft industry into the North American and other markets and even though only a few remain in service as the 1990s progress, some will certainly survive into the next millennium.

Britain seemed to have a substantial lead in airliner technology with the appearance of the Comet in 1949, the world's first jet airliner. Early service seemed to support this, but a series of tragic accidents soon ended the dream and resulted in the grounding of the aircraft and the loss of any advantage briefly enjoyed by the British industry.

The crash investigations resulted in a vast increase in knowledge of the hitherto grey area of airframe fatigue, the results of which were passed on to other manufacturers for the benefit of all who have flown in airliners since then.

A 'second generation' of Comets appeared in the late 1950s, and although they gave many years of safe and reliable service, by then the advantage had been well and truly lost to American manufacturers. Only 112 Comets were flown, but the aircraft remains one of the most important airliners in the history of aviation because of what it was and what it could have been.

'Technical triumph and commercial disaster' is the description most commonly applied to the Concorde, the only supersonic transport to have achieved the status of regular airline service.

Although just 20 were built and then operated only by the national airlines of the two sponsoring countries, Concorde is truly one of the most remarkable aircraft ever built, performing routinely what even military jets find difficult – cruising over long distances at twice the speed of sound, all with 100 passengers in the cabin sipping champagne!

Much new technology had to be invented in order to allow Concorde to perform its intended role, with aerodynamics, airframe and engine design all stretching the limits of available knowledge. Concorde has now been in service for more than two decades and plans are in place which will probably see the aircraft still flying the airways 40 years after it first carried paying passengers. With no successor in sight, Concorde will probably remain the world's only operational supersonic transport for many years yet.

As is always the case with a book such as this, it would have impossible to finish without the help of many people. I therefore gratefully acknowledge the efforts and support of some people with whom I have been long associated: Philip J Birtles, Mike Kerr, Juanita Franzi, Dennis Newton, Eric Allen, Gerard Frawley, Jim Thorn and Maria Davey in particular plus Rolls-Royce's John Gunn and Air France.

Stewart Wilson
Buckingham 1996

Published by Aerospace Publications Pty Ltd (ACN: 001 570 458), PO Box 3105, Weston Creek, ACT 2611, publishers of monthly *Australian Aviation* magazine.
Production Manager: Maria Davey

ISBN 1 875671 21 8

Proudly printed in Australia by Pirie Printers Pty Ltd, 140 Gladstone Street, Fyshwick 2609
Distributed throughout Australia by Network Distribution, 54 Park Street, Sydney 2000. Fax (02) 264 3278
Distribution in North America by Motorbooks International, 729 Prospect Ave, Osceola, Wisconsin 54020, USA.
Fax: (715) 294 4448. Distribution throughout Europe and the UK by Airlife Publishing Ltd, 101 Longden Rd, Shrewsbury SY3 9EB, Shropshire, UK, Fax (743) 23 2944.

CONTENTS

Front cover (top to bottom): Comet 4 G-APDB of Dan-Air; Viscount 756D VH-TVH of Trans-Australia Airlines; Concorde G-BOAA of British Airways. *(not to scale)*

THE BRITISH AIRLINER SINCE 1945

The three aircraft covered in this volume – the Vickers Viscount, de Havilland Comet and BAC/Aerospatiale Concorde – in many ways sum up the British commercial aircraft industry in the postwar era. It has been a story of technical innovation in many areas combined with all too few examples of commercial success, especially in comparison with the USA's industry.

The Viscount is an example where commercial success did accompany technical innovation. The world's first turboprop airliner to enter service, Viscount production amounted to 444 aircraft and the type remains Britain's best selling indigenous airliner. It was exported in large numbers including to the lucrative US market and in its day offered a new standard of economy of operation and passenger comfort in a world used to piston engined airliners.

A look at the Viscount's production history reveals some interesting figures, particularly the relatively short time it was in large scale production: seven full years between 1953 and 1959. Although the last Viscount was delivered in 1964, some 95 per cent of them had been handed over by 1960, with production running at only a trickle after that. This short production cycle is in marked contrast to most airliners of the turbine age. Continuity was lost when the Viscount's larger successor, the Vanguard, turned out to be a commercial failure with only 44 built. The

last Vanguard was flown 19 months *before* the ultimate Viscount.

The de Havilland Comet was the world's first jet airliner and at the time of its introduction to service in 1952 looked to have the world at its feet. But with technical innovation often comes risk, and for the Comet, this proved fatal. A series of accidents early in the aircraft's career stalled the programme for three years, allowing initially Boeing and then Douglas to gain a foothold in the market which they then dominated with the 707 and DC-8, respectively.

The heavily revamped Comet 4 appeared in 1958 but by then the larger and longer ranging American jets were flying with the 707 in fact entering service at about the same time as the British aircraft. Douglas suffered to some extent by hesitating slightly in its decision to develop the DC-8 and it entered service a year after the 707.

The result was the manufacture of 878 707s and 154 closely related 720s over many years along with 557 DC-8s. By comparison, production of all Comet variants reached just 112 aircraft (plus two unsold airframes completed as prototypes for the Nimrod maritime patrol aircraft) with the last aircraft delivered in early 1964 at a time when 707 and DC-8 production was near its peak.

The Comet was certainly unlucky and the lessons learned from the accident investigations were shared

with other manufacturers, including Boeing and Douglas, to everyone's (especially the travelling public's) benefit.

The Anglo-French Concorde represents superb engineering and application of technology in combination with commercial disaster. Undoubtedly one of the two or three most remarkable aircraft ever built, it remains the only supersonic transport (SST) to enter 'proper' service. A qualification is needed here: Concorde was, of course beaten into the air by the Soviet Tupolev Tu-144 and also into service of sorts, although this was limited to freight runs and a very brief period of passenger carrying before the project was abandoned. Concorde has been in successful, routine and major incident-free service since early 1976.

Regardless of Concorde's undoubted technical triumphs, the fact remains that only 20 were built including prototypes and pre production aircraft and the taxpayers of Britain and France saw no tangible return on their investment. There were undoubtedly intangible benefits associated with Concorde – such as prestige – but the commercial aspects of the programme remained firmly in the red.

All sorts of things conspired against Concorde including the oil crisis of the early 1970s, the rise of environmentalism at about the same time (Concorde is undeniably noisy

Technical triumph and financial disaster is the description most often applied to the BAC/Aerospatiale Concorde supersonic transport. Regardless, more than two decades after entering service, Concorde continues to give safe and reliable service at the limits of airline travel. (via Philip J Birtles)

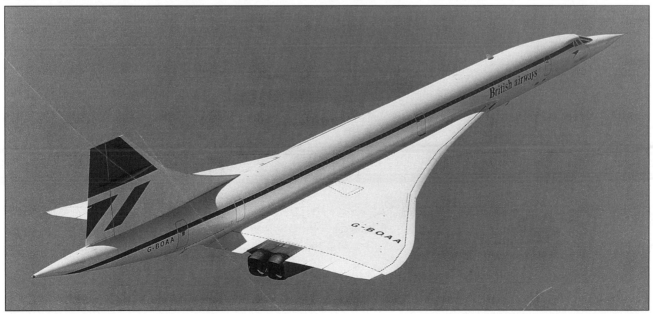

The Vickers Viscount, the world's first turboprop airliner and still Britain's most numerically successful commercial transport. (D Fraser)

and thirsty), the entry to service of the Boeing 747 with its cheap seat-mile costs and therefore lower fares, and the cancellation of the USA's own SST projects which conveniently coincided with an American change in attitude towards supersonic transports generally. This negative attitude did nothing for Concorde's sales prospects with the result that only the state owned flag carriers of the sponsoring nations (BOAC/British Airways and Air France) ever took delivery of the type.

Advantage or Illusion?

When the Viscount and Comet were entering service, it appeared that Britain had gained a substantial advantage over its US rivals in the design and manufacture of airliners. Britain also appeared to have an advantage in this field in the 1920s and early 1930s but this quickly disap-

peared in the five or six years before the outbreak of war when the Americans came up with truly innovative designs such as the Boeing 247, the pressurised Boeing Stratoliner and the Douglas DC-2 and DC-3. All were monoplanes, all were made of metal and all featured retractable undercarriage.

The Douglas pair in particular revolutionised the airline industry, the DC-3 capable of making money without subsidy and while Douglas was turning them out by the hundred, British airlines were in the main still flying biplanes with fixed undercarriages. Excluding the efficient fleet of Shorts flying boats (which catered for an entirely different and uniquely British market) there were exceptions, but these were too late and too few to stem the tide of Douglas airliners which began to dominate European skies in the second half of the 1930s.

The outbreak of World War II in September 1939 further inhibited Britain's development of airliners.

With this in mind it is perhaps surprising to see Britain apparently leading the world in airliner development in the years immediately after the war. Or did it? Were the Viscount and Comet the result of a British advantage or was that advantage an illusion?

Both had come about as a result of the wartime Brabazon Committee (discussed below) which was established in 1942 with the sole purpose of planning Britain's postwar civil aviation needs. Both also resulted from the lead Britain held in the field of gas turbine engine development in the late 1940s and early 1950s.

In the field of airframe development as it applied to airliners, the Americans gained a substantial advantage during the war years. An oft-quoted agreement allegedly existed

The world's first jet airliner, the de Havilland Comet. Its lead was swept away by a series of accidents and subsequent grounding for several years and by the time the second generation of Comets appeared – illustrated by this Series 4B of British European Airways – it was too late. (Philip J Birtles)

between Britain and the USA whereby design and construction of transport aircraft would rest solely with American manufacturers while hostilities continued.

Interestingly, there is no hard evidence that any such arrangement existed, at least formally, although it must be said that British industry was hard pressed during the war and fully occupied building combat aircraft and it is doubtful that there was much spare capacity to be used on transports. This doesn't mean that no transport aircraft were developed in Britain at the time but types such as the Lancastrian were conversions of Lancaster bombers (mainly performed postwar anyway) and the Avro York utilised the Lancaster's wings, powerplants, undercarriage and tail in combination with a new fuselage.

More significant modern transport types such as the Douglas DC-4 and Lockheed Constellation were built in the USA during the war and equally important were the innovations being developed by Boeing in particular. The company's involvement in large aircraft production placed it in good stead for the postwar airliner market, especially through the high levels of technology incorporated in the B-29 Superfortress strategic bomber, which in turn evolved into the C-97 Stratofreighter transport/tanker and its civil equivalent, the Stratocruiser.

From there, the available technology flowed easily to the Boeing 707 jet and its close relative, the KC-135 tanker for the US Air Force via the Model 367-80 prototype of 1954. Boeing's cause was helped to a very substantial degree by the USAF's ordering of hundreds of KC-135s in the 1950s, something which did no harm at all to Boeing's balance sheet when it came to ammortising the development costs of the civil 707. This direct government support to Boeing's commercial aircraft programmes might put the company's recent bleatings about the subsidisation of Airbus Industrie into some sort of proper perspective!

Jet engine technology was initially imported into the USA from Britain but before long American engine makers were developing their own powerplants and manufacturing them in large numbers.

First thoughts for the postwar British airliner business centred around interim types such as the Avro Lancastrian, a conversion of the Lancaster bomber. This is the prototype conversion.

An interim but successful type was the Vickers Viking, utilising the wings, powerplants and undercarriage of the Wellington bomber in combination with a new fuselage. Production amounted to 163, many of them for export.

(bottom right) One of the great wastes of British time and money, the ill-conceived Saro Princess flying boat, first flown in 1952 and abandoned shortly afterwards.

The Vickers Vanguard – only 44 built for just two customers. (BA)

Hawker Siddeley Trident production reached only 117 aircraft compared with the rival Boeing 727's total of 1,831. (Stewart Wilson)

It would be easy to conclude, therefore, that Britain's apparent lead in commercial aviation in the immediate postwar years through the Comet and Viscount was indeed an illusion, exacerbated by the Comet's early problems; the failure to fully exploit the Viscount's successes by quickly following it up with a viable replacement; and insisting on building several designs which were always going to be 'white elephants' such as the two giants, the Princess flying boat and the Brabazon trans-Atlantic airliner. Another notable commercial failure of the 1950s was the Bristol

Britannia large turboprop which had its production restricted to 85 examples, a quarter of them for the Royal Air Force.

The problems continued into the 1960s with several commercial failures such as the Vickers VC-10 and the Hawker Siddeley Trident. The VC-10 was a superb aeroplane but it appeared later than desirable and was then subject to fatal vacillations by its launch customer, BOAC. Only 54 VC-10s were built including 14 for the RAF.

The Trident should have sold many times as many as it did but in the end

only 117 were built. This compares most unfavourably with the Trident's closest rival, the Boeing 727, which reached a production tally of 1,831 aircraft, at the time the highest for any jet airliner.

Like the VC-10, the Trident's problem was the customer for which it was developed, in this case British European Airways (BEA), state owned like BOAC. Originally developed by de Havilland before it became part of the nationalised Hawker Siddeley, the Trident (or DH.121 as it was first known) was intended to be a larger aircraft than finally emerged, very

The VC10 is generally recognised as a superb aeroplane but it was too late to make an impact. Production was just 54 of which 14 went to the Royal Air Force. (BAe)

The BAC One Eleven has been one of the more successful British airliners of the modern era with about 240 built but the design was not properly developed and its American rivals (which remain in production in developed versions) have outsold it many times over.

similar in fact to the Boeing 727 which was more than a year behind, flying in 1963.

BEA then insisted on downsizing and amazingly, the manufacturer agreed despite realising that this was going to make export sales much more difficult to achieve. In Seattle, Boeing's salespeople must have laughed themselves silly when they heard the news! The result was that Hawker Siddeley spent most of the remainder of the Trident's relatively brief production life trying to make it carry more and further. By the time the stretched Trident 3 appeared in 1969 the horse had bolted and Boeing had cornered the market with the original and further developed versions of the 727.

When BOAC and BEA combined to form British Airways (BA), the policy of causing difficulties for the local industry seemed to continue by completely ignoring the products of Airbus Industrie. For many, BA stands for 'Boeing Always', or 'Boeing Airways'!

Other British airliners achieved more commercial success. The BAC One Eleven short/medium range twinjet sold moderately well (232 built in the UK plus a few in Romania) but again this figure compares unfavourably with its American opposition, the Boeing 737 and Douglas DC-9/MD-80 families. Both of these were beaten to the market by the British aircraft but were developed into large families over several generations and sold in substantial numbers. Both remain in production and between them sales totalled about 5,600 aircraft by 1995.

The One Eleven's problem was the failure to develop it properly, and like the Trident, a stretched version was introduced too late to fully capitalise on the early models' market inroads.

The Avro/Hawker Siddeley HS.748 twin turboprop regional transport is Britain's second biggest selling airliner with 382 built between 1960 and 1988 including licensed assembly in India. Its British rival, the Handley Page Herald, reached a production tally of only 50, while that market was dominated by the Dutch Fokker F27, nearly 800 of which were built by the parent company and under licence by Fairchild in the USA.

Placing the HS.748 in second place assumes excluding the de Havilland Dove (544 built but really a light aircraft) and BAe Jetstream 31 from the equation. Including earlier Handley Page built aircraft, Jetstream production has reached about 430 aircraft and although a light regional airliner, for the purposes of this discussion it is too small.

Challenging the HS.748's produc-

The Avro/Hawker Siddeley/BAe 748 regional turboprop sold reasonably well with 382 built including licence production in India. Sales of its major rival, the Fokker F27 Friendship, reached nearly 800. (BAe)

Another British success story, the BAe Jetstream 31 of which about 430 have been built including earlier Handley Page variants. (BAe)

tion total is the BAe 146/RJ family of four engined regional jet transports. By late 1995 sales had reached about 320 examples of what could well be the last wholly British airliner and if production continues into the 21st century (which seems likely), the 146 could well eventually topple the Viscount from the top of the production tally tree.

Britain's commercial aircraft future lies in European collaboration with Airbus Industrie (in which BAe is a full partner) and through other joint deals including the recently announced AI(R) involving BAe's various regional aircraft programmes (the 146/RJ and Jetstream) in conjunction with the Franco-Italian ATR consortium.

The Airbus story is in itself remarkable, growing from an idea in the 1960s and the maiden flight of its first aircraft in 1972 (with very few orders to back it up) to a company which in the mid 1990s offers a large range of airliners from 120 seat narrowbody jets to widebodies capable of carrying up to 440 passengers. In 1994, Airbus sold more airliners than Boeing and has emerged as the second force on the world market behind the American giant, displacing McDonnell Douglas to a distant third.

With orders for about 320 by late 1995, the BAe 146/RJ family could eventually topple the Viscount as Britain's best selling airliner.

Britain's commercial aviation future appears to be in co-operation with European industry. As a full partner in Airbus Industrie, British Aerospace built the wings for this Airbus A300-600R. (AI)

The Brabazon Committee

Even though Britain was not seriously engaged in the development and production of transport aircraft during World War II, it was realised at a relatively early stage that plans would have to be made for when peace finally came.

The result was the establishment in late 1942 of a series of committees to "advise on the design and production of transport aircraft". The chairman was the immediate past Minister of Aircraft Production, Lord Brabazon of Tara (formerly J T C Moore-Brabazon, the pioneer airman). As was the case with most such committees, this one quickly assumed the name of its chairman and thus became known as the Brabazon Committee. More than one committee was actually involved, but the singular form of the name became common usage.

The original committee was at first titled the Transport Aircraft Committee and comprised mainly senior public servants. A second committee was established in 1943 – again under the chairmanship of Lord Brabazon – and had as its members a wide range of aviation industry and airline representatives including Captain Geoffrey (later Sir Geoffrey) de Havilland.

The original committee had as its terms of reference the preparation of outline specifications of several aircraft types needed for postwar air transport and to select which manufacturers might be invited to submit designs as soon as urgent work permitted. The committee was also tasked to examine which existing military types were most suitable for conversion to civil transport use and to prepare a plan for "the immediate use of spare design and production capacity while the industry was in transition from war to peace".

First recommendations were to develop transport versions of the Short Sunderland flying boat and the Halifax bomber plus promoting production of the new Avro York transport (which had already flown) and the Short Shetland flying boat. All but the latter achieved a degree of success, the Sunderland conversion becoming known as the Sandringham.

The Brabazon Types

In 1943, the Brabazon Committee issued basic specifications for five new types of aircraft it considered would be needed by British operators in the postwar years. Of note is the fact that none of them was for a flying boat at a time when this was still the preferred method of long range flying by the British. The five Brabazon types were:

Type 1: A large pressurised airliner powered by six to eight engines capable of flying nonstop between London and New York at a cruising

The Bristol Brabazon, named after the chairman of the committee which spawned it. The one and only flying prototype is seen here in company with a rather more successful Bristol product, the Freighter.

Built to the same requirement as the Viscount, the Armstrong Whitworth Apollo was restricted to a production run of only two. (BAe)

speed of 275mph (442km/h) at 20,000 feet (6,100m). Range was specified at 5,000 miles (8,046km).

This requirement emerged in 1949 as the Bristol Brabazon powered by eight 2,500hp Bristol Centaurus radial piston engines driving four sets of contra-rotating propellers. With a wing span of 230 feet (70.1m), a length of 177 feet (53.9m) and a maximum weight of 290,000lb (131,544kg), the Brabazon was a very large aircraft capable of carrying 100 passengers across the Atlantic.

Unfortunately, it turned into one of British industry's 'white elephants' and can be regarded as a waste of resources. Development was difficult and first flight was continually postponed due to these troubles, the one and only prototype first flying in September 1949. A second aircraft was not completed and the programme was abandoned in 1952.

Type 2: The original proposal was for an unpressurised DC-3 replacement to operate on European and Empire feeder routes carrying 20 passen-

gers. A cruising speed of 200mph (322km/h) and a range of up to 1,750 miles (2,816km) was specified.

The Type 2 requirement was eventually split into two parts, and as is usually the case in airliner development, the hardware which eventuated was larger, heavier and capable of carrying greater payloads than originally envisaged. The revised Type 2A requirement emerged as the Airspeed Ambassador powered by two Bristol Centaurus piston engines and capable of carrying between 28 and 50 passengers. The first Ambassador flew in July 1947 and although only 20 production aircraft (plus prototypes) were built for BEA, the type served the airline well as an interim type on European routes until the turboprop Viscount came along. The Ambassador's good operating economics were particularly attractive.

The Brabazon Type 2B specification was for a pressurised 24 seater powered by turboprop engines. This was satisfied by the Vickers Viscount, one of the subjects of this book. The

first Viscount was flown in July 1948 and after a lengthy development period entered service with BEA and other operators in 1953 as a 43 to 53 seater. The Viscount was developed through several variants over the years and the 444th and last aircraft was delivered in 1964.

The Armstrong Whitworth Apollo was also developed in response to the Type 2B requirement and flown in April 1949. A series of airframe and engine problems caused its cancellation in 1952 after two had been built.

Although not formally built for the Brabazon Type 2 requirement, the Vickers Viking more or less filled it and served BEA as a useful interim type from 1946. Capable of carrying 21-24 passengers in an unpressurised cabin, the Viking cruised at 210mph (338km/h), had a range of up to 1,700 miles (2,734km) or 600 miles (965km) with full passenger load and served BEA well until the Viscount came along. The Viking also formed the backbone of many British independent operators' fleets and 163 were built of which many were exported.

The Viking utilised the Wellington bomber's Bristol Hercules powerplants, geodetic structure outer wings and landing gear in combination with a new stressed skin fuselage. The prototype flew in June 1945 and all 163 had been built by the end of 1947.

Type 3: The original specification called for a four engined long range (for the time) airliner for Empire routes capable of cruising at more than 225mph (362km/h) over a range of up to 3,500 miles (5,632km). Passenger capacity was specified at 20 with sleeping accommodation. The Type 3 specification went through numerous changes and permutations (generally getting larger as time went by) before being cancelled in 1947. As such, it was the only one of Brabazon 'types' not to be built, but in the same year

Built to meet the Brabazon Committee's Type 2A requirement, the pressurised Airspeed Ambassador was well liked and successful in service but only 20 production aircraft were built. It was usurped by the turboprop Viscount.

BOAC issued a specification for a medium range Empire transport which emerged in 1952 as the Bristol Britannia.

Type 4: An interesting and for the time radical requirement for a "jet propelled mailplane" capable of flying across the Atlantic with a ton of payload at 400mph (644km/h) with the crew accommodated in a pressurised cabin. This basic specification underwent considerable development and revision over the next few years and finally emerged as the de Havilland Comet, the world's first jet airliner.

Type 5: A small twin engined feederliner capable of carrying 8-12 passengers and cruising at more than 175mph (281km/h) over a range of up to 1,000 miles (1,609km). Initial thoughts centred around re-engining the prewar DH Flamingo all metal shoulder wing airliner, but the requirement was then split into two parts.

The Type 5A evolved as a larger, 14 seat offsider for the original Type 5, which was then redesignated the Type 5B. Out of the Type 5A came the Miles (later Handley Page) Marathon powered by four de Havilland Gipsy Queen engines. Early problems (including the collapse of Miles, the crash of the first prototype and the failure of the expected major customer, BEA, to order it) did little for its prospects. In the event only 40 were

The Bristol Britannia was vaguely connected with the Brabazon Type 3 requirement. Much delayed and overtaken by the jets, the 'Whispering Giant' managed a production run of only 85 aircraft, a quarter of them for the RAF.

built between 1948 and 1951, most of these ending up in RAF service.

The Type 5B requirement ended up with the most successful of all the Brabazon Committee aircraft, certainly in terms of numbers built. The first de Havilland Dove was flown in September 1945 (as the first British civil aircraft to fly after the end of WWII) and the 544th and last was completed in 1967, although series production had ended well before then.

Although military orders accoun-

ted for about 40 per cent of all Dove production, the type still served its intended purpose with civilian operators around the world. Of interest is a parallel with the Viscount's production history: ie large numbers built over a relatively short time, followed by a longish period of low rate production. In the case of the Dove, production had reached 400 by early 1953, the rate then declining to bring the tally to 500 by the end of 1957. After that, new Doves appeared infrequently.

A successful product of the Brabazon Committee, the de Havilland Dove feederliner and corporate aircraft was produced in large numbers over a period of more than 20 years. (Stewart Wilson)

VICKERS
VISCOUNT

VICKERS VISCOUNT

Nearly five decades after the maiden flight of the prototype, the world's first production turbine powered airliner – the Vickers Viscount – remains Britain's most numerically successful airliner.

Ordered by some 60 operators around the world, the Viscount was very much an aircraft of its time, bringing revolutionary standards of comfort to its passengers and outstanding operating economics to its owners. The resale of second hand examples added substantially to the number of operators who flew Viscounts at some stage, the tally finally reaching over 200, including many military and corporate operators. At its peak, it was estimated that somewhere in the world, a Viscount was taking off or landing every 27 seconds.

The key to the Viscount's success was the significant number of export sales it achieved. Possibly the most important were the November 1952 contract for 15 for Trans Canada Airlines and the 1954 orders from Capital Airlines for 60. The TCA order (which was followed up by another for 36 aircraft) opened up North America to the Vickers sales teams; the Capital contracts allowed British industry a foot in the US market's door. This not only helped in selling other Viscounts to US operators but it also helped aircraft which followed such as the BAC One Eleven and BAe 146 families.

With the arrival of pure jets on internal trunk routes in the 1960s, the reign of the Viscount as front line equipment began to diminish as firstly Caravelles and Boeing 727s and then the Douglas DC-9, BAC One Eleven and Boeing 737 began to take over. This resulted in the second wave of Viscount sales, that of second hand aircraft to smaller airlines operating on secondary routes or charter services. The release of Viscounts from the major operators also resulted in a number of aircraft being put to work as corporate transports, particularly in the USA.

Viscount numbers inevitably diminished through the 1970s and '80s until by late 1995 only 14 remained in service. With the end in sight for this fine and successful airliner, it's worth remembering that in its day, the Viscount gave millions of passengers their first experience of smooth, turbine powered and 'over the weather' pressurised flight.

Vickers Ltd

Vickers was well placed to tackle the development of what at the time was an advanced and revolutionary aeroplane. One of Britain's industrial giants, the company comprised 17 separate subsidiaries by the early 1950s with interests in not only aircraft manufacture but also shipbuilding and other heavy industries.

The company had been building aircraft since 1911, one of its better known products from those early days being the Vimy heavy bomber of 1917 which subsequently became fa-

mous for the long distance flights it achieved. The first crossing of the Atlantic by air (from Newfoundland to Eire) was in a Vimy flown by Capt John Alcock and Lt Arthur Whitten-Brown in June 1919, while five months later another Vimy, flown by brothers Capts Ross and Keith Smith and two other crewmembers, travelled from England to Australia for the first time.

The World War I period saw Vickers produce several fighter aircraft, notably the FB.5 and FB.9 'Gunbus' series of pusher biplanes.

The company's aviation interests were reorganised in July 1928 when a separate aircraft manufacturing subsidiary – Vickers (Aviation) Ltd – was formed, this in turn talking over the Supermarine Aviation Works later in the same year. The resulting Vickers-Supermarine organisation went on to produce several significant aircraft, not the least of which was the Spitfire fighter of World War II.

Further reorganisation occurred in October 1938 when both Vickers (Aviation) and Supermarine were taken over by Vickers-Armstrongs Ltd.

Between the wars, Vickers produced numerous civil and military aircraft including commercial versions of the Vimy plus the Vulcan, Viastra, Vanguard, Vellore and Vellox airliners. Military activity included the Victoria, Vernon and Valentia transports, Vildebeest single engined torpedo bomber and its Vincent general purpose derivative, the Virginia bomber

Elegant from any angle. An early production BEA Viscount 701 above the clouds. (BA)

and the Wellesley single engined day and night bomber monoplane of 1936, the first RAF aircraft to incorporate the geodetic construction technique devised by Barnes Wallis and later applied to the Wellington bomber.

The Vickers Wellington twin engined medium bomber first flew in 1936 and entered RAF service in 1938. Able to carry almost as much as the four engined Boeing B-17 Fortress bomber over a similar range, the Wellington was the mainstay of RAF Bomber Command strength in the early years of World War II until the four engined 'heavies' – notably the Avro Lancaster – became available in numbers. Wellington production reached 11,641 in a dozen major versions.

Other Vickers wartime aircraft included the Warwick (basically an enlarged Wellington), the Windsor four engined heavy bomber which flew in prototype form only and the Type 432, a pressurised twin engined high altitude fighter which was also restricted to prototype status.

Postwar, Vickers products included the Viking interim airliner, the Viscount, the Valiant jet bomber, the Valetta and Varsity twin engined transport/crew trainers developed from the Viking, the Vanguard large turboprop airliner and the VC10 jet transport.

The Interim Viking

Often overlooked when the history of British commercial aviation is discussed, the Viking was nevertheless an extremely important part of the story as it was Britain's first postwar airliner and provided the basis of British European Airways' network and operating procedures until the Viscount began to replace it in 1954. After that, several British independent airlines and overseas operators found the Viking a reliable and useful part of their fleets and the last example remained in service until 1971. Also of importance was the Viking's contribution to Britain's postwar exports. Of the 163 aircraft built, some 65 were sold to overseas operators.

Among Vickers' between the wars products was the Wellesley single engined bomber, the first RAF aircraft to incorporate Barnes Wallis' geodetic construction technique.

Vickers took over the Supermarine Aviation Works in 1929 and its best known product – the Spitfire – appeared seven years later.

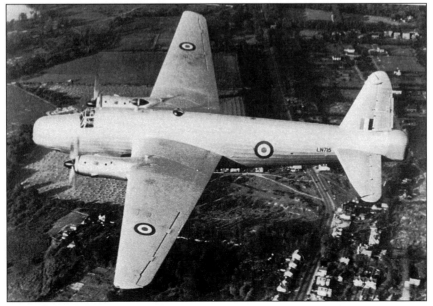

(bottom left) The Vickers Wellington was RAF Bomber Command's mainstay in the early years of World War II. This Wellington X (LN715) is photographed in 1948 as an engine testbed fitted with two Rolls-Royce Dart turboprops.

The Viking was officially an interim type and as such did not come under the direct auspices of the Brabazon Committee. Instead, it was designed to Specification 17/44 under the company designation VC1 (Vickers Commercial 1). Derived from the Wellington bomber, it combined that aircraft's Bristol Hercules powerplants, wings and undercarriage in combination with tail surfaces from the Warwick and a new stressed skin fuselage. The wings retained their geodetic structure and fabric covering initially but metal covering followed.

The first Viking was flown on 22 June 1945 and the last aircraft in April 1949. Two basic versions were produced: the Viking 1 with standard accommodation for 24 passengers and the slightly longer 1B with 27 seats. In later high density configurations up to 36 passengers could be carried.

BEA operated 49 Vikings from September 1946 and the first service flown was between Northolt and Copenhagen. By the time BEA started to replace its Vikings with Viscounts, the earlier aircraft had flown 65 million miles (104.6m kilometres), 414,000 hours and carried more than 2.7 million passengers.

First Concepts

It was at the 59th meeting of the second Brabazon Committee that the chain of events which eventually led to the emergence of the Vickers Viscount began. At that meeting, a study paper on a 30,000lb (13,600kg) gross weight airliner was examined, the paper comparing the operating economics of such an aircraft powered by either Rolls-Royce Merlin piston engines, turbojets or Armstrong Siddeley Mamba turboprops.

It was decided that the turboprop route was the best way to go, and accordingly, Lord Brabazon recommended that steps be taken to develop such an aircraft as quickly as possible. The aircraft would meet the Brabazon Committee's Type 2 requirement, originally for an unpressu-

Two shots of the Vickers Viking airliner, an important postwar interim type of which 163 were built. First flown in June 1945, the Viking provided the basis of BEA's European network until the Viscount came along in 1954. Independent British airlines such as Channel Airways also found the Viking a useful and reliable part of their fleets. (Stewart Wilson/AA Collection)

The Vickers Valiant, the first of Britain's V-bomber trio which included the Avro Vulcan and Handley Page Victor.

rised DC-3 replacement for European and Empire routes carrying 20 passengers up to 1,750 miles (2,800km) at 200mph (320km/h).

This requirement was subsequently split into two parts: Type 2A for a piston engined airliner (eventually emerging as the Airspeed Ambassador) and Type 2B for a pressurised turboprop aircraft carrying 24 passengers.

At the time, Vickers was well advanced on the construction of Britain's first postwar airliner, the piston engined unpressurised Viking as described previously. Even before this aircraft had flown, the company was working on a possible successor designated Type 453 or VC2 under the direction of Vickers-Armstrongs' chief designer, Rex Pierson.

With publication of the Type 2B requirement in April 1945, work on a new design to fill it began in earnest. In September of the same year, Rex Pierson was promoted to chief engineer of Vickers-Amstrongs and his role of chief designer was taken over by G R (later Sir George) Edwards who would guide the Viscount's progress from then.

Vickers submitted its first firm proposal for the VC2 aircraft in June 1945. Its major features were a portly 'double bubble' pressurised fuselage seating 24 passengers three abreast, a maximum weight of 24,500lb (11,113kg), a cruising speed of 297mph (478km/h) at 20,000 feet and a range of 1,040 miles (1,674km) carrying a 7,500lb (3,400kg) payload. Wing span was 88 feet (26.8m) and length 63ft 9in (19.4m), while power would be provided by four Rolls-Royce Dart turboprops each of 1,030 equivalent horsepower (ehp), a measure of power taking into account the engine's basic shaft horsepower (shp) rating and an allowance for residual jet thrust. Although shaft horsepower (shp) is the standard turboprop engine measure of power these days, ehp was the most common used for the Dart throughout its life and it is this figure which will be mainly used in this book.

Although Vickers specifically mentioned the Dart when presenting the VC2, provision was made in the design for other turboprops which were under development at the time, inclu-

ding the Napier Naiad and Armstrong Siddeley Mamba. Nevertheless, the Dart was always Vickers' favoured choice, despite the Naiad promising greater power and the Mamba appearing to be maturing more quickly for a time.

There had been some discussion between Vickers and the Ministry earlier in 1945 as to whether or not pressurisation was in fact necessary or desirable in the VC2 design. The use of turboprop engines settled the issue, as they would be uneconomical at lower altitudes and have good operating economics higher up.

Additionally, Vickers already had some useful experience with pressurisation under its belt through the Wellington V and VI of 1940/41, experimental versions of the bomber developed to investigate the feasibility of bombing from very high altitudes. This work provided Vickers with considerable insight into the art and science of pressure cabins which it would be able to quickly apply to civil projects such as the VC2.

The Design Firms

Progress on the VC2 Type 453 project was regarded as slow by the Brabazon Committee and in October 1945 the newly established Ministry of Supply (renamed from the former Ministry of Aircraft Production) asked four other companies – Shorts, Blackburn, Handley Page and Armstrong Whitworth – to submit designs to meet the Brabazon Type 2B requirement. Of these, Armstrong Whitworth's AW.55 Avon design was selected and two prototypes ordered as insurance against the failure of the Vickers VC2. Renamed Apollo to avoid confusion with the Rolls-Royce axial flow turbojet engine, the first aircraft was flown in April 1949 but problems with its airframe and Mamba engines plus the fact that the VC2 proved successful meant this insurance wasn't needed and only two were built.

Now under the leadership of George Edwards, the VC2 design team carried out a detailed study of their aircraft in late 1945 and some fundamental changes were made. The major one was replacing the double bubble fuselage design with a more conventional circular section one. The external diameter of this new fuselage design was 10ft 8in (3.25m), this dimension remaining constant throughout the Viscount's life and allowing comfortable four abreast seating initially and adequate width for five abreast arrangements later on.

Other design features incorporated at this time – the equally tapering wings, dihedral tailplanes, elliptical

The Vickers Vanguard large turboprop airliner was produced in much smaller numbers than its illustrious predecessor.

cabin windows, oval doors and cockpit roof shape – resulted in an aircraft which looked very much like the definitive Viscount.

In March 1946, the Ministry of Supply awarded Vickers a contract for two prototype VC2s worth £1.8m and the following month issued Specification 8/46 to the company.

The specification's major points were: a short-medium range 24 to 28 seater powered by four turbine engines; a freight/baggage capacity of 274cu ft (7.76m³), interior noise levels no greater than 70 decibels (cockpit) and 60 decibels (cabin); a cabin pressure differential of 6.5lb sq in allowing a cabin altitude of 8,000 feet (2,438m) while the aircraft was flying at 30,000 feet (9,144m); the ability to carry a 7,500lb (3,400kg) payload for 700 nautical miles (1,297km) at 240 knots (445km/h) at 20,000 feet (6,096m); a maximum range of 1,200 nautical miles (2,220 km); and takeoff and landing runs of no more than 1,200 yards (1,097m).

Interestingly, the Armstrong Siddeley Mamba was the officially preferred powerplant over the Dart because it was considered to be further advanced than the Rolls-Royce product. Vickers remained convinced that the Dart was the proper choice and the engine nacelles were designed to accept both engines.

There would be further changes to the basic design before construction of the prototypes began at Vickers' Foxwarren experimental workshop in late 1946. This workshop was located midway between the company's Weybridge and Wisley facilities in Surrey and both aircraft were relocated to the latter for final assembly and their initial flights.

The changes came from a British European Airways requirement for a 32 seater and resulted in a larger aeroplane with its length increased from 65ft 6in (19.96m) to 74ft 6in (22.70m) and the span up to 89ft 0in (27.13m) with a commensurate increase in wing area to 885sq ft (82.2m²). The maximum takeoff weight was set at initially 38,170lb (17,314kg) and then 39,500lb (17,917kg). The Mamba was still the specified engine.

This new VC2 specification was dubbed the Type 609 and given the name Viceroy.

From Viceroy to Viscount

While construction of the prototypes was underway at Foxwarren, further studies into alternative powerplants were undertaken by the Ministry of Supply in 1947 including a version with four Naiad or two Double Naiad turboprops and even one with a pair of Dart turboprops on the inner engine positions and Nene jets outboard.

Vickers finally got its way as to the choice of powerplant for the Viceroy in August 1947 when the Ministry instructed the manufacturer to install Darts on the aircraft. This resulted from further investigation into the Dart's status and the discovery that considerable development work and redesign had been incorporated and that good progress was being made. Darts were flight tested by Rolls-Royce in the nose of a Lancaster and by Vickers in both normal engine positions on a Wellington.

The change from Mamba to Dart power resulted in a new Type number for the prototypes, 630.

One more nomenclature change had to be made before 1947 was out, in the interests of an early example of 'political correctness'. 1947 saw the independence and partition of India and the redundancy of its ruling British Viceroy as a result. A new name had to be found which continued Vickers' traditional 'V' alliteration, and the suitably noble 'Viscount' was chosen.

Doom and Gloom

1947 was also the year in which the entire Viscount project came into great jeopardy, thanks to BEA placing an order for 20 Airspeed Ambassadors in December. The first Ambassador had flown five months earlier and had been built to meet the Brabazon Committee's Type 2A require-

Darts on the wing. This superb engine was a key part of the Viscount's and other aircrafts' success. Power was more than trebled over the years as the Dart was developed.

The world's first all turboprop powered aircraft, the Trent-Meteor. The aircraft was first flown in its new configuration in September 1945. (Rolls-Royce)

ment. It featured piston engines (which enabled it to be flown earlier than the Viscount) and a comfortable pressurised cabin. A lengthy development period meant it didn't enter service until 1952 (by which time the enlarged Viscount 700 was well into its own test programme) but in 1947 it offered serious competition to the Viscount.

BEA had begun to question the economic viability of the Viscount during 1947 and was behind further studies into alternative powerplants and options. BEA's basic need was for a larger aircraft with higher oper-

ating weights. From these studies came several Viscount projects including the Type 652 with the 630's fuselage but a pair of Bristol Hercules piston engines and a bigger wing; and the Type 653 with its fuselage stretched to carry 40 passengers, enlarged wing and four Darts. Vickers had itself previously studied the Type 640 'Viscount Mk.II' with Naiad engines and increased gross weight for more range.

None of these proposals found any favour and by April 1948 – when construction of the two prototypes was well advanced – one of the most

advanced and potentially great airliner designs in existence had no customer. One impractical scheme to come out of this was to build a stretched Viscount initially powered by two Bristol Hercules piston engines which would be replaced by four Darts of suitable power at a later date.

The effect of this uncertainty was to slow down the Viscount programme, including abandoning plans to build a third prototype which would be financed by the manufacturer. At the same time, it was decided that the second prototype Viscount would be modified as a testbed with two Rolls-Royce Tay turbojets replacing the original four Darts as the Type 663. The purpose of this aircraft was to conduct high altitude research into the control systems of the forthcoming Vickers Valiant bomber.

The Viscount Flies

At this point, the Viscount programme was at its lowest ebb with no airline orders, disinterest by what should have been its first and one of its largest customers, and a rival aircraft on order instead.

Several factors saved the Viscount: the ability of Rolls-Royce to quickly and reliably develop the Dart so a larger Viscount could be planned, the failure of the Ambassador to enter service quickly so any time advantage could be commercially exploited (BEA's 20 aircraft were the only ones ordered by a customer), and the ability of the Viscount to show its capabilities and the level of its advances once it was in the air.

Vickers' spirits rose in early July 1948 when the first V.630 Viscount was rolled out of its Wisley hangar. Registered G-AHRF, the aircraft was flown for the first time on the 16th of the month with Captain J 'Mutt' Summers in command. Summers had an illustrious history as a test pilot, his achievements including flying the prototype Supermarine Spitfire on its maiden flight in March 1936. The second (Tay powered) Viscount prototype first flew on 15 March 1950 carrying the military serial VX217. Both these aircraft and their careers are discussed in more detail in the following chapter.

The Durable Dart

Fundamental to the success of the Viscount and many other aircraft was its powerplant, the Rolls-Royce Dart turboprop. This extraordinary engine began life producing just 990ehp and was subsequently developed through nine families each comprising several subvariants. By the time its development had peaked, some Dart ver-

The primary characteristics of the Rolls-Royce Dart.

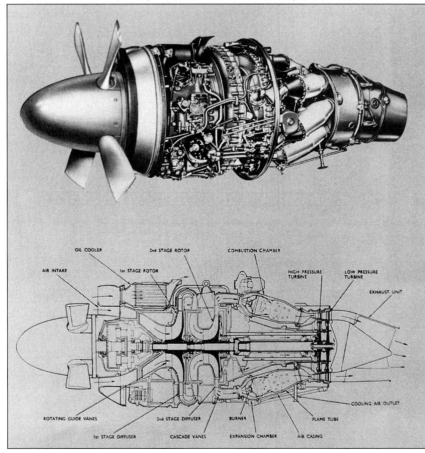

sions were capable of producing over 3,400ehp.

The first Dart was bench tested in 1946 and by the time production ended 40 years later about 7,100 had been built and accumulated some 110 million hours in the air. Millions more hours have been added since then.

The Dart has powered some of the postwar era's best known and most successful transport aircraft apart from the Viscount, among them the Fokker F27 Friendship, Hawker Siddeley HS.748, Hawker Siddeley Argosy, Handley Page Herald, Grumman Gulfstream I, NAMC YS-11 and Convair 600. A purely military application was France's Breguet Alizé shipborne anti submarine aircraft.

Rolls-Royce began developing what would emerge as the Dart in April 1945, the third of the company's turboprop projects of the time. The first was the Clyde, a very powerful engine designed to produce up to 4,000shp. The first Clyde tested in August 1945 but after some 1949 flight trials in a Westland Wyvern was abandoned as no permanent application could be found for it.

The second project involved converting an existing centrifugal flow turbojet (the Derwent) to a basic propeller turbine engine by fitting an extended turbine compressor shaft and reduction gearing to which was fitted a five bladed propeller. Called the Trent, two of the new engines were installed in a Gloster Meteor fighter and flown in that configuration for the first time in September 1945. The Trent-Meteor therefore became the world's first turboprop aircraft. The combination provided invaluable information and experience to Rolls-Royce, all of which could be applied to the Dart.

Initially known as the RB.53, the Dart's basic configuration comprised a two stage centrifugal compressor, seven combustion chambers and a

One of the two BEA Dakotas converted to Dart power in 1951 and used on commercial freight services for two years. They taught the airline, the engine manufacturer and the airworthiness authorities much about turboprop operations and helped pave the way for a smooth introduction to service for the Viscount.

two stage turbine. A three stage turbine appeared later on as part of the never ending quest to find more power.

The engine was a disappointment at first, early bench testing producing only about 600shp when 1,000 was the target. Additionally, the weight of the engine was over 1,100lb (500kg), some 30 per cent greater than the target. The use of magnesium alloys for many of the castings got the weight down to acceptable levels, while redesigning the compressor and turbine improved the power output and reliability.

Flight testing got underway in October 1947 in a Lancaster with a Dart installed in its nose, while a Wellington powered by two Darts in place of the normal pair of Bristol Hercules piston engines followed in early 1948. This was the first aircraft to fly exclusively powered by the Dart. Other aircraft were also fitted with Darts for testing including an Airspeed Ambassador and in 1949, an Avro Athena advanced trainer and the first of three Douglas DC-3 Dakotas.

One was an ex RAF Dakota and the other two were BEA aircraft. After testing, this pair was returned to the airline for operation as commercial

freighters for two years from 1951. As such, they were the world's first turbine powered aircraft to be put into revenue earning service. This gave the BEA some useful practical experience in turboprop operations ahead of the introduction of the Viscount (and the Dart a chance to prove itself in service) and the 3,870 hours logged by the Dakotas was achieved without the need for a single premature engine removal.

This performance undoubtedly helped convince many within the airline and aircraft manufacturing industries plus the airworthiness authorities that gas turbine engines had the potential to provide reliability and time between overhauls only dreamt of in the world of piston engines. And so it proved to be.

Stories surrounding the Dart-Dakotas and their considerably enhanced performance figures over the standard aircraft are legendary. Although most of them are undoubtedly somewhat exaggerated (including jet fighters cruising at 50,000 feet with a Dakota flying alongside!), the aircrafts' ability to happily operate at 25,000 feet or so did result in some bemusement on the part of pilots and air traffic controllers.

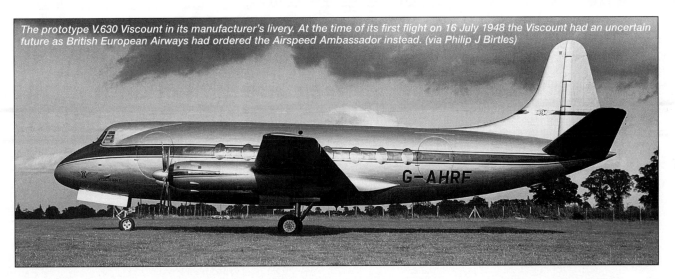

The prototype V.630 Viscount in its manufacturer's livery. At the time of its first flight on 16 July 1948 the Viscount had an uncertain future as British European Airways had ordered the Airspeed Ambassador instead. (via Philip J Birtles)

Two ex BEA Viscount 806s in later service: Guernsey Airlines' G-BLOA (top) and British Air Ferry's G-APEY.

Botswana Airlines' sole Viscount (top), an ex TAA V.756D; and G-AOHT (bottom) an ex BEA Viscount 806 of Euroair. (Eric Allen)

Union of Burma Airways Viscount 761D XY-ADF (top) at Rangoon in March 1964; and New Zealand NAC V.807 ZK-NAI (bottom) at Sydney in February 1967. (Eric Allen)

Antipodean Viscounts: TAA V.756D VH-TVH (top) taxying at Sydney Airport in July 1965; and Ansett-ANA V.812 VH-RMK (bottom) cleaning up after takeoff from the same airport two years later. (Eric Allen)

United Airlines Viscount 745D N7454 (top) following the takeover of Capital Airlines. Manx Airlines' G-AOYM (bottom) is a former BEA Viscount 806 photographed at Heathrow in June 1985. (United Airlines/Rob Finlayson)

V.737 CF-GXK (top), one of two Viscounts operated by the Canadian Department of Transport between 1955 and 1982. Another ex BEA Viscount 802 is G-AOHT (bottom), operated by Virgin Atlantic in 1985. (Eric Allen)

More Antipodean Viscounts: TAA V.816 VH-TVQ (top); and a scratchy but interesting shot (bottom) of Ansett-ANA V.720 VH-TVF shortly after transfer from TAA in 1958 and still wearing the latter's basic livery. (Eric Allen)

BEA Viscount 806 G-AOHI (top) on approach to Heathrow in February 1970; and the former RAAF VIP Viscount 836 A6-435 (bottom) photographed in November 1969 with the very temporary American registration N40NA before its aborted delivery to the Alda Corporation. Note the slipper tanks. (Eric Allen)

VISCOUNT VARIANTS

V.630 VISCOUNT

The prototype V.630's first flight from Wisley on 16 July 1948 with 'Mutt' Summers and G R (Jock) Bryce at the controls lasted 20 minutes and was very successful, the pilot describing the new airliner as "the smoothest and best I have ever known". The only problem was a faulty fuel flow gauge.

Despite the euphoria of that maiden flight, the overall mood within the Viscount team matched the weather of the day – dull and gloomy – as the aircraft still had no customer. It's potential became obvious even in the earliest flight trials and it would not be long before a developed version would be attracting orders.

Registered G-AHRF, the prototype Viscount was smaller than the variants which would follow. Powered by four 1,380ehp Dart 502s, it could carry 32 passengers at up to 300mph (483km) and over a range of about 900 miles (1,448km). Its maximum takeoff weight of 43,000lb (19,505kg) was less than three-quarters of that of the production Viscount 700 which would follow.

Nevertheless, the general characteristics of later Viscounts were there: large oval windows which would prove so popular with passengers; four bladed Rotol propellers designed specifically for the Dart (their modest diameter allowing a shortish undercarriage to make servicing the engines from the ground easier); an engine installation design which al-lowed an interchangeable 'power egg' configuration, all metal struc-ture; dual wheels on the steerable nose (forward retracting) and main (retracting forwards into the inboard engine nacelles) undercarriage units; a 6.5lb sq in cabin pressure differen-tial which was the highest of any air-liner at the time; interconnected bag-type fuel tanks in the wings; oval passenger entry doors on the port side of the fuselage; and the tail-plane's 14deg dihedral.

There is a bit of a story behind the Viscount's passenger windows. Their generous size originally came about following a 1945 international airwor-thiness organisation suggestion that the minimum size for an emergency exit should be 26 inches (66cm) high by 19 inches (48cm) wide. Vickers re-alised that windows of that size would add to passenger appeal and if they were of a proper shape would not cause any structural or design problems. The result was the Vis-count's familiar oval cabin windows which in early production aircraft all doubled as emergency exits! Twenty emergency exits was soon judged as a little excessive and this was re-duced to just three or four per side.

There were three main systems on the Viscount – pressurisation (engine driven by three Roots superchargers); hydraulic (for landing gear, nose wheel steering and brakes); and elec-trical (for lighting, radio, the double slotted flaps and trimming operations plus propeller de-icing and other services). A pneumatic system was also installed, its sole function being to inflate the seals around the doors in the pressure cabin.

Flying controls were all manually operated by push-pull rods and bag-gage space was provided at the front and rear of the cabin plus in the air-craft's belly.

Proving The Concept

After having completed the man-datory 15 flying hours, G-AHRF ap-peared at the Society of British Aircraft Constructors (SBAC) show at Farnborough in September 1948, the sleek turboprop offering a marked contrast to the piston engined airlin-ers of the day and creating consider-able interest.

Vickers knew it had a potential winner on its hands and began a comprehensive sales and public rela-tions campaign starting later in Sep-tember 1948 when the prototype was flown to Villacoublay, near Paris, for its first overseas venture. Continued test flying revealed few, if any prob-lems and the manufacturer realised that if it could build a larger, more commercially viable Viscount the world's airlines would queue up to buy it. The opportunity to do this came in late 1948 when Rolls-Royce was able to offer a 40 per cent more powerful version of the Dart which would allow higher weights and greater seating capacity.

The prototype Viscount photographed during 1949 operating on behalf of the British Ministry of Supply and carrying the military serial VX211. Both starboard engines are stopped and the propellers feathered. (via Philip J Birtles)

The prototype Viscount takes off from Wisley on its maiden flight – 16 July 1948.

G-AHRF's flying programme continued in the meantime, now carrying the RAF serial VX211 for operation on behalf of the Ministry of Supply. The Viscount achieved a major milestone on 15 September 1949 when, after completing 160 flights and 290 hours in the air, the prototype was awarded a restricted Certificate of Airworthiness, the first turbine powered aircraft to achieve this.

The CofA was restricted as substantial testing still had to be carried out; tropical operations and use of the pressurisation and innovative thermal de-icing systems were not covered. The pressurisation system was not installed in the aircraft until mid 1949 and it would not be until 27 July 1950 that G-AHRF was awarded its full CofA, allowing the carriage of fare paying passengers under all conditions. Hot weather trails were conducted at Eastleigh Airport (Nairobi) in Kenya the previous month, including extensive testing of the water-methanol injection system Rolls-Royce had developed to help restore power lost by high temperatures and altitudes.

Winning Hearts and Minds

G-AHRF had in the meantime been on tours and demonstration flights which convinced many – including the all important British European Airways – that here was an aircraft which should be purchased.

In March and April 1950 the aircraft was taken on a major European tour. Significantly, it was painted in BEA colours (and remained in them for the rest of its days) and the pilot in command was BEA's Captain Wakelin. The airline had not yet formally ordered any Viscounts (that was still four months away), but the close co-operation between manufacturer and major customer which would play such an important part in the aircraft's future development was already in place.

The Viscount's European tour took in eight capital cities and 61 hours in the air. The purpose of the exercise was not just publicity, but also to gain some operational experience on routes the aircraft was likely to fly once in service. An interesting experiment carried out during the tour was

that of descending and landing on two engines in order to save fuel at low altitudes, where a turboprop engine is not very fuel efficient. The technique was also used when the aircraft was holding in the landing pattern and although successful, the idea was not adopted for service use as it increased the pilots' workloads and compromised safety and performance if a missed approach was necessary.

On 29 July 1950 – two days after the Viscount's full CofA had been awarded, history was made when the prototype flew from London's Northolt Airport to Le Bourget at Paris with 26 passengers on board. Of those, 14 were fare paying and the remainder guests of the airline and manufacturer. The 230 mile (370km) flight was commanded by Captain Richard Rymer and took 57 minutes to complete, resulting in a block speed of 242mph (389km/h). Cruising speed was 273mph (439km/h) at 18,000 feet (5,490m).

BEA committed itself to purchase 20 larger Viscount 700s in August 1950, the first prototype of which would fly later in the same month. G-AHRF was immediately put to work by the airline, flying scheduled services for a period of just under four weeks until 23 August 1950.

The aircraft flew between Northolt and Le Bourget until 14 August, during which time 36 return trips were made and then eight return journeys were flown between London and Edinburgh between 15 and 23 August.

The Viscount 630 in Vickers livery and carrying its civil registration G-AHRF. (Rolls-Royce)

G-AHRF undertook a tour of European cities in March and April 1950 and in August of the same year flew scheduled services with BEA. It is photographed here at Schiphol Airport, Amsterdam, during the European tour and contrasts greatly with the piston engined DC-3s and Constellation in the background.

The V.663 Tay-Viscount on the ground. First flown on 15 March 1950, this aircraft was used for high altitude development of the Vickers Valiant control system and other tasks.

The Tay-Viscount at the 1950 SBAC Show at Farnborough where it caused a sensation with its speed and rate of climb.

Combined, these flights carried 1,815 passengers and 124hr 35min flying time was logged. They went a long way towards proving the reliability of the turbine engine but equally importantly, the Viscount's quiet, smooth and vibration free 'above the weather' flight proved extremely popular with passengers, as did those large windows and the view they afforded. Millions of other passengers would shortly appreciate those virtues as well.

G-AHRF returned to Vickers at the completion of the BEA trials, by which time the first V.700 was only five days away from its maiden flight. After a shaky start, the success of the Viscount project now seemed much more assured with first orders in the book and a high level of passenger acceptance already demonstrated.

The prototype continued test flying until 27 August 1952 when it suffered an undercarriage collapse during a practice forced landing in the Sahara Desert near Khartoum and was damaged beyond repair. It had 931 flying hours in its logbook.

> **VISCOUNT 630**
> **Powerplants:** Four Rolls-Royce Dart R.Da.1 Mk.502 turboprops each rated at 1,380ehp for takeoff. Dowty-Rotol four bladed propellers of 10ft 0in (3.05m) diameter. Fuel capacity 1,400imp gal (6,364 l) in wing tanks.
> **Dimensions:** Wing span 89ft 0in (27.12m); length 74ft 6in (22.70m); height 26ft 3in (8.00m); wing area 885sq ft (82.2m²).
> **Weights:** Max takeoff 43,000lb (19,505kg); max zero fuel 36,000lb (16,330kg); max landing 40,000lb (18,144kg); empty equipped 27,000lb (12,247kg); max payload 9,000lb (4,082kg).
> **Accommodation:** 32 passengers four abreast.
> **Performance:** Max cruise 261kt (483km/h); economical cruise 237kt (439km/h); initial climb 1,100ft (335m)/min; engine out climb 650ft (198m)/min; takeoff field length 4,600ft (1,402m); range (max payload and reserves) 609nm (1,126km); range (6,000lb payload and reserves) 957nm (1,770km).

V.663 TAY-VISCOUNT

With the slowdown of the Viscount development programme over the northern winter of 1947-48 came the decision to complete the second V.630 prototype as a testbed powered by two 6,250lb thrust Rolls-Royce Tay centrifugal flow turbojets in place of the usual four Dart turboprops. Redesignated the Type 663, this aircraft flew for the first time from Vickers' Wisley airfield on 15 March 1950 carrying the military serial number VX217. The allocated civil registration G-AHRG was not taken up.

VICKERS VISCOUNT
PROTOTYPES

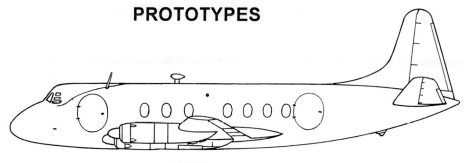

V.630
First prototype (G-AHRF/VX211), originally named Viceroy and to seat 24/32.

V.663 TAY-VISCOUNT
Second prototype 630 used as a flying test bed for two Rolls-Royce R.Ta.1 Tay turbojets.

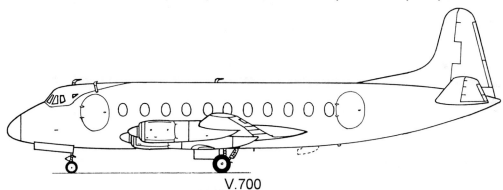

V.700
Prototype for production series. The first production Viscount was the V.701 - 40/47 seater.

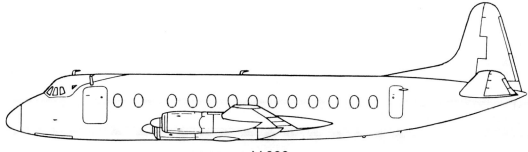

V.800
Basic designation of the stretched 44/70 seater version of the 700 series. There was no prototype as such - the first to fly was the V.802 (G-AOJA) on 27 July 1956.

D Newton

VICKERS VISCOUNT
SERIES 800/810

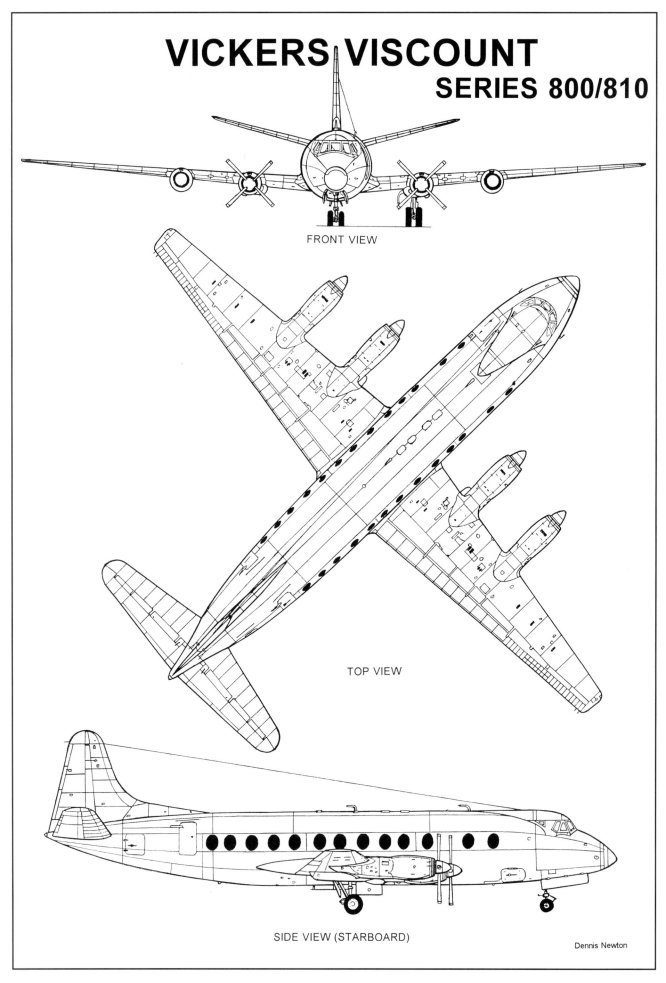

FRONT VIEW

TOP VIEW

SIDE VIEW (STARBOARD)

Dennis Newton

VICKERS VISCOUNT
SERIES 800/810

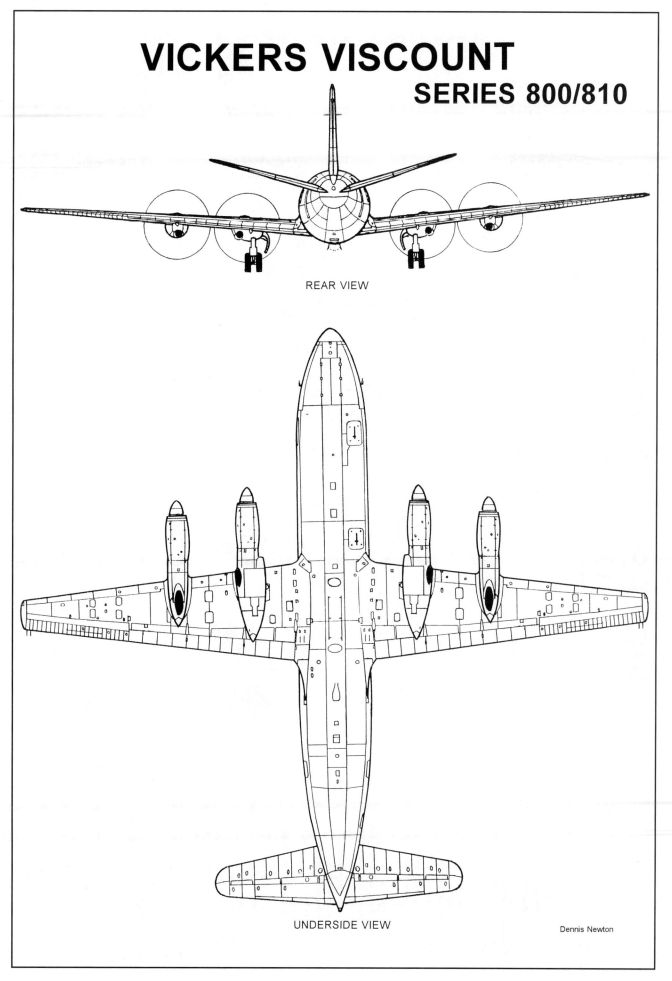

REAR VIEW

UNDERSIDE VIEW

Dennis Newton

VICKERS VISCOUNT
810/840 Series

© Dennis Newton

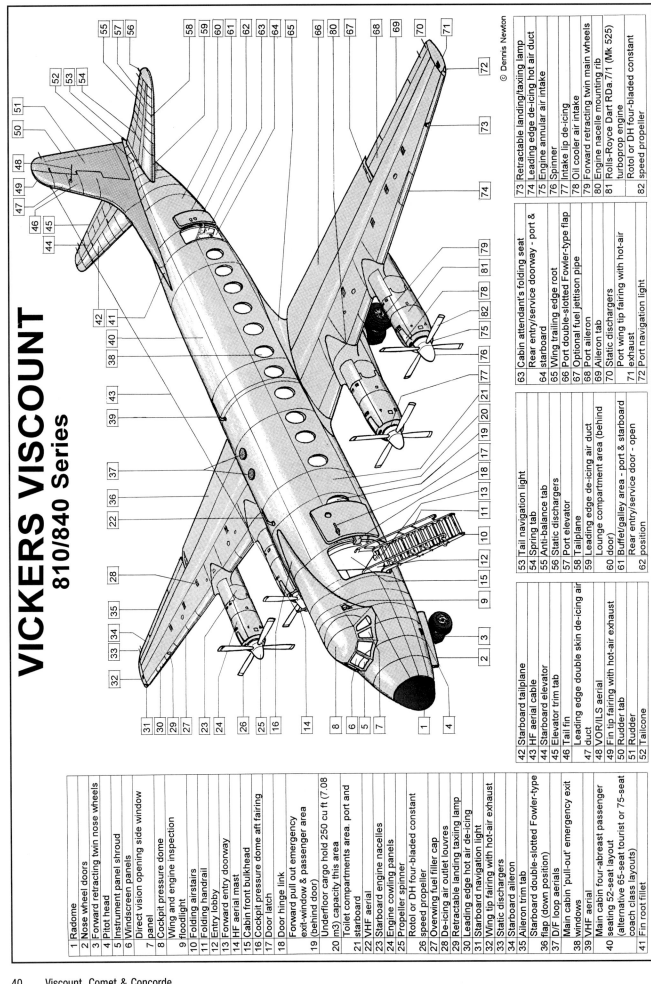

1 Radome
2 Nose wheel doors
3 Forward retracting twin nose wheels
4 Pitot head
5 Instrument panel shroud
6 Windscreen panels
7 Direct vision opening side window panel
8 Cockpit pressure dome
9 Wing and engine inspection floodlight
10 Folding airstairs
11 Folding handrail
12 Entry lobby
13 Forward entry doorway
14 HF aerial mast
15 Cabin front bulkhead
16 Cockpit pressure dome aft fairing
17 Door latch
18 Door hinge link
19 Forward pull out emergency exit-window & passenger area (behind door)
20 Underfloor cargo hold 250 cu ft (7.08 m3) capacity this area
21 Toilet compartments area. port and starboard
22 VHF aerial
23 Starboard engine nacelles
24 Engine cowling panels
25 Propeller spinner
26 Rotol or DH four-bladed constant speed propeller
27 Overwing fuel filler cap
28 De-icing air outlet louvres
29 Retractable landing taxing lamp
30 Leading edge hot air de-icing
31 Starboard navigation light
32 Wing tip fairing with hot-air exhaust
33 Static dischargers
34 Starboard aileron
35 Aileron trim tab
36 Starboard double-slotted Fowler-type flap (down position)
37 D/F loop aerials
38 Main cabin 'pull-out' emergency exit windows
39 VHF aerial
40 Main cabin four-abreast passenger seating 52-seat layout (alternative 65-seat tourist or 75-seat coach class layouts)
41 Fin root fillet

42 Starboard tailplane
43 HF aerial cable
44 Starboard elevator
45 Elevator trim tab
46 Tail fin
47 Leading edge double skin de-icing air duct
48 VOR/ILS aerial
49 Fin tip fairing with hot-air exhaust
50 Rudder tab
51 Rudder
52 Tailcone
53 Tail navigation light
54 Spring tab
55 Anti-balance tab
56 Static dischargers
57 Port elevator
58 Tailplane
59 Leading edge de-icing air duct
60 Lounge compartment area (behind door)
61 Buffet/galley area - port & starboard
62 Rear entry/service door - open position

63 Cabin attendant's folding seat
64 Rear entry/service doorway - port & starboard
65 Wing trailing edge root
66 Port double-slotted Fowler-type flap
67 Optional fuel jettison pipe
68 Port aileron
69 Aileron tab
70 Static dischargers
71 Port wing tip fairing with hot-air exhaust
72 Port navigation light
73 Retractable landing/taxing lamp
74 Leading edge de-icing hot air duct
75 Engine annular air intake
76 Spinner
77 Intake lip de-icing
78 Oil cooler air intake
79 Forward retracting twin main wheels
80 Engine nacelle mounting rib
81 Rolls-Royce Dart RDa.7/1 (Mk 525) turboprop engine
82 Rotol or DH four-bladed constant speed propeller

The 663 retained the same overall dimensions as the V.630 Viscount prototype, the changes incorporated revolving around the installation of the two Tays which were mounted in underwing pods each incorporating a revised main undercarriage design. The Tay-Viscount made only one public appearance, at the 1950 SBAC show at Farnborough where it caused something of a sensation with the turn of speed and rate of climb it displayed. Performance figures were never published.

The aircraft was used by the Ministry of Supply for various tests and trials including high altitude tests of the Boulton Paul powered control system for the Vickers Valiant bomber. It then became the first aircraft in the world to fly with an electrically signalled flight control system (fly-by-wire these days) and was also used by the Decca Navigator company.

The Tay-Viscount survived until 1958 when it was damaged beyond repair in a hydraulic fire having logged just 110 very useful flying hours.

V.700 VISCOUNT

The promise of more power from a new member of the Rolls-Royce Dart family, the R.Da.3, encouraged Vickers to start work on a 'stretched' Viscount in January 1949. Under the Type 700 designation, production versions of the new variant differed from the prototype in several significant ways, including lengthening the fuselage by 6ft 8in (2.03m) in equal parts fore and aft of the wing allowing an increase in passenger capacity to 40, 44 or 48 four abreast or up to 53 utilising some five abreast seating (later high density configurations accommodated up to 63 passengers); the wing span was increased by 5ft 0in (1.52m) by adding a new inner section (which also moved the engines further away from fuselage; and

Viscount 700 G-AMAV in the air. By the time it was awarded a full Certificate of Airworthiness in June 1952, 53 Viscounts had been ordered by five customers.

G-AMAV wearing race number 23 for its successful participation in the 1953 London–New Zealand air race. It was also the first turboprop aircraft to cross the Atlantic.

The first production Viscount 701, BEA's G-ALWE. This aircraft flew for the first time on 20 August 1952.

BEA's second Viscount 701, G-ALWF. Note the front integral airstairs and the oval passenger doors.

maximum takeoff weight went up to initially 58,000lb (26,309kg), subsequently 60,000lb (27,216kg) and 63,000lb (28,577kg) later.

The R.Da.3 Darts were housed in redesigned cowlings of the 'petal' design allowing complete access to the engines for maintenance; the undercarriage suspension was made softer; more positive nosewheel steering was incorporated; the de-icing system was modified; the fin fillet was larger to compensate for the V.630 prototype's tendency to yaw slightly in rough weather and for the 700's longer fuselage; the choice of conventional or anti skid brakes was offered; and the main undercarriage legs were mounted offset in the inner nacelles.

The fuel system was modified to increase capacity to 1,720imp gal (7,819 l) and an early production modification was the optional addition of further fuel cells within the wings bringing internal capacity to 1,900imp gal (8,637 l) if the optional water-methanol injection for the engines was fitted and 1,950imp gal (8,865 l) if it wasn't. Two slipper tanks mounted under the outer wing leading edges were also subsequently offered as an option, each carrying 145imp gal (659 l) of fuel and bringing the V.700's capacity up to 2,240imp gal (10,183 l). A further modification was later developed for VIP and corporate Viscounts which required even

Viscount 701s on the production line at Weybridge with BEA's second aircraft in the foreground. This line closed in 1954 to make way for the Valiant bomber but a new assembly line for Viscounts soon had to be built.

more range, this involving the installation of a 450imp gal (2,045 l) tank in the underfloor freight hold.

The powerplant for production Viscount 700s was initially the Dart 505 of 1,547ehp for takeoff, this being replaced by the Mk.506 which offered a similar takeoff rating but had slightly more power at the recommended cruise rating. Early Viscount 700s originally fitted with Dart 505s were subsequently given 506s and this became the standard powerplant for the basic 700 series aircraft.

The First 700

The first Viscount 700 was built to a Ministry of Supply contract placed

Nearly two-thirds of all Viscounts were built on Vickers' new Hurn (Bournemouth) production line. These are V.724s for Trans Canada Airlines in 1955 with c/n 50 in the foreground. The signs in the background (No 605 etc) relate to TCA fleet numbers.

Asymmetry in extremus! The first Viscount 701 (G-ALWE) at Farnborough in 1952 with only the starboard outer Dart turning. Rudder control was undoubtedly a bit course!

with the manufacturer in February 1949, a few weeks after Vickers had decided to go ahead with this larger version of the airliner which at this stage was still without a customer.

A year earlier, construction of a third, company funded Viscount prototype had been abandoned following British European Airways' decision to order the Airspeed Ambassador and some components from this aircraft were used in the manufacture of the first 700. The aircraft's wings were constructed at Itchen and the fuselage at South Marston (both of these being Supermarine facilities) and the components were brought together for final assembly at Weybridge to fly from the associated Brooklands airfield, the first turbine powered aircraft to do so.

Flown for the first time on 28 August 1950 by Jock Bryce, the prototype Viscount 700 was painted in BEA livery and registered G-AMAV. It differed from production 700s in having a lower maximum takeoff weight of 50,000lb (22,680kg) and was initially powered by Dart 504s of similar rating to the 505s which would be installed on early production models. G-AMAV's first public appearance was at Farnborough in September 1950 when it made a spectacular low level pass with three of its four Darts feathered.

The usual testing programme was carried out with hot weather trials conducted in South Africa during October and November 1951 and icing trials early the following year. These trials usually resulted in the opportunity being taken to demonstrate the aircraft to potential customers in the region in which they were being carried out.

An innovation which was tested during this time was one of the first applications of the 'stick shaker' stall protection device now in widespread use. The system instigates a violent oscillation of the control column about 10 knots (18km/h) above the stall, leaving the pilots in no doubt as to what was about to happen.

G-AMAV was awarded an interim Certificate of Airworthiness in June 1952 and in the same month the aircraft was demonstrated in India and Pakistan. By then, Vickers had received orders for 53 production Viscounts from five customers: BEA (26), British West Indian Airlines (4), Aer Lingus (4), Air France (12) and Trans-Australia Airlines (7). By the end of the year Trans Canada Airlines had also signed up for an initial 15 aircraft and provided Vickers with the extremely important breakthrough into the North American market. TCA eventually ordered 51 Viscounts.

The next step was achieving a full Certificate of Airworthiness so that fare paying passengers could be carried. Although experience on the Viscount airframe could only be achieved by the aircraft itself, its powerplant could build up service hours on other aircraft and this was gained between 1951 and 1953 by the two Dakotas mentioned previously. Re-engined with Rolls-Royce Darts, the aircraft were flown on regular freight services within the BEA network, building up a bank of operating knowledge for not only the airline but also Vickers, the engine manufacturer and airworthiness authorities.

Bugs were ironed out, operating procedures refined and by the time a full CofA was awarded to the Viscount, much had been learned about its powerplant. G-AMAV flew several hundred hours on BEA route proving flights over the winter of 1952-1953 and was joined by the first two production Viscount 701s for BEA (G-ALWE and 'WF) in February.

The Viscount was awarded its full Certificate of Airworthiness on 17 April 1953 and BEA inaugurated the world's first regular turboprop airliner service the following day, V.701 G-AMNY flying from London Heathrow to Cyprus via Rome and Athens. Captains A S Johnson and A Wilson were on the flightdeck for this first of countless thousands of Viscount passenger flights which would take place over the next half a century.

UK to New Zealand

While early production Viscounts were establishing themselves in service during 1953, plans were afoot to run a major international air race between London and Christchurch in New Zealand. The race had first been mooted five years earlier and initial interest had been high, as had the number of aircraft on the provisional entry list. As time went on, the list

TAA's first Viscount 720, the first variant with increased fuel capacity. This aircraft was delivered in October 1954 – the first outside Europe – but crashed only 26 days later in a training flight accident. (via Philip J Birtles)

became smaller and when the race was held in October 1953 there were only eight starters and public interest was nowhere near as great as previous marathon air races.

The race was a chance, however, for Vickers to show off the Viscount in new parts of the world. Of the eight aircraft which did compete, five were Canberra jet bombers (three RAF and two RAAF) contesting the speed section for outright victory. The transport section (which was to be decided on handicap) comprised the prototype Viscount 700, G-AMAV, a KLM Douglas DC-6B and a Royal Air Force Handley Page Hastings.

The original intention had been to enter a production British European Airways Viscount 701 in the race but they were all needed for their regular duties. G-AMAV was therefore seconded, flying in BEA colours with the name *Endeavour* and carrying the race number 23.

The Viscount was really unsuitable for the event being a medium range aircraft and it was modified accordingly by having bag fuel tanks installed in the cabin bringing fuel capacity up to 2,850imp gal (12,956 l) and maximum range to over 3,600 miles (5,800km). The Viscount was operated at weights of up to 64,500lb (29,257kg), considerably heavier than standard.

The field departed London on 8 October 1953 and travelling the 12,367 miles (19,903km) route via Bahrain, Negombo, Cocos Island and Melbourne (including some remarkably fast turnaround times, 14 minutes at Bahrain, for example) G-AMAV arrived at Christchurch 40 hours and 41 minutes later. This beat the DC-6 by over nine hours, but the piston engined airliner was given handicap honours. The Hastings retired after an engine failure and the outright winner was an RAF Canberra PR.3.

Although a low key affair, the race did the Viscount's image no harm as it had demonstrated excellent reliability, beaten a piston engined airliner to the line and shown off the aircraft to the public in parts of the world the Viscount had not as yet ventured to.

Models and Production

The first production Viscount 701 (G-ALWE) for BEA was flown on 20 August 1952 and was joined by the second aircraft (G-ALWF) in early December of the same year. The first handover to BEA took place in January 1953 and by the time services were inaugurated in April, BEA's first six aircraft had been flown of which five had been handed over. The first V.708 for Air France was flown on 11 March 1953 and delivered in May.

The Viscount's second customer was Air France, which took delivery of 12 V.708s from May 1953. F-BGNK was the first of them.

Vickers offered Viscount purchasers a high degree of customisation in their aircraft with the result that individual type numbers were allocated to each customer. As noted above, BEA's aircraft were V.701s and Air France's V.708s, while other early variants were the V.702 for BWIA and V.707 for Aer Lingus. A full list of Viscount type numbers is presented at the end of this chapter.

There were a couple of external changes made to the aircraft relatively early in its production run including replacing the external ventral intake scoop for the air conditioning system with a flush intake and some revision to the cockpit window design. All Viscounts had a three piece windscreen with a flat panel at the extreme front but the prototypes and some production aircraft had a single

The cockpit of a TAA Viscount 756D, up to the minute technology in its day.

BEA's first Viscount 701 in the airline's engineering hangar at London Heathrow. Note the Airspeed Ambassadors in the background. (Rolls-Royce)

side piece with two horizontal frames surrounding an opening section. Later aircraft had two smaller side windows (split by a vertical frame) in its place.

The first 24 production Viscounts (18 for BEA and six for Air France) were built at Weybridge but the decision was made to end production at that site due to the space being needed for the Valiant bomber. A new line was established at Hurn (Bourne-mouth) to take over Viscount production, the first aircraft from that source (V.701 G-AMOO for BEA) flying on 1 December 1953.

Necessity resulted in full production being resumed at Weybridge on a new assembly line due to the strong demand for Viscounts from operators all over the world. By the end of 1954 orders had been received for over 220 Viscounts (including the crucially important one for 60 aircraft from the USA's Capital Airlines) and a year later the total had been increased to nearly 300.

The new Weybridge line was originally intended to handle smaller orders for a handful of aircraft or less, with Hurn looking after the larger orders. After the introduction of the stretched 800 series in 1956, Weybridge took responsibility for the manufacture of most of this model with Hurn concentrating on the Vis-

The V.724 for Trans-Canada Airlines was an important subvariant, introducing numerous modifications which would become standard equipment on all Viscounts as well as introducing the aircraft to the North American market. This is CF-TGI, the airline's first Viscount.

count 700. This was the general but certainly not inflexible rule, examination of the full Viscount production list elsewhere in this publication will showing there was considerable variation on this, particularly with 700s coming out of Weybridge.

The manufacture of Viscount wings was subcontracted to Saunders-Roe and overall production peaked at about 10 per month in 1957, a record for any British airliner. Vickers could boast of having more than a "mile of production lines" in operation between its two assembly sites.

Production was finally divided thus: of the 444 Viscounts built, two (the V.630 and V.663 prototypes) emerged from Wisley, 284 from Hurn and 158 from Weybridge. The last Viscount to fly (c/n 456, a V.843 for China's CAAC) was built at Hurn and flown on 2 January 1964 while Weybridge's last was Austrian Airlines' V.837 OE-LAM c/n 442 on 22 July 1960.

The following table provides a summary of Viscount production over the years and illustrates well the buildup to the peak of 1956-58 and then the rapid decline after that. As can be seen, production was at very much a trickle over the last few years.

A Viscount 784D of Central African Airways. The V.700D series introduced the more powerful Dart 510 engine along with higher operating weights and speeds and improved payload-range performance.

VISCOUNT FIRST FLIGHTS	
1948	1
1949	0
1950	2
1951	0
1952	2
1953	22
1954	22
1955	43
1956	82
1957	111
1958	93
1959	38
1960	7
1961	9
1962	6
1963	5
1964	1

Improving The Breed

The basic Dart 506 powered Viscount evolved over the years as modifications and improvements were offered, two subvariants in particular summarising most of those changes. The first was the Viscount 720 for Trans-Australia Airlines (TAA), an initial quantity of seven of which were ordered in June 1952. Deliveries began in October 1954, making TAA the first airline outside Europe to operate the aircraft.

The V.720 was the first to incorporate additional fuel cells in the wings, increasing internal capacity from 1,720imp gal (7,819 l) to 1,950imp gal (8,865 l) and pioneered the use of the two 145imp gal (659 l) slipper tanks under the wings. TAA needed this additional fuel capacity so it could carry an economical payload on the 1,380 miles (2,220km) Adelaide-Perth sector against the prevailing substantial westerly wind.

Of even greater importance to the evolution of the Viscount was the V.724 for Trans-Canada Airlines, which, when ordering its aircraft, suggested some 250 modifications be incorporated. Some of these were the result of the nature of TCA's operations – fuselage ice guard panels for example – but many others would be of benefit to subsequent Viscount operators and become standard equipment.

The list of modifications incorporated in the 724 included the fitting of Maxaret anti skid brakes, a two crew cockpit which eliminated the radio operator, automatic propeller synchronisation, improved interior heating, a revised four tank fuel system giving each engine an individual supply (with crossfeed naturally available), a strengthened undercarriage allowing an increase in maximum weight to 60,000lb (27,216kg), improved cabin soundproofing, thicker window panels, the incorporation of automated equipment in many areas (most of it of American origin) and numerous other detail changes. The 724 was also the first variant to dispense with the ventral air conditioning intake scoop and replace it with a flush unit.

Another important change which first appeared on the Viscount 724 was the fitting of an improved wing spar design which would have a much longer life. Early Viscounts could fly only 17,000 hours before their spars' 'safe life' had expired. The modifications incorporated resulted in the new Viscount wing spar having a safe life of 30,000 hours.

Alternative seating arrangements for the Viscount 700 series. Five abreast arrangements were also possible for 53 or later up to 63 passengers.

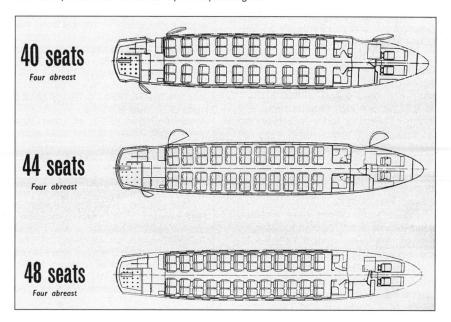

40 seats Four abreast

44 seats Four abreast

48 seats Four abreast

A Viscount 760D of Hong Kong Airways with under wing slipper fuel tanks installed.

Viscount 700D

The generic designation V.700D was given to Viscount 700 series aircraft powered by the Rolls-Royce Dart R.Da.3 Mk.510 engine producing 1,740ehp for takeoff and driving new paddle bladed propellers, the combination allowing higher cruising speeds and a further increase in maximum takeoff weight to 64,500lb (29,257kg). This in turn resulted in improved payload-range performance.

Other generic designations associated with the series were the V.770D for the North American market and the V.771D executive version. As before, each customer was allocated an individual type number for its aircraft.

The first customer for the 700D was the USA's Capital Airlines which placed a series of orders in 1954 for no fewer than 60 Viscounts, all but the first three of which were built to 'D' standards as the Viscount 745D. At the time, the Capital orders represented the biggest ever placed with a British aircraft manufacturer. Worth $US67m, the orders were of vital importance to the Viscount programme as they established the aircraft in the US market and followed on from the 'toe in the North American' door achieved when Trans Canada Airlines ordered the first of eventually 51 Viscount 700s in late 1952.

The V.745D incorporated other modifications which would subsequently be offered as standard equipment including a fuel jettison system (a mandatory US requirement), the fitting of weather radar (which added 8 inches/20cm to the nose of the aircraft), hydraulically operated forward airstairs to help speed up turnaround time and Freon airconditioning to reduce the Viscount's dependence on ground equipment.

Capital's operations often dictated the flying of short 'commuter' stages, sometimes over distances of little more than 100 miles (160km). This type of operation meant the aircraft would be completing a high ratio of operating cycles to hours flown with much of it conducted at lower than usual altitudes where the air tends to be more turbulent. This translates into extra wear and tear on the airframe and to help combat it, the new wing spar design first incorporated into TCA's V.724s was combined with much heftier lower spar booms. The result was a Viscount which could be equally at home on short hops or trunk routes of 1,500 miles (2,410km) or more.

Capital's first Viscount 745D (N7405 c/n 103) was flown from Hurn on 3 November 1955 and deliveries began immediately. The airline had taken delivery of its three standard model Viscount 744s four months earlier.

Production of the various 700 series Viscounts reached 288 aircraft comprising 138 V.700s and 150 V.700Ds. The last of them (a V.739 for Misrair) was flown on 21 March 1960.

Local Service Viscount

An interesting Viscount 700 variant which did not achieve production was the V.790, conceived as a 'local service' version mainly for the US market. Promoted in 1958, the V.790 project featured Dart 506 engines combined with the new and more efficient propellers developed for the Viscount 745D. Due to the lower altitudes at which the 790 would fly over its short stage lengths, the maximum cabin pressure differential was planned to be lower at 4.5lb/sq in instead of the standard 6.5lb/sq in.

It was intended specifically for short stages and a high number of operating cycles while remaining as independent as possible from complicated ground support backup. Airfield requirements were modest, several stages could be flown without

---

VISCOUNT 700/700D

Powerplants: *Four Rolls-Royce R.Da.3 Dart Mk.506 (V.700) each rated at 1,547ehp for takeoff or Dart Mk.510 (V.700D) each rated at 1,740ehp for takeoff. Rotol or De Havilland four bladed propellers of 10ft 0in (3.05m) diameter. Fuel capacity (early V.700) 1,720imp gal (7,819 l); later V.700/D 1,900imp (8,637 l) or 1,950imp gal (8,864 l); optional underwing slipper tanks total capacity 290imp gal (1,318 l); additional 450imp gal (2,046 l) tank in belly hold optional for executive versions.*

Dimensions: *Wing span 93ft 8.5in (28.56m); length (standard nose) 81ft 2in (24.74m), length (radar nose) 81ft 10in (24.94m); height 26ft 9in (8.15m); wing area 963sq ft (89.5m²); wheelbase 24ft 10.5in (7.58m); wheel track 23ft 10in (7.26m).*

Weights: *(V.700) Max takeoff 60,000-63,000lb (27,216-28,577kg); max landing 58,500lb (26,536kg); max zero fuel 49,000lb (22,226kg); basic empty (40 seats) 36,859lb (16,719kg); max payload 12,141lb (5,507kg).*

Weights: *(V.700D) Max takeoff 64,500lb (29,257kg); max landing 58,500lb (26,536kg); max zero fuel 50,168lb (22,756kg); basic empty (40 seats) 37,918lb (17,200kg); max payload 12,250lb (5,557kg).*

Accommodation: *40-53 passengers (later 60-63) depending on layout and seat pitch; cabin length 45ft 0in (13.71m), max width 9ft 7in (2.92m), height 6ft 6in (1.98m); baggage/freight capacity 370cu ft (10.48m³) in underfloor and rear cabin holds.*

Performance: *(V.700) Max cruise 282kt (521km/h); economical cruise 275kt (508km/h); takeoff field length 5,500ft (1,676m); initial climb 1,200ft (366m)/min; engine out climb 732ft (223m)/min; service ceiling 28,500ft (8,690m); max payload range (with reserves) 844nm (1,562km); max fuel range (40 passengers, reserves) 1,044nm ((1,931km) with 1,720imp gal fuel or 1,260nm (2,028km) with 1,950imp gal fuel.*

Performance: *(V.700D) Max cruise 290kt (537km/h); economical cruise 282kt (521km/h); takeoff field length 5,600ft (1,707m); initial climb 1,400ft (426m)/min; engine out climb 750ft (228m)/min; service ceiling 27,500ft (8,382m); max payload range (with reserves) 1,157nm (2,140km); max fuel range (43 passengers, reserves) 1,496nm (2,768km), max fuel range (slipper tanks, reserves) 1,627nm (3,010km), max fuel range (slipper and belly tanks, reserves) 2,131nm (3,943km).*

Viscount 700 production: *138 V.700, 150 V.700D, total 288.*

refuelling or any maintenance, airstair doors were fitted and a high density 65 passenger interior was proposed.

Despite an active marketing campaign and the promise of seat-mile costs ten per cent lower than the Douglas DC-3, operators decided to stick with piston engined airliners on short routes and no Viscount 790s were sold. It wasn't until the twin turboprop Fokker F27 and Hawker Siddeley HS.748 came along that turbine aircraft started to move into the 790's intended market.

V.800 VISCOUNT

Investigations into an enlarged Viscount began in early 1952 when Rolls-Royce announced the uprated R.Da.5 family of Dart engines which promised 1,690ehp for takeoff. Development began under the Type 800 designation, initial investigations being carried out around a fuselage stretch of 13ft 3in (4.04m) compared with the Viscount 700 providing accommodation for up to 86 passengers in a high density configuration. Maximum takeoff weight was 65,000lb (29,484kg).

This design involved numerous compromises, the most serious of which were a decrease in the estimated cruising speed to below 300mph (483km/h) and substantial reductions in payload-range perform-

G-AOJC, BEA's third Viscount 802, delivered in January 1957. This first stretched variant offered increased seating capacity and lower seat-mile operating costs at the expense of range.

THE VISCOUNT'S DARTS

Dart Type	Max T-O	Max Cont	Cruise	Application
R.Da.1 Mk.502	1380ehp	–	–	V.630
R.Da.3 Mk.505	1547ehp	1190ehp	890ehp	V.700
R.Da.3 Mk.506	1547ehp	1190ehp	955ehp	V.700
R.Da.6 Mk.510	1740ehp	1435ehp	1025ehp	V.700D, V.802-805
R.Da.7 Mk.520	1890ehp	1655ehp	1145ehp	V.806-808
R.Da.7 Mk.525	1990ehp	1745ehp	1325ehp	V.810
R.Da.7 Mk.530	2030ehp	1745ehp	1325ehp	V.833 only

Note: Mks.520, 525 and 530 derated by approximately 100shp.

A New Zealand NAC Viscount 807 showing the rectangular passenger doors fitted to all V.800/810 models. This is ZK-BRE and the photograph was taken at Wellington in December 1973. (Michael Maton)

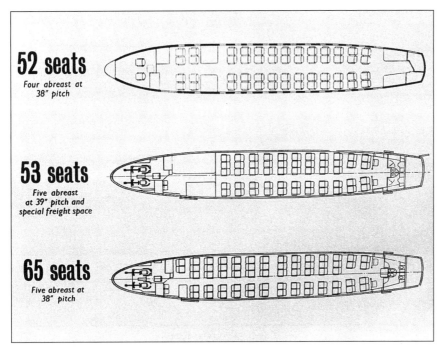

52 seats
Four abreast at 38" pitch

53 seats
Five abreast at 39" pitch and special freight space

65 seats
Five abreast at 38" pitch

Some of the seating arrangements available for the Viscount 800/810.

ance. Despite this, British European Airways saw the new Viscount as being ideal for its short range services where traffic was heavy – notably on trunk routes to some western European centres such as Paris and Amsterdam – and in February 1953 ordered 12 aircraft under the designation Viscount V.801.

Further studies by both the manufacturer and customer over the next year resulted in considerable revision of this initial Viscount 800 design. It was decided that it had too much capacity for projected traffic requirements and the anticipated performance penalties were too severe.

A new, smaller Viscount 800 therefore emerged, featuring the 1,740ehp Dart 510 which would shortly appear on the Viscount 700D in combination with that model's 64,500lb (29,257kg)

maximum weight and a fuselage stretched by only 3ft 10in (1.17) forward of the wings. Inside, the cabin was lengthened by 9ft 3in (2.82m) thanks to the rear pressure bulkhead being moved aft. The V.800's higher empty weight and similar maximum weight to the V.700D meant there were compromises in payload-range performance but on the shortish routes BEA had in mind for it this was compensated for by its lower seat-mile operating costs.

The result was a Viscount capable of carrying between 52 and 65 passengers depending on the layout and seat pitch, although up to 71 could be accommodated in a high density layout. The cabin interior was modernised and an extra four inches (10cm) width was found thanks to some resculpturing of the sidewalls.

Other changes incorporated in the Viscount 800 included replacing the original oval passenger entry doors with rectangular ones which lay flat against the fuselage when opened, thus eliminating the difficulties experienced with the 700's doors when they were opened in a strong wind.

The forward cabin door was made larger than necessary so it could double as a freight door, providing an early example of what would now be called a QC (quick change) configuration. With an eye on the aircraft's ability to carry a mixed freight/passenger load if necessary, the 800's floor was made 50 per cent stronger than before. When BEA ordered this revised Viscount 800 it specified seats which could be folded against the cabin walls so the aircraft could be quickly turned into a freighter.

BEA changed its original order for the V.801 to the new variant – dubbed V.802 – in April 1954, ordering 12 and taking up options on 10 more. These options were converted to firm orders in 1955 and two more were later added to the tally, bringing the number up to 24. Other airlines to order this first version of the Viscount 800 were KLM (V.803), Transair/British United (V.804) and Eagle Aviation (V.805).

There was no prototype Viscount 802 as such, the first aircraft (G-AOJA) also being the first for BEA. It was flown 29 September 1956 and deliveries to BEA began in January 1957, immediately after certification was awarded. Services (initially London-Paris) began in February.

Viscount 806

The Viscount 806 was an subvariant of the basic V.800, developed to take advantage of the extra power provided by a new series of Dart engines, the R.Da.7. Featuring three

Aer Lingus Viscount 808 EI-AKO (formerly EI-AKJ). The Irish national airline operated 21 Viscounts over the years and was an early customer.

Close up of the engine installation, main undercarriage and slipper tanks on G-AOYF, Vickers' demonstrator Viscount 806. This aircraft first flew in August 1957 but was written off just two months later. The 806 was the first to use the R.Da.7 Dart.

turbine stages instead of two, the R.Da.7 promised over 2,000ehp, although in its initial Mark 520 form as fitted to the Viscount 806 it produced 1,890ehp for takeoff, derated slightly to maintain performance in higher temperatures.

As such, the 806 was a stepping stone between the 802-805 and the definitive 810 which would shortly follow. It retained the operating weights of the earlier 800 series Viscounts but the more powerful Darts resulted in a faster cruising speed and improved climb and takeoff performance.

BEA ordered 19 Viscount 806s in January 1956 and other operators were New Zealand National Airways Corporation (V.807) and Aer Lingus (V.808), a total of 29 aircraft out of the overall V.800 production tally of 86.

The first V.806 (G-AOYF) was flown on 9 August 1957 in Vickers house livery and carrying the legend 'Viscount 806-810' on the fuselage, the intention being for it to be used in the certification programme for the latter. Unfortunately, G-AOYF had a short life and was damaged beyond repair after a heavy landing, undercarriage collapse and quickly extinguished fire sustained during a simulated emergency landing demonstration at Johannesburg in October 1957. Components from the damaged aircraft were subsequently used in the construction of V.806 G-APOX (c/n 418) which in April 1959 became the last Viscount delivered to British European Airways.

VISCOUNT 802

Powerplants: *Four Rolls-Royce Dart R.Da.3 Mk.510 turboprops each rated at 1,740ehp for takeoff. Four bladed Rotol or De Havilland propellers of 10ft 0in (3.05m) diameter. Fuel capacity 1,940imp gal (8,819 l).*

Dimensions: *Wing span 93ft 8.5in (28.56m); length (standard nose) 85ft 0in (25.91m), (radar nose) 85ft 8in (26.11m); height 26ft 9in (8.15m); wing area 963sq ft (89.5m²); wheelbase 28ft 8.5in (8.75m).*

Weights: *Max takeoff 64,500lb (29,257kg); max landing 58,500lb (26,536kg); max zero fuel 55,000lb (24,948kg); basic empty 41,200lb (18,688kg); max payload 13,700lb (6,214kg).*

Accommodation: *52-71 passengers; baggage/freight capacity 370cu ft (10.48m³); cabin length 54ft 0in (16.46m), width 9ft 11in (3.02m); height 6ft 6in (1.98m).*

Performance: *Max cruise 283kt (523km/h); economical cruise 270kt (499km/h); takeoff field length 5,450ft (1,661m); initial climb 1,220ft (372m)/min; engine out climb 680ft (207m)/min; service ceiling 27,000ft (8,230m); max payload range (with reserves) 600nm (1,110km); max fuel range (43 passengers, reserves) 1,165nm (2,156km).*

V.806 supplementary data: *Four 1,890ehp Dart 520; max cruise 291kt (539km/h); econ cruise 283kt (523km/h); initial climb 1,400ft (427m)/min.*

Viscount 800 production: *68.*

V.810 VISCOUNT

The final expression of the Viscount's development to achieve production, the V.810 was built for customers who wanted the increased passenger capacity of the V.800 series without the compromises in payload-range performance and at higher speeds. The Viscount 800 had been only modestly successful and the 810 represented the logical next step – combining the V.800's stretched fuselage with the more powerful R.Da.7 Dart and higher operating weights.

The Viscount 800's maximum takeoff weight had been the same as the smaller 700D but on the 810 as originally proposed this was increased by 3,000lb (1,361kg) to 67,500lb (30,618kg). By the time the Viscount 810 entered service it had increased again to 69,000lb (31,298kg) and subsequently to 72,500lb (32,886kg).

Some beefing up of the structure was required to cater for the higher weights: the wing rib, spar structures, fin and rear fuselage were strengthened, and the engine mountings and nacelles were also made stronger to cope with the more powerful engines.

Power was provided by Dart Mk.525s rated at 1,990ehp for takeoff and derated by about 110ehp. This was the standard Viscount 810 powerplant, the only exceptions being a trio of V.833s built for Hunting Clan in 1959. These aircraft were fitted with Dart 530s which were similar

The V.810 became the major Viscount production variant from 1958, although the last V.700 was not flown until early 1960. The last Viscount to fly (and the 86th V.810) was a V.843 for China's CAAC on 2 January 1964.

The USA's Continental Airlines was the launch customer for the definitive Viscount 810, which combined the 800's increased passenger capacity with more powerful engines and higher operating weights. Continental ordered 15 V.812 Viscounts with deliveries beginning in May 1958.

but developed slightly more (2,030ehp) maximum power.

More efficient '160 activity' propellers were fitted to take full advantage of the extra power, resulting in improved takeoff and climb performance along with faster cruising speeds. The Viscount 810's 365mph (587km/h) maximum cruising speed was 30mph (48km/h) higher than the V.700D and V.806 and was the fastest of the series. As before, water-methanol injection was available to restore power in hot and high conditions, although without it, maximum power was available up to 21deg C (70deg F).

Other modifications introduced to the V.810 included a slightly narrower front passenger door (still of the rectangular type introduced on the 800), rudder power was enhanced by allowing greater deflection angles and

the braking system was made more effective.

The first Viscount 810 (G-AOYV c/n 316) was retained by Vickers for development and demonstration flying and recorded its maiden flight on 23 December 1957. The loss of the first V.806 in South Africa two months earlier caused some minor delays in the certification process but this was quickly achieved without problems. A US FAA Type Certificate was awarded in April 1958, allowing the launch customer, Continental Airlines, to begin services in late May, initially between Chicago and Los Angeles.

Continental had ordered 15 aircraft (as the V.812) as early as December 1955 and other customers quickly followed. Among them were major operators such as South African Airways, Lufthansa, Trans-Australia Airlines and All Nippon Airways.

VISCOUNT 810

Powerplants: *Four Rolls-Royce Dart R.Da.7 Mk.525 turboprops each rated at 1,990ehp for takeoff. Four bladed Rotol or De Havilland propellers of 10ft 0in (3.05m) diameter. Fuel capacity 1,900imp gal (8,637 l), provision for two 145imp gal (659 l) or 250imp gal (1,135 l) underwing slipper tanks.*

Dimensions: *Wing span 93ft 8.5in (28.56m); length (radar nose) 85ft 8in (26.11m); height 26ft 9in (8.15m); wing area 963sq ft (89.5m²); wheelbase 28t 8.5in (8.75m); wheel track 23ft 10in (7.26m).*

Weights: *Max takeoff 72,500lb (32,886kg); max landing 64,000lb (29,030kg); max zero fuel 57,500lb (26,082kg); basic empty 43,200lb (19,596kg); max payload 14,300lb (6,486kg).*

Accommodation: *52-71 passengers; baggage/freight capacity 370cu ft (10.48m³); cabin length 54ft 0in (16.46m), width 9ft 11in (3.02m), height 6ft 6in (1.98m).*

Performance: *Max cruise 318kt (587km/h); economical cruise 305kt (565km/h); takeoff field length 6,100ft (1,860m); initial climb 1,650ft (503m)/min; engine out climb 770ft (235m)/min; service ceiling 27,000ft (8,230m); max payload range (with reserves) 1,110nm (2,052km); range with max fuel (70 passengers, reserves) 1,175nm (2,172km); range with slipper tanks (50 passengers, reserves) 1,523nm (2,816km).*

Viscount 810 production: *86*

Nice portrait of Ansett-ANA's Viscount 832 VH-RMG, delivered in March 1959.

SUMMARY OF VISCOUNT VARIANTS AND ORDERS

Model	Customer	Date	No	Dart	Notes
V.453	–	–	–	–	initial design studies
V.609	–	–	–	–	Viceroy project, Mamba engines
V.630	Ministry of Supply	03/46	1	502	ff 16/07/48 c/n 1
V.640	–	–	–	–	Napier Naiad engines, project
V.652	–	–	–	–	2 x Hercules engines, project
V.653	–	–	–	–	stretched project with Darts
V.663	Ministry of Supply	03/46	1	–	2 x Tay, ff 15/03/50 c/n 2
V.700	Ministry of Supply	11/48	1	505	ff 28/08/50 c/n 3
V.701	BEA	08/50	20	505	40-47 pax, later Dart 506, airstairs
V.701	BEA	–	7	506	60-63 pax from 1960, airstairs
V.702	BWIA	06/53	4	506	44-53 pax, increased fuel
V.703	BEA	–	–	–	53 pax project
V.707	Aer Lingus	11/51	4	505	53 pax, later Dart 506
V.708	Air France	11/51	12	505	49 pax, later Dart 506
V.720	TAA	06/52	7	506	44 pax, slipper tanks
V.721	Aust National A/W	–	–	506	project only
V.723	Indian Air Force	11/53	1	506	VIP interior
V.724	TCA	11/52	15	506	44-48 pax, anti skid brakes, fuselage ice guard panels, two crew cockpit
V.728	Cyprus Airways	–	–	506	project only
V.730	Indian Air Force	11/53	1	506	same as V.723 except interior
V.731	KLM	–	–	506	project only
V.732	Hunting Clan	05/53	3	506	52 pax, slipper tanks, square tipped props
V.734	Pakistan Air Force	03/55	1	506	VIP interior, slipper tanks
V.735	Iraqi Airways	07/53	3	506	44-53 pax
V.736	Fred Olsen	01/54	2	506	48 pax
V.737	Canada Dept of Int	04/54	1	506	VIP interior
V.739	Misrair	03/54	6	506	40 pax
V.740	RAF Queen's Flight	–	–	506	staff transport, project only
V.741	RAF Queen's Flight	–	–	506	VIP interior, project only
V.742D	Braathens-SAFE	09/54	1	510	del to Brazilian AF, VIP
V.744	Capital Airlines	06/54	3	506	48 pax
V.745D	Capital Airlines	08/54	37	510	48 pax, first 9 with Dart 506, airstairs
V.745D	Capital Airlines	12/54	20	510	48 pax, airstairs
V.746	East African A/W	–	–	506	project only
V.747	Butler Air T'port	06/54	2	506	40 pax
V.748D	Central African AW	07/54	5	510	47-59 pax, slipper tanks
V.749	LAV	05/54	3	506	40 pax
V.754D	Middle East A/W	06/55	6	510	44-48 pax
V.755D	Airwork	12/55	3	510	del to Cubana, 48 pax
V.756D	TAA	04/55	7	510	44 pax, slipper tanks
V.757	TCA	08/54	36	506	44-48 pax, anti skid brakes, fuselage ice guard panels
V.759D	Hunting Clan	11/54	2	510	53 pax, slipper tanks
V.760D	Hong Kong Airways	10/54	2	510	40-44 pax, slipper tanks
V.761D	Union of Burma A/W	05/55	3	510	48 pax
V.763D	Howard Hughes	06/55	1	510	del to TACA, 48 pax
V.764D	US Steel Corp	06/55	3	510	VIP interior, slipper and belly tanks, airstairs
V.765D	Standard Oil Corp	06/55	1	510	similar to V.764D
V.766	Fred Olsen	–	–	510	built as V.779D
V.767	BOAC	–	–	–	project only
V.768D	Indian Airlines	07/55	10	510	44 pax
V.769D	PLUNA	09/56	3	510	48 pax, slipper tanks
V.770D	–	–	–	510	generic designation of V.700D for North American market
V.771D	–	–	–	510	executive version of V.770D
V.772	BWIA	06/55	4	506	48 pax
V.773	Iraqi Airways	03/56	1	506	48 pax
V.776D	Kuwait Oil Co	08/58	1	510	built as V.745D, converted
V.779D	Fred Olsen	06/55	4	510	48 pax
V.780D	–	–	–	510	V.700D in VIP configuration
V.781D	South African A F	03/56	1	510	VIP interior, slipper tanks
V.782D	Iranian Airlines	03/56	3	510	48 pax convertible to VIP
V.784D	PAL	04/56	3	510	48 pax, slipper tanks
V.785D	LAI (Alitalia)	05/56	10	510	48 pax
V.786D	Lloyd Aereo C'bia	09/56	3	510	48 pax, slipper and belly tanks
V.789D	Brazilian AF	09/56	1	510	VIP interior, slipper and belly tanks
V.790	–	–	–	506	project, local service variant
V.793D	Royal Bank Canada	/58	1	510	built as V.745D, VIP interior
V.794D	Turk Hava Yollari	07/57	4	510	48 pax
V.795	TWA	–	–	506	project only
V.797D	Canadian DoT	/57	1	510	built as V.745D and converted
V.798D	Northeast Airlines	07/57	10	510	48 pax
V.800	–	–	–	510	generic designation
V.801	BEA	–	–	510	revised as V.802
V.802	BEA	04/54	24	510	53-57 pax, later 66-71 pax
V.803	KLM	06/55	9	510	53 pax, later 66-71 pax
V.804	Transair (BUA)	06/55	4	510	65 pax
V.805	Eagle Aviation	05/57	2	510	70 seats
V.806	BEA	01/56	19	520	58 pax, later 66-71 pax
V.807	New Zealand NAC	11/55	4	520	60 pax
V.808	Aer Lingus	03/56	6	520	70 pax
V.810	Vickers	–	1	525	prototype c/n 316, ff 23/12/57
V.812	Continental	12/55	15	525	56 pax, airstairs
V.813	SAA	03/56	7	525	56 pax, later 66 pax
V.814	Lufthansa	05/56	11	525	64 pax
V.815	PIA	05/56	5	525	51 pax
V.816	TAA	01/59	2	525	56 pax
V.818	Cubana	06/56	4	525	52 pax
V.819	Niarchos	–	–	525	not built, order cancelled
V.821	Eagle Aviation	–	–	525	not built, order cancelled
V.823	California Eastern	–	–	525	not built, order cancelled
V.825	Black Lion Avn	–	–	525	not built, order cancelled
V.827	VASP	05/57	6	525	56 pax
V.828	All Nippon Airways	04/60	9	525	60 pax, TV monitors in cabin
V.829	TAP	–	–	525	not built, order unconfirmed
V.831	Airwork	04/58	3	525	60 pax, slipper tanks
V.832	Ansett-ANA	05/58	4	525	56 pax
V.833	Hunting Clan	05/58	3	530	60 pax, later 80 pax
V.834	LOT	–	–	525	project only
V.835	Tennessee Gas	/59	1	525	converted from V.818, VIP
V.836	Union Carbide	09/59	1	525	converted from V.816, VIP
V.837	Austrian Airlines	02/60	6	525	60 or 70 pax
V.838	Ghana Airways	04/60	3	525	60 pax
V.839	Iranian Government	02/60	1	525	converted from V.816, VIP
V.840	–	–	–	541	project for '400mph Viscount'
V.842	Iraqi Airways	–	–	541	lapsed with V.840 project
V.843	CAAC	12/61	6	525	last Viscount order, 52 pax
V.844	Govt of Liberia	–	–	541	lapsed with V.840 project
V.850	–	–	–	–	Viscount Major project, R.Da.8 Darts, stretched

Notes: The 'date' column reflects the date on which orders were placed and applies to the initial order only; subsequent reorder dates (where appropriate) are not noted. The 'No' (number) column includes any reorders. The exceptions to these comments occur in the Capital Airlines listings.

THE 400mph VISCOUNT

Of the several Viscount 810 projects which failed to develop beyond the drawing board, the V.840 perhaps came closest to reality. First promoted in 1958, the Viscount 840 combined the 810's airframe and operating weights with four Dart R.Da.11 Mk.541 engines heavily derated to produce 2,350ehp for takeoff. The result was promoted as the '400mph Viscount', indicative of the V.840's maximum cruising speed.

Vickers proposed both building new 840s and converting existing 810s to the new configuration as the unmodified airframe was already more than capable of handling the extra power and higher speeds. Other performance figures published for the 840 included a nine per cent reduction in the amount of runway required for takeoff. Range figures were similar to the 810.

There was some airline interest in the Viscount 840, BEA taking an op-

tion on 12 and Iraqi Airways and the Government of Liberia also reserving delivery positions. In the event, none were built new and none were converted from existing aircraft.

Other 'paper' Viscounts included the V.850 Viscount Major with a stretched fuselage and R.Da.8 Darts and the V.870, a larger and completely new design which was part of the evolutionary process which led to the V.950 Vanguard.

The first of Lufthansa's 10 Viscount 814s (D-ANUN) during a test flight over England in September 1958.

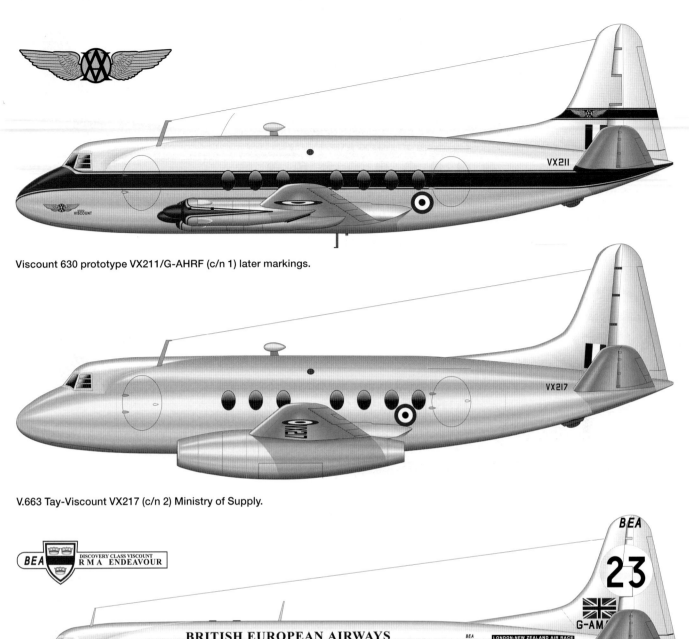

Viscount 630 prototype VX211/G-AHRF (c/n 1) later markings.

V.663 Tay-Viscount VX217 (c/n 2) Ministry of Supply.

Viscount 700 prototype G-AMAV 'RMA Endeavour' (c/n 3) London-New Zealand Air Race colours October 1953.

Viscount 701 G-ALWF (c/n 5) Cambrian Airways 1966-71. Ex BEA, Channel Airways.

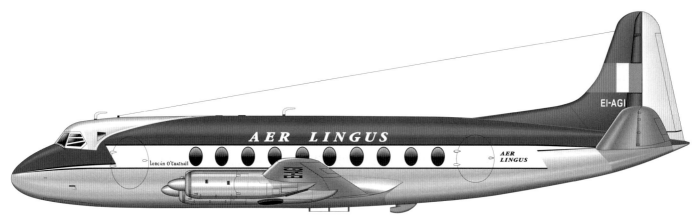

Viscount 707 EI-AGI 'St Lorcan O'Tauthail' (c/n 34) Aer Lingus 1954-60.

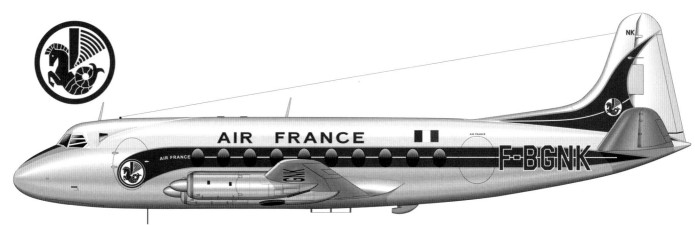

Viscount 708 F-BGNK (c/n 8), first for Air France delivered May 1953.

Viscount 724 CF-TGI (c/n 40), first for Trans-Canada Airlines delivered December 1954.

Viscount 724 CF-TGI, same aircraft as above, leased to Trans Air by TCA 1963-64.

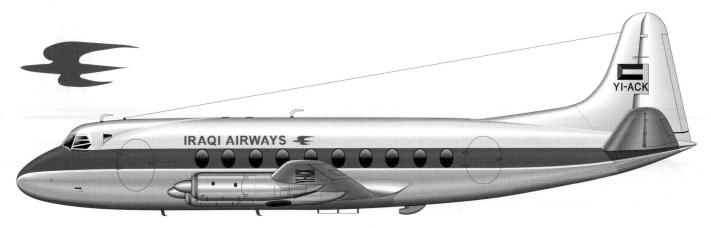

Viscount 735 YI-ACK (c/n 67) first for Iraqi Airways delivered October 1955.

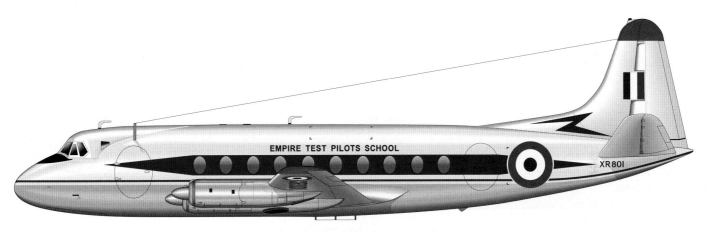

Viscount 744 XR801 (c/n 89) Empire Test Pilots School 1962-71. Ex Capital Airlines N7403.

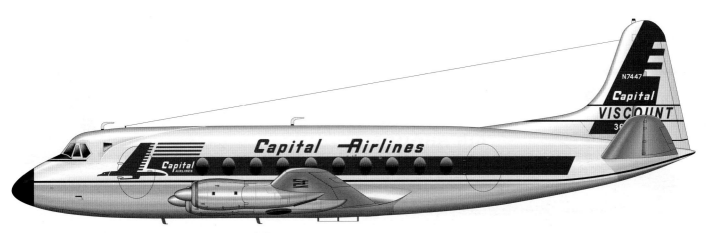

Viscount 745D N7447 (c/n 203) Capital Airlines 1956-61.

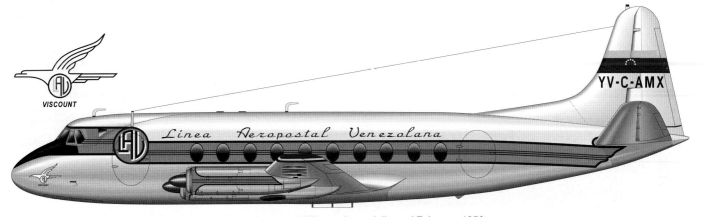

Viscount 749D YV-C-AMX (c/n 94) first for Linea Aeropostal Venezolana, delivered February 1956.

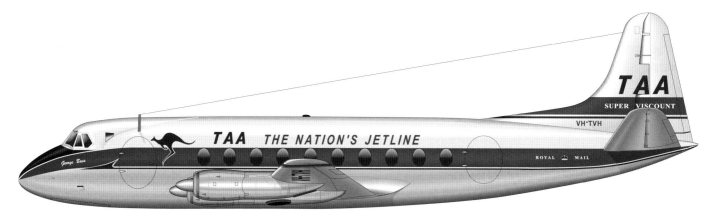

Viscount 756D VH-TVH 'George Bass' (c/n 146) Trans Australia Airlines 1956-70.

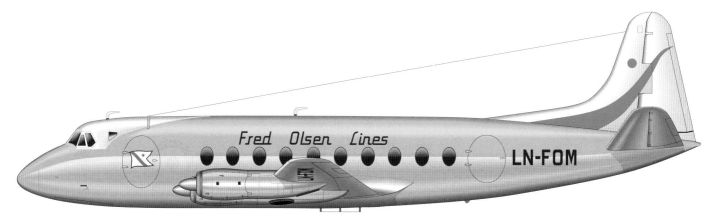

Viscount 779D LN-FOM (c/n 247), markings at time of delivery to Fred Olsen Flyselskap April 1957.

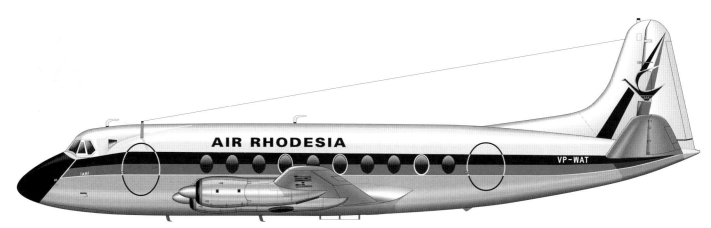

Viscount 782D VP-WAT (c/n 298) Central African Airways/Air Rhodesia. Purchased 1966 from Iranian Airlines.

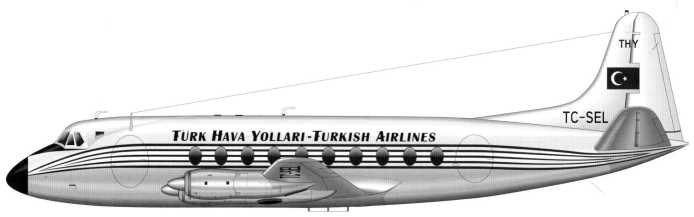

Viscount 794D TC-SEL (c/n 430) Turk Hava Yollari – Turkish Airlines 1958-71.

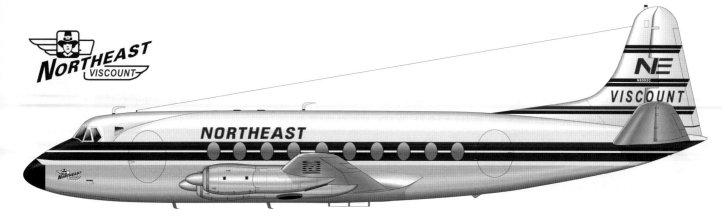

Viscount 798D N6592C (c/n 234) Northeast Airlines (USA) 1958-61.

Viscount 806 G-AOYJ (c/n 259) British Airways 1974-81, ex British European Airways.

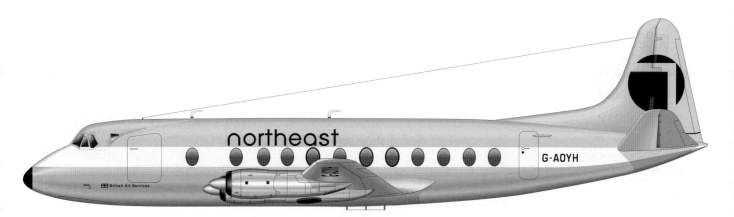

Viscount 806 G-AOYH (c/n 311) Northeast Airlines (UK) 1970-74, ex BEA.

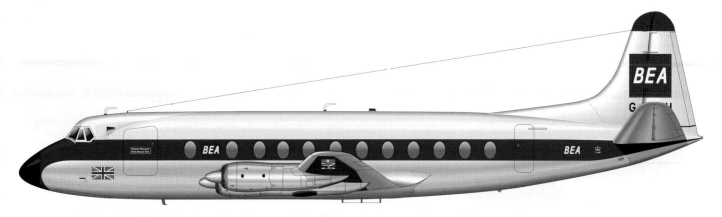

Viscount 802 G-AOHH 'Sir Robert McClure' (c/n 157) British European Airways 1957-74. Markings circa 1969.

Viscount 815 G-AVJB (c/n 375) delivered British Air Ferries 1981. Ex Pakistan International, Luxair, British Midland, Nigeria Airways, British Airways, Jersey European.

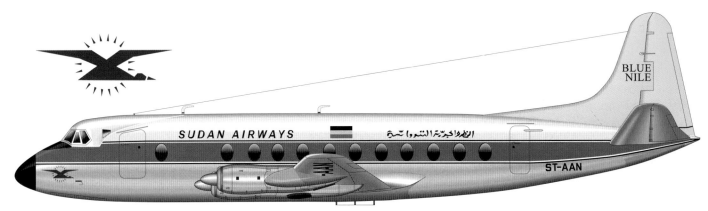

Viscount 831 ST-AAN (c/n 419) Sudan Airways leased from Airwork 1959-62.

Viscount 832 VH-RMI (c/n 416) Ansett-ANA 1959-66.

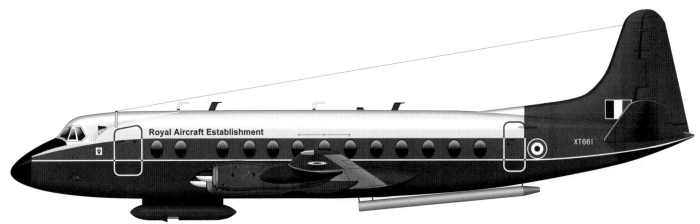

Viscount 838 XT661 (c/n 371) Royal Aircraft Establishment Farnborough, delivered 1965, used for radar calibration and testing. Ex Ghana Airways.

VISCOUNT IN SERVICE

The Viscount Revolution

More than four decades after the Viscount first entered service, the memory has faded a little and its easy to forget the impact the world's first turboprop airliner made on its operators and passengers during its early days of service. The aircraft received 'rave reviews' by all and sundry, the likes of which are rarely if ever heard today if only because of the modern familiarity of air travel. To the average traveller, one airliner seems much like any other.

Vickers' promotional literature naturally played up the Viscount's passenger appeal, promoting its smoothness with gimmicks such as claiming it was possible to balance pencils on their ends and coins on their edges while in flight. Illustrations 'proving' these facts were commonplace, but anyone reading this who has flown in a Viscount has ever actually been able to perform these feats, the writer would love to know! Gimmicks aside, the Viscount *did* offer passengers smooth and (relatively) vibration free flight which could not be matched by piston engined airliners.

More seriously, Vickers also made extensive use of positive quotes from airline executives, pilots, passengers and the press in its promotional material for the Viscount and it's worth repeating some of them to help paint the picture of enthusiasm for the airliner in its early years of operation. Some of the following quotes clearly indicate the extent of the revolution created by the Viscount, both in the operational and passenger acceptance senses.

"During the last four months of 1955 since the Viscounts completely replaced piston aircraft on the New York routes, our passenger traffic has increased by 67 per cent." – D V Richardson, TCA District Manager.

"The Viscounts gave a definite fillip to traffic. Without them the Aer Lingus return would have been considerably less favourable, and Ireland's competitive position might have been jeopardised." – J F Dempsey, Aer Lingus GM.

"The Viscount has met or exceeded every contract guarantee – the aircraft has caused less trouble than any new type of aircraft." – J T Dyment, TCA Director of Engineering.

"Experience has shown that when Viscounts are introduced, traffic automatically rises by 25 to 30 per cent." – Air France official statement.

"You can converse in conversational tones anywhere in the cabin. You put a finger on the big oval window of the Viscount and can barely feel a ripple." – New York Journal American.

"Popular acceptance of the Viscount has increased its percentage of seats sold to the highest point in the country's history." – NY World Telegram & Sun.

"The sleek silver and red Viscount was photographed more often than Niagara Falls on a holiday weekend." – Toronto Telegram

"We can say 'well done' to a friendly competitor and be thankful that the genius which produced this fine airplane is on our side in democracy's struggle." – Memphis Press-Scimitar.

"The Viscount alters all one's current ideas of flying – it was like riding in electric after steam." – Sydney Sun.

"The Viscount load factor of 86.5 per cent for the year was amazingly high and easily the best figure ever recorded for any aircraft operating Australian domestic routes. The best salesmen for Viscounts are ordinary passengers who describe the virtues of propeller turbine flight to their friends." – J Borthwick, Commercial Director Trans-Australia Airlines.

It is impossible to describe the operations of all Viscount operators in the space available, so in order to paint a general picture of the airliner's service life – concentrating on the impact it had in the early days – we'll examine several specific operators instead. A table listing the vast majority of Viscount operators over the years accompanies the text.

BEA

As the first and eventually most numerous operator of the Viscount, British European Airways was obviously also a vitally important customer in the sense that many future sales depended on BEA's success or otherwise with the type.

BEA took delivery of its first Viscount 701 in January 1953 and the world's first regular turboprop service was flown on 18 April of the same year, between London and Cyprus via Rome and Athens. A London to Istanbul service was introduced the following day. It's interesting to note that BEA decided to put its new aircraft into service initially on two of its longest routes, rather than at first concentrating on services which

I-LIZT, one of 10 Viscount 785Ds Alitalia ordered in 1956.

Air Rhodesia/Air Zimbabwe operated 11 Viscounts between 1968 and 1971, this one (VP-WAT) an ex Iranian Airlines V.782D.

didn't radiate quite so far out from London.

BEA's full fleet of 20 Viscount 701s had been delivered by mid 1955, by which time the route network had built up to include Oslo, Stockholm, Copenhagen, Dusseldorf, Paris, Geneva, Zurich, Milan, Vienna, Amsterdam, Lisbon, Madrid, Palma, Gibraltar, Rome, Athens, Istanbul, Cyprus and Beirut. Within the United Kingdom, BEA put its Viscounts to work on services to Belfast, Glasgow, Edinburgh, Birmingham and Manchester. The 20 Viscounts were usually scheduled thus: 14 on services, four in maintenance and two on standby.

BEA Viscounts held official and unofficial speed records on just about every European route, several of them recording average speeds as high as 360mph (579km/h) presumably with the help of substantial tailwinds. That speed was even achieved on the very short 151 miles (242km) hop between London and Manchester.

BEA's Viscounts achieved some impressive operating statistics during their first two-and-a-half years in operation with BEA. Utilisation reached 8.5 hours per day during the peak summer months; the breakeven load factor to cover direct costs on all Viscount services (including the high cost internal routes) was only 31.1% or 15 passengers assuming the normal 47 seat layout; BEA recorded its first ever net profit £52,000 in 1955 and the Viscount was given much of the credit for this; in 1956 the airline's net profit increased nearly tenfold to £500,000; between April 1953 and December 1955, with an average effective fleet for the period of 16.3 aircraft, BEA's Viscounts made a net profit of over £2.25m.

The Viscount Jump

As BEA was the first operator of the Viscount, it was on its services that the phenomenon known as the 'Viscount jump' – a steep rise in passenger traffic – was first observed. Prior to the introduction of the Viscount, BEA was carrying less than one-third of the total traffic on Scandinavia/Britain services. Five months after the introduction of the Viscount the airline's share jumped to more than 50 per cent. In the 12 months period to March 1954, BEA's Swiss traffic went up by 68 per cent, Scandinavian by 58 per cent, Iberian by 49 per cent and Mediterranean by 41 per cent. During the winter in which BEA Viscounts first operated to Scandinavia (1953-54), the airline's traffic increased by a remarkable 110 per cent. Most important is the fact that these increases were sustained – traffic didn't begin to drop off after the 'novelty' factor of the Viscount had begun to wane.

Viscounts Everywhere

The Viscount remained BEA's front line 'workhorse' through the 1950s, its influence starting to diminish only later in the decade and early 1960s when larger capacity aircraft with longer ranges were needed on some of the major trunk routes into Europe. This need was filled by the Comet 4B and the Vickers Vanguard, the latter accommodating well over 100 passengers in what was an early attempt to create an 'airbus' concept with low seat-mile operating costs and therefore lower fares.

BEA in the meantime began taking delivery of larger Viscount 800s in early 1957, the airline's total Viscount fleet eventually exceeding 70 aircraft, including a few leased in from time to time. At their peak, BEA Viscounts served 53 destinations throughout Europe, the UK, Scandinavia and the Middle East. With the introduction of Comets and Vanguards they were more often used on domestic and 'thin' European services.

Most of the Viscount 701s were disposed of in 1963, leaving a substantial fleet of 800s in service with BEA until the early 1970s when some of these were also sold. The remainder served mainly with the airline's Scottish and Channel Islands Divi-

G-AOYK, a BEA Viscount 806 pictured here at the start of its lease to Cyprus Airways in October 1965. (via Philip J Birtles)

The former BEA Viscount 802s and 806s appeared in the livery of numerous operators after they were sold from the early 1970s. This V.806 (G-AOYG) flew with Cambrian Airways, Alidair, British Airways and British Air Ferries before being leased to Virgin Atlantic in 1987-88. (Rob Finlayson)

British European Airways' Viscount 701 G-AMNY was third production aircraft delivered in February 1953. (via Philip J Birtles)

After leaving mainline service, BEA's remaining Viscounts flew with its Scottish and Channel Islands divisions. This is V.802 G-AOJB. (Philip J Birtles)

A view of BEA's Engineering Base at London Heathrow in the 1950s with Viscount 701s predominant. The airline operated more than 70 Viscounts over a period of 31 years including with British Airways.

sion. With the amalgamation of BEA and BOAC into British Airways in 1973, some 37 Viscounts were still in the fleet. The last was finally retired in 1984, ending more than 30 years' service with the British national carrier.

AIR FRANCE

Air France was the second airline to order Viscounts, placing a contract for 12 V.708s in November 1951 and starting services in September 1953. It has been suggested that Air France bought Viscounts only because it feared the threat posed by BEA and its aircraft. Even if this is the case, the Air France board was obviously smart enough to realise the Viscount's potential and like most other operators, immediately found it had a winner on its hands.

Like BEA, Air France quickly started to gain substantial benefits from the Viscount in terms of traffic figures. Initial services were on the Paris-Milan-Rome-Athens-Istanbul route which had been averaging load factors of a modest 52 per cent. The first year of Viscount operations saw this jump to 67 per cent and in 1955 it was 74 per cent. A more accurate assessment of the Viscount's early impact on Air France operations is provided by the increase in tonnes-kilometres of 12 per cent recorded on that route.

In November 1954, Air France switched the whole of its European network to Viscount operations, the passenger response causing the airline to state that: "when Viscounts are introduced, traffic almost automatically increased by 25 to 30 per cent" – another example of the 'Viscount jump'.

In the first six months of 1955 the total traffic on the Paris-London route increased by 14 per cent, and of that new traffic Air France's Viscounts could claim three-quarters. Interestingly, at that stage BEA did not use Viscounts on this service. The average number of passenger carried per trip on the Paris-London service had previously been 29.3 (using Douglas DC-4s), rising to 36.5 in the last two months of 1954 with the Viscount and to 40 passengers in the whole of 1955 and despite increased frequencies.

Other Air France routes onto which Viscounts were introduced showed equal and sometimes greater improvements, particularly on services to Geneva and Zurich where traffic increased by nearly half between 1954 and 1955.

By April 1958 Air France's Viscounts had flown some 36,000 hours and the average passenger load factor was 80 per cent over the entire network which stretched from Paris to London, Geneva, Milan, Nice, Rome, Barcelona, Madrid, Athens, Istanbul, Zurich, Munich, Vienna, Dusseldorf, Hamburg, Copenhagen and Stockholm.

Despite this success, the Viscount had a brief career in Air France colours as the locally designed and built Caravelle jet began to enter service in 1959. Viscount operations continued until 1963 when the last of them was sold.

AER LINGUS

The airline of the Irish Republic ordered four Viscount 707s in November 1951, receiving them in March and April 1954 and starting services from Dublin to London, Paris, and Amsterdam (via Manchester) immediately. Aer Lingus went on to become a major Viscount operator, taking delivery of six new V.808s in 1957-59 as well as acquiring second hand V.803s from KLM in 1966 (the Dutch opera-

Air France's fourth Viscount 708, the newly delivered F-BGNN, embarks a load of passengers at a wet Heathrow in December 1953. (via Philip J Birtles)

F-BGNM, Air France's third Viscount 708, delivered in September 1953. (Air France)

tor's entire fleet) and other used V.800s from other sources. This brought the airline's total to 21 aircraft, operated until 1970 when they were replaced by BAC One Elevens and Boeing 737s.

Aer Lingus was the source of a genuine 'quick change' (QC) Viscount variant during the 1960s when several V.808s were converted to 808C configuration with a large 89in (2.26m) wide front door, strengthened floor and roller guides fitted, allowing the loading and carriage of up to nine 53 x 88in (134 x 223cm) pallets. A movable cabin bulkhead was incorporated, allowing mixed passenger-freight combinations to be carried.

Aer Lingus' early Viscount operations followed the pattern set by BEA and Air France, with the 'Viscount jump' immediately apparent. In its first full year of operations, the airline's four Viscounts carried over 52,000 passengers, generating a traffic increase of 26 per cent compared with that attained by the previously used DC-3s. Average load factor was 75 per cent and the Viscount was certainly responsible for Aer Lingus turning its £62,000 loss in 1954-55 into a £25,000 profit the following year.

The airline's Viscount 707s were removed from service in 1960 and sold following the arrival of Fokker F27 Friendships for use on the 'thinner' routes while the 800s were put to work on the higher density services. The longest sector these aircraft plied was now Dublin to London, a distance of 378 miles (608km).

An interesting Aer Lingus Viscount story took place in 1958 when all four V.707s were equipped as flying hospitals to take 100 invalids to Lourdes in France where they were hoping to be miraculously cured of their ills. The Viscounts were fitted with 14 stretchers and seats for 35 others, the conversion to and from this configuration

taking less than 90 minutes. There is no record of whether or not the patients gained relief from their problems.

TRANS-AUSTRALIA AIRLINES

TAA's Viscounts were the first to be operated outside Europe. The first of the initial order for six V.720s arrived in Australia in October 1954 but unfortunately was written off less than three weeks later in a training accident when a three engined take-off was attempted. This didn't prevent the airline from starting scheduled operations by mid December 1954, by which time two more Viscounts had been delivered.

TAA's Viscounts were responsible for other 'firsts'. They were the first fitted with more powerful Dart 506 engines, the first with increased internal fuel capacity and also the first to have external slipper tanks installed. This extra fuel was necessary to cope with what was at the time the longest stage flown by any Viscount in regular service, the 1,380 miles (2,220km) between Adelaide and Perth, invariably against a stiff headwind.

TAA eventually ordered 14 Viscounts, comprising seven V.720s, five

V.756Ds and two V.816s. A further four were obtained second hand at various times. The effect of the Viscount in Australia was similar to other parts of the world – great interest was created by what was seen as a revolution in air transport and this interested quickly translated into increased passenger numbers.

By May 1955 the aircraft had achieved an average load factor of 85.5 per cent and the fleet of five aircraft was collectively recording 300 flying hours per week. By July of the same year TAA Viscounts held ten speed records between centres in Australia (including Perth-Adelaide at an average speed of 425mph including a healthy 105mph tailwind), a figure which had increased to 16 by the end of the year. Load factors remained in the 85-86 per cent area for some considerable time, while during 1955 average daily utilisation averaged just under nine hours per day.

TAA's management was obviously pleased with the Viscount as the airline's profit doubled in the 1954-55 financial year compared to the previous 12 months. TAA's chairman, G P N Watt, said: "The Viscounts have had

VH-TVH, a Viscount 756D from the second batch of aircraft ordered by Trans-Australia Airlines in 1955.

TAA took delivery of two new Viscount 816s in 1959. VH-TVQ was the 419th Viscount built out of 444.

a significant effect on developing TAA's business and improving its finances. They have been a potent factor in producing increased passenger figures". The 'Viscount jump' had struck again!

Two Airline Policy

One of the characteristics of Australian commercial aviation from 1951 was the Two Airline Policy, a policy of strict control over interstate air services which limited the number of airlines contesting this market to two. Fleet purchases had to be approved by the government, as did changes in air fares and the introduction of new routes. It was highly regulated and although it was intended to promote competition it really had the opposite effect.

Fleets were virtually identical for many years, as were schedules and fares. To the outsider, it appeared that government owned TAA was constantly being held back in order to help its privately owned opposition. An example was in the late 1950s when TAA wanted buy Caravelles but was denied permission to do so. These would have been the first jets on Australian domestic routes but that important occasion had to wait until 1964 when both airlines introduced Boeing 727s on the

same day and the same route in a carefully stage managed exercise.

The two players in Australia's two airline game were the government owned TAA (established in 1946) and originally the privately owned Australian National Airways (ANA). When ANA got into financial difficulties in 1957 it was taken over by Ansett Airways, becoming Ansett-ANA. The name was changed again to Ansett Airlines of Australia in 1968.

Australia's Two Airline Policy ended in 1990 and a deregulated market was introduced, allowing other operators to join in if they wished. By then, TAA had become Australian Airlines but it was later taken over by Qantas prior to privatisation and now operates under that name. This brief background is presented to set the scene for an interesting slice of airline history in which the Viscount played a major role ... or rather the *lack* of Viscounts played a major role. It could be argued that ANA's demise resulted from the airline not ordering Viscounts.

When TAA's Viscounts began flying in Australia, ANA's main type was the pressurised but piston engined Douglas DC-6B. ANA had taken out an option on six Viscounts at around the same time TAA had placed its order, but TAA acted more quickly and

secured earlier delivery positions than its rival. ANA's hierarchy then had what might be these days described as a 'dummy spit', cancelled its Viscount options and ordered DC-6Bs instead. Although they were able to be put into service a year earlier than TAA's Viscounts, they were no match for the turboprop airliner when it did arrive, being far less economical and having little passenger appeal by comparison.

In The Name of Competition

The Australian Viscount saga moved into a new phase when Ansett-ANA was established. At the time of merger it had no Viscounts, although it acquired two with the purchase of New South Wales operator Butler Air Transport the following year. Four new Viscount 832s were ordered at the same time for delivery in 1959.

In the meantime, the Australian government decided that in order to maintain equilibrium (in the name of competition) TAA should be forced to hand over some of its Viscounts to Ansett-ANA. In return, the government airline had to take some of Ansett's DC-6Bs! To say they weren't wanted is a gross understatement!

Ansett-ANA took over four of TAA's Viscount 720s as part of this arrangement and eventually operated 11 aircraft including the V.832s, V.720s, the Butler V.747s, an ex Continental V.812 and an ex Cubana V.818.

Both airlines used the Viscount as their front line equipment until firstly Lockheed Electras were introduced in 1959 and then Boeing 727s in 1964. The arrival of Douglas DC-9s in 1967 saw the beginning of the end for Viscounts in Australia, TAA and Ansett retiring the last of them in 1970.

The Viscount 700s had been permanently grounded the previous year following the crash of an Ansett oper-

Viscount 720 VH-TVF, one of the aircraft originally delivered to TAA but subsequently transferred to Ansett-ANA. This photograph was taken at Sydney Airport in 1965. (Vance Ingham)

ated, ex TAA V.720 at Port Hedland WA in December 1968. The aircraft – being operated under lease by MacRobertson Miller Airlines, had broken up in flight and was the last of several crashes by Australian Viscounts.

The aircraft's starboard wing had failed due to fatigue cracks emanating from an engine nacelle attachment bolt on the lower boom of the main spar. The spar was well within the manufacturer's safe life limits but some poor maintenance work in the hangar had over a period of time eventually resulted in a crack forming. The Viscount involved was the highest time example in Australia with 31,800 hours logged.

Structural Integrity

The structure of the Viscount – particularly of the wings in earlier aircraft – was possibly its major failing, despite its numerous other positive features. John Hopkins, TAA's Director of Engineering, was one of the world's most respected men in his field. He described it like this:

"Where the Viscount fell down was in its structure, the materials used in its structure and the philosophy used in justifying the safety of the structure. The Viscount was made of zinc bearing light alloys [as were the early de Havilland Comets] which turned out to be rather prone to stress corrosion for one thing and also to have a rather poor fatigue life under repeated stress.

"The major load bearing elements like the main wing spars and the tail

Ansett-ANA operated 11 Viscounts between 1958 and 1970, of which two V.832s were purchased new. VH-RMI was one of them.

unit were designed to a load spectrum that was calculated and checked by strain gauged aeroplanes in flight and then converted into an expected lifetime of loading conditions. Then by test methods in the structures laboratory, it was converted to an expected safe life before you would get a fatigue failure occurring in any of these members.

"It is terribly difficult to take into account all the million and one variations in the life experience of an aeroplane and the minute differences in manufacturing quality between test specimens and the run of the mill factory production. The unfortunate fact is that you can't be certain of a calculated safe life, and this began to show up in the Viscount at a fairly early age and we had to change spar booms and all sorts of components. We changed then several times over; that meant pulling the whole structure to bits when putting in a new spar boom.

"You can't live with that for long, but it was the only way to keep the aeroplanes safe. So they had to go, there was no way you could keep a Viscount operating indefinitely. It just became too expensive and time consuming to keep on replacing the parts you were doubtful about".

NORTH AMERICAN TRIUMPH

Trans Canada Airlines

When Trans Canada Airlines placed an order for 15 Viscount 724s in November 1952, it was recognised by Vickers as being of extreme importance because it gave the Viscount that vital toe in the door of the North American market.

The V.724 was itself an important subvariant of the aircraft as it introduced numerous new features to the aircraft which would become standard on future models, a two crew cockpit, increased operating weights, improved systems and upgraded cabin environment among them.

A mixture of technologies at Melbourne's Essendon Airport in the early 1960s as Ansett-ANA Viscount 832 VH-RMG departs behind a Douglas DC-3 and a Bristol Freighter. (Kevin Gleeson)

SUMMARY OF VISCOUNT OPERATORS

Notes: The table attempts to provide a comprehensive – but by no means complete – list of Viscount operators over the years including airline, military, government and some corporate. Although not tracing the histories of individual aircraft, the listing of the Viscount models which flew with various operators gives some opportunity to trace second hand sales over the years.

Operator	Country	Dates	No	Types/Notes
Aden Airways	Aden	1963-67	2	760
Aer Lingus	Ireland	1954-70	21	707 803 805 806 808
Aerolineas Condor	Ecuador	1980	1	745
Aerolineas TAO	Colombia	1968-75	3	745 785
Aerosierra de Durango	Mexico	1973-74	1	745
Aerospeca Colombia	Colombia	1971-88	4	745 798
Air Botswana	Botswana	1977-81	2	745 761
Air Commerz	W Germany	1970-72	2	808
Air Ferry	UK	1968	2	812
Air France	France	1953-63	12	708, lsd 3 1967-68
Air Inter	France	1960-75	15	708 724
Air International	UK	1971-72	1	702
Air Laos	Laos	1976-	1	786
Air Malawi	Malawi	1967-80	2	748 754
Air Tourisme Alpin	Switz'd	1972	1	808
Air Ulster	UK	1969	1	803, lsd from Aer Lingus
Air Vietnam	Vietnam	1961-63	2	708, lsd from Air France
Airwork	UK	1958-60	4	736 832, merged BUA 1960
Air Rhodesia/Zimbabwe	Zimbabwe	1968-91	11	748 745 756 782 838 839
Alidair	UK	1972-83	13	708 724 735 812 814 831
Alitalia	Italy	1957-71	18	745 785 798
All Nippon Airways	Japan	1960-70	11	744 828
Aloha Airlines	USA	1963-71	4	745 754 798
Ansett-ANA	Australia	1958-70	11	720 747 812 818 832
Aqua-Avia Society	New Zealand	1981-82	1	802, lsd from BAF
Arkia	Israel	1969-80	9	814 819 825 831 833
Austrian Airlines	Austria	1958-71	12	745 779 837
Austrian Air Transport	Austria	1964-70	2	837
Aviaco	Spain	1965	1	831
Bahamas Airways	Bahamas	1961-68	7	701 702 707
Baltic Airlines	UK	1988-89	7	813 814
Baltic Aviation	Sweden	1986-90	1	815
BKS Air Transport	UK	1967-73	16	701 702 707 708 745 776 786 798 806; 3 lsd 1961; named Northeast A'lines 1970-73
Botswana Nat'l Airways	Botswana	1969	1	756
Bouraq Indonesia	Indonesia	1983-96	5	812 843
British Air Ferries	UK	1981-96	33	802 806 807 808 812 813 814 815 836; British World Airlines 1993
British Airways	UK	1973-84	37	701 802 806 814
British Caledonian	UK	1985	1	806, lsd from BAF
British Eagle	UK	1958-68	17	701 707 732 739 755 805
BEA	UK	1953-73	75	701 732 736 779 802 806
Forca Aerea Brasilia	Brazil	1957-70	2	742 798
British Midland Airways	UK	1967-88	24	702 736 755 760 785 813 814 815 831 833
BOAC	UK	1972-74	2	701, lsd from Cambrian
Boulton Paul Aircraft	UK	1950-57	1	663, research
British International	UK	1958-60	1	776
British United Airways	UK	1960-69	14	708 736 804 831 833
BWIA	Trin/Tob	1955-70	8	702 772
Butler Air Transport	Australia	1955-58	2	747, merged Ansett 1958
CAAC	China	1963-83	6	843, last Viscounts built
Cambrian Airways	UK	1963-72	20	701 806, merged BA
Capital Airlines	USA	1955-61	60	744 745, merged United
Capital Airlines	UK	1989	1	806, lsd from BAF
Central African Airways	Rhodesia	1956-67	8	784 754 782
Channel Airways	UK	1962-72	21	701 702 707 812
Chinese Air Force	China	1970-	3	734 843
Condor Flugdienst	W Germany	1961-69	4	814, Lufthansa subsidiary
Continental Airlines	USA	1958-67	15	812
Cubana	Cuba	1956-62	7	755 818
Cunard Eagle Airways	Bermuda	1960-62	2	755
Cyprus Airways	Cyprus	1965-76	10	708 806 812 813 814
Dan-Air Services	UK	1975-81	7	708 804 808 838 839
Department of Transport	Canada	1955-82	2	737 797
Eagle Airways	Bermuda	1958-73	4	707 805
ETPS	UK	1962-72	2	744 745
Euroair	UK	1984-85	4	802 804 806
Falconair Charter	Sweden	1967-70	3	784
Far Eastern Air T'port	Formosa	1970-79	12	806 812 816 818 832
Filair	Zaire	1987-92	3	754 757
Fred Olsen Air T'port	Norway	1955-63	6	736 779, all leased out
Gambia Air Shuttle	Gambia	1988-90	2	813 814, lsd from BAF
Ghana Airways	Ghana	1961-75	3	838
Gibraltar Airways	UK	1974-88	1	807, GB Airways from 1981
Grupo Cydsa	Mexico	1971-75	1	764, corporate
Guernsey Airlines	UK	1977-86	6	708 724 735 806
Hawaiian Airlines	USA	1963-64	2	745 798
Hong Kong Airways	Hong Kong	1957-59	2	760
Hunting Clan	UK	1954-60	6	732 833, merged BUA 1960
Icelandair	Iceland	1957-70	2	759
Indian Airlines	India	1957-76	16	723 730 768 779
Indian Air Force	India	1955-67	2	723 730
Intra Airways	UK	1976-79	5	708 724 814 815
Invicta Airways	UK	1968-69	2	755, merged BMA 1969
Iranian Airlines	Iran	1958-66	3	782 839
Iraqi Airways	Iraq	1955-78	4	735 773
Janus Airways	UK	1983-84	3	708 724
Jersey Air Ferries	UK	1983	1	806, BAF subsidiary
Jersey European Airways	UK	1979-80	1	815, Intra renamed
Jordanian Airways	Jordan	1961-64	2	754 (3 x 831 lsd 1966-67)
Kestrel International	UK	1972	1	815, lsd from BMA
KLM Royal Dutch	Holland	1957-66	9	803
Kuwait Airways	Kuwait	1958-67	8	702 707 745 754 761, all leased
Kuwait Oil Co	Kuwait	1958-62	1	776
Lao Air Lines	Laos	1969-	1	806
LAV	Venezuela	1956-75	7	701 702 749
Lineas Aereas Canarias	Spain	1985-91	2	806
Lineas Aereas La Urraca	Colombia	1971-72	3	837
LANICA	Nicaragua	1958-59	2	786
Lloyd Aereo Colombiano	Colombia	1957-58	1	786
London European Airways	UK	1985-86	1	806
LOT – Polish Airlines	Poland	1962-67	3	804
Lufthansa	W Germany	1958-71	11	814
Luxair	Luxembourg	1966-69	1	815
MacRoberston Miller	Australia	1968	3	720 747, Ansett subsidiary

Operator	Country	Dates	No	Types/Notes	Operator	Country	Dates	No	Types/Notes
Maitland Drewery Avn	UK	1960-61	3	708	Somali Airlines	Somalia	1968-79	3	745 785
Malayan Airways	Malaysia	1959-63	2	760	South African A F	Sth Africa	1958-91	1	781
Mandala Airlines	Indonesia	1970-95	10	806 812 816 832	South African Airways	Sth Africa	1958-72	8	813 818
Manx Airlines	UK	1982-88	3	806 813 816	Southern International	UK	1974-81	4	807 808 814
Maritime Central	Canada	1959-62	1	806	Standard Oil Corp	USA	1957-75	1	765, corporate
Merpati Nusantara	Indonesia	1970-92	8	812 816 818 828 832	Starways	UK	1961-63	2	707 708
Mexican Electricity	Mexico	1972-75	1	798	Sudan Airways	Sudan	1959-62	1	831
Middle East Airlines	Lebanon	1955-70	12	732 736 754	Sultan of Oman A F	Oman	1971-79	5	808 814 836
Ministry of Supply	UK	1948-58	2	630 663	Tennessee Gas	USA	1959-66	1	835, corporate
Ministry of Technology	UK	1964-	2	837 838, Royal Radar Est	Tradair	UK	1960-62	2	707
					TAA	Australia	1954-71	18	720 745 756 816 818
Misrair/United Arab	Egypt	1956-65	8	732 739	TransAir	Canada	1963-64	1	724, lsd from TCA
MMM Acro Services	Zaire	1984-86	2	708	Transair	UK	1957-60	5	736 804, merged BUA
Nigeria Airways	Nigeria	1968-69	1	815, leased					
NZ National Airways	New Zealand	1958-75	5	807	Trans Canada Airlines	Canada	1955-74	51	724 757, Air Canada from 1964
Nora Air Services	W Germany	1971-72	6	814					
Northeast Airlines	USA	1958-63	10	798	Trans Florida Airlines	USA	1977-88	1	745, not in serv 1979-83
Pakistan Air Force	Pakistan	1956-70	1	734					
Pakistan International	Pakistan	1959-66	5	815	TACA International	El Salvador	1957-76	6	745 763 784 786 798
Pearl Air	Guiana	1975-78	1	804					
Pelandok Airways	Malaysia	1972-73	1	832	TAC Colombia	Colombia	1971-87	4	828 837
Philippine Airlines	Philip'es	1957-67	4	745 784	Treffield International	UK	1967	2	812, lsd from Channel A/W
PLUNA	Uruguay	1958-82	8	745 769 810 827					
Polar Airways	UK	1983	3	802 806	Turk Hava Yollari	Turkey	1958-71	5	794
Progressive Airways	UK	1971	1	803, failed before deliv	Turkish Air Force	Turkey	1971-92	3	794
					Union of Burma Airways	Burma	1957-76	3	761
RAAF	Australia	1964-69	2	836 839	Union Carbide	USA	1960-64	1	836, corporate
SA de Transport Aerien	Switzer'd	1969-72	2	803 808, lsd from Aer Lingus	United Aircraft	Canada	1972-89	1	757, engine testbed
					United Airlines	USA	1961-69	47	745, Capital takeover 1961
SAS	Norway	1960-61	4	779, lsd from Fred Olsen					
					US Steel Corporation	USA	1956-70	3	764, corporate
Scibe Airlift Cargo	Zaire	1976-83	2	808	VASP	Brazil	1958-75	17	701 827
Seulawah Air Services	Indonesia	1970-71	1	806	Virgin Atlantic Airways	UK	1985-89	4	802 806 814, all leased
Silver City Airways	UK	1961	3	708, didn't enter service					
					West African Air Cargo	Ghana	1977-78	1	814
Skyline Malmo	Sweden	1971-78	6	784 814, some for spares	Winner Airways	Taiwan	1969-71	1	806
					Zaire Aero Service	Zaire	1978-84	5	757
SAETA	Ecuador	1969-79	4	745 785 798	Zairean Airlines	Zaire	1981-96	2	757

After BEA and Capital, Trans Canada Airlines (Air Canada from 1964) was the operator of the third largest fleet of Viscounts in the world with 51 aircraft entering service. This is V.757 CF-THJ, delivered in May 1957. (Air Canada)

After their retirement, many of Air Canada's Viscounts found useful employment with other operators and in other roles. This V.757 (C-FTID-X) was used as a testbed for the Pratt & Whitney Canada PT6A-50 turboprop engine as fitted to the DHC Dash 7 regional airliner. P&WC operated the Viscount between 1972 and 1989. (DHC)

TCA subsequently placed further orders for 36 Viscount 757s which were similar to the original aircraft. The first V.724 was delivered in October 1954 and by February 1956 all 15 had been delivered. The 36 V.757s followed between 1956 and 1959.

The first TCA Viscount service was flown in April 1955 between Toronto and New York and within a year the aircraft was being used on most of the airline's major trunk routes which spread from Toronto, Ottawa and Montreal in Canada's east across the country through Winnipeg, Calgary and Edmonton and other ports to Vancouver in the west. Services to the north-eastern USA centres of New York, Cleveland and Chicago were of vital importance to both TCA and the Viscount as they gave Americans there first chance to sample the new airliner.

Once again, the 'Viscount jump'

was evident: on the Toronto-New York service TCA's share of the total traffic increased from 42 per cent to 54 per cent in one month; the number of passengers carried in the first four weeks of Viscount services increased by 57 per cent over the period immediately prior; in February 1956 TCA Viscounts carried 85 per cent more passengers to New York from Montreal and Toronto than were carried in the same month of the previous year (using Canadair North Stars); and overall Viscount load factor for the first year of operation was 81 per cent.

The arrival of Vickers Vanguards in late 1961 saw Viscounts gradually being taken off TCA's major routes and put on smaller city pair routes where the jump in traffic previously experienced was repeated. TCA became Air Canada in 1964 and even the arrival of Douglas DC-9 jets in 1966 did not mean the immediate

end of the Viscount as some of the ports it was serving did not yet justify the larger aircraft.

As late as 1973 Air Canada still had 10 Viscounts in its fleet, five of them serving in the airline's eastern region and five others on standby. The last was finally retired in 1974, like most of the others sold to other operators.

Capital Airlines

This was the big one for the Viscount programme, a series of orders placed in 1954 for a total of 60 Viscounts by one of the USA's major airlines, Capital. The first three were Viscount 744s to basically the same specification as the aircraft which had previously been delivered to operators in Europe, Canada and elsewhere, the remainder were the first orders placed for the Viscount 700D variant with more powerful engines,

The Capital Airlines orders for 60 Viscounts was a major coup for Vickers. This is the first of three V.744s (N7402) which preceded the main order for V.745Ds. N7402 was delivered in June 1955. (via Philip J Birtles)

increased operating weights and improved performance. Capital's aircraft were designated V.745Ds.

Deliveries began in June 1955 when the first V.744 arrived. The V.745Ds were delivered between November 1955 and June 1958 with the bulk of them (47) handed over during the course of 1956 and accounting for more than 60 per cent of all Viscount deliveries in that year.

Capital was in the mid 1950s the USA's fifth largest carrier in terms of passenger volume and was a purely regional airline, operating an extensive network covering some 60 cities in the eastern half of the United states stretching from Miami in the south to Minneapolis in the north. Its headquarters was in Washington DC and the 44 seat Viscounts were used to replace 55 seat Lockheed Constellations.

The airline embarked on a massive public relations-cum-educational programme prior to the introduction of the Viscount with the intention of letting the American travelling public know as much about this new and radical airliner. "Swift, smooth, silent and sure" were the catchcries used and great emphasis was put on the fact that the aircraft was powered by Rolls-Royce engines – "a symbol of perfection".

Capital's marketing campaign had everything. The image of the Viscount was everywhere – in trade and national magazine advertisements, on billboards, calendars, packs of playing cards, posters, coins, telephone directories, matchboxes, air mail stickers and handouts. There were framed pictures, postcards, newspaper advertisements, brochures, booklets, information kits, display models (in several sizes with wing spans ranging from one to seven feet) and even a massive pantechnicon which toured the land displaying a full size Dart mockup and a Viscount cabin section mockup inside. A fortune was spent selling the Viscount to the American people.

Services began in July 1955, initially operating between Washington and Chicago. Within three months Capital was the top carrier on this route, often operating with 100 per cent load factors. Using Constellations, average load factors had been 40 per cent (22 passengers); with the Viscount it rose to an average of 85 per cent, or 37 passengers per flight. It was the 'Viscount jump' yet again.

By March 1956 Capital had 16 Viscounts in service and was by now operating many services out of Washington, Chicago and New York. At this time the Viscount fleet was averaging overall load factors of 80 per cent compared with 58 per cent

The signing of the Capital contract in 1954 with senior representatives of the airline and manufacturer present. Left to right: Capital's C H Murchison (chairman), J H Carmichael (president), R G Lochiel (vice president and treasurer); plus Vickers' Sir James Reid Young, George Edwards and R P H Yapps.

for the rest of the Capital fleet. On the hotly contested Washington-Chicago service the airline increased its frequency from two to six nonstop services each day while the major competitor (American Airlines) was forced to reduce its daily services from five to four and remove its Douglas DC-7s to another market.

Things looked rosy for Capital but despite the success of the Viscount and the profits it was generating, the airline was in financial difficulties. It had been so well before the Viscount was introduced, the nature of its short stages proving difficult to operate profitably regardless of how much traffic was being generated. From 1955, only one type in Capital's fleet was making money, and that was the Viscount. The DC-3s, DC-6s and Constellations were losing steadily. Capital had been trying to sell its grossly unprofitable Constellations but had been unable to find a buyer, thus adding to its problems.

Too rapid expansion and the drain on capital also took its toll. The airline was in the difficult position where it had to spend a lot of money on new turbine engined equipment in order to survive, but it didn't have the money to spend.

In July 1956 Capital ordered 15 more Viscounts and some de Havilland Comets. Both orders were eventually cancelled, the Viscounts' completion either being delayed or in the case of those already built, stored until other buyers could be found. At this stage Capital owed Vickers a lot of money and over the next couple of years numerous payment deadlines were missed. Finally, in April 1960, Vickers was forced to foreclose.

Enter United

Rescue came in the form of United Airlines which took over Capital in July 1961. Fifteen of the Viscounts were returned to Vickers, and part of the settlement was a parcel of United

Capital Airlines Viscounts on the production line at Hurn in 1955.

Zambia Airways Viscount 754D carrying the Rhodesian registration VP-YTE. This is an ex Middle East Airways aircraft.

Intra Airways Viscount 724 G-BDRC, a former TCA aircraft. The Jersey based carrier flew five Viscounts between 1976 and 1979.

Indonesia's Mandala Airlines was operating this ex TAA Viscount 816 as late as 1995, flying as PK-RVS. This aircraft is subject to an extensive effort by Australian enthusiasts to preserve it.

Airlines stocks and shares which allowed the British manufacturer to recover about 75 per cent of the money it was owed. Such was the demand for the Viscount, these 15 aircraft were quickly sold, as were the other 15 aircraft from the previously cancelled order.

United retained 41 of Capital's Viscounts and these were largely operated on the routes they had been flying before the takeover. United quickly developed a liking for the aircraft and repurchased six of the aircraft which had been returned to Vickers!

United Airlines kept gradually diminishing numbers of Viscounts in service throughout most of the 1960s, the final service by the British airliner taking place on 14 January 1969.

Continental Airlines

Continental Airlines was the second US operator to purchase Viscounts and the first airline in the world to order the V.810 model. As the V.812, 12 were ordered in December 1955 and a further three in February 1956 with deliveries starting in May 1958. Services started in the same month, initially between Los Angeles, Denver and Chicago.

As had been the case with Capital Airlines, a heavy publicity campaign preceded Continental's introduction of the Viscount. Other services were quickly added and once again the Viscount proved to be profitable and popular with passengers on Continental's mainly US west coast network.

Continental lost two Viscounts in accidents and two more were sold in 1960. The remainder stayed in service until 1967 when they were replaced by DC-9s. The entire fleet was purchased by Britain's Channel Airways.

ZK-BRE, one of five new Viscount 807s operated by New Zealand National Airways Corporation between 1958 and 1975. NAC was the only non European customer for the 800 series Viscount.

Northeast Airlines

The third US purchaser of new Viscounts, Northeast ordered 10 V.798Ds in July 1957 and deliveries began in May 1958. Northeast intended using the Viscounts on its US east coast routes linking Boston, New York, Philadelphia and Montreal, the Boston-New York service getting underway first.

Once again, the Viscount proved to be an instant hit and a moneymaker, but Northeast had some similarities with Capital, the most important of which was that it was in financial difficulties before the Viscounts were delivered. Despite the Viscount's profitability and the increased traffic and load factors it generated, its days as an operator of the turboprop airliner were numbered.

Like Capital, Northeast owed Vickers a considerable sum of money and failure to meet its obligations caused the manufacturer to start action to repossess the aircraft in June 1963. The action was delayed for three months to allow the Viscounts to be used during the peak summer season. They were returned to Vickers (which also had a lien on the airline's nine DC-6Bs and six DC-3s) in September 1963 and were quickly resold.

ASSORTED VISCOUNTS

About 70 airlines, military operators, governments and corporations ordered new Viscounts over the years and these are listed in the 'Summary of Viscount Variants and Orders' table in the previous chapter. As the original owners disposed of their fleets, a second generation of operators emerged, mostly smaller airlines who built up their early turbine engined fleets around second hand Viscounts. Other established Viscount operators also scoured the used aircraft market to add to their own fleets.

The disposal of the larger fleets obviously created the best opportunities for the purchase of used Viscounts. When the Capital/United Viscounts became available there were many aircraft to choose from and the same applied to the BEA, TCA, Continental and Lufthansa

Gibraltar Airways (or GB Air from 1988) operated this single ex New Zealand NAC Viscount 807 (G-BBVH) between 1974 and 1988 before its career ended with a landing accident at Tangiers. It is photographed here at London Gatwick in 1988. (Dave Fraser)

UK independent airline British Eagle operated a mixture of Viscount marks for a decade from 1958, most of them second hand. This is G-AOCC, a former Cubana V.755D. (Evan Jones)

KLM's nine new Viscount 803s served for nine years from 1957 until they were replaced by Douglas DC-9s. The whole fleet was sold to Aer Lingus.

British West Indian Airways was an early Viscount customer, ordering four V.702s in 1953 for use on its Caribbean services. They were delivered in 1955 and a further four V.772s were added to the fleet in 1957-58.

Lufthansa was one of the major new customers for the Viscount 810 series, ordering 10 V.814s for delivery in 1958-59. The last had been retired by 1971, replaced by Boeing 737s, for which Lufthansa was the launch customer. Viscount 814 D-ANUN is illustrated.

fleets. Many Viscounts changed hands six or seven times during their careers.

The introduction of V.800/810 series helped start a new round of ordering in the second half of the 1950s, these increased capacity models bringing new customers such as Continental, South African Airways, Lufthansa, Pakistan International, Cubana and All Nippon Airways to the fold as well as generating new orders from established users such as BEA, TAA and KLM.

One of the more interesting Viscount orders was the very last one placed in December 1961 by China's CAAC for six V.843s. These were the last Viscounts built and were delivered between July 1963 and April 1964.

This was the first sale of a Western aircraft to Red China and as such created a lot of interest around the world. Vickers also received criticism from some quarters for doing business with the communists. The strongest opposition came from the USA which had trade embargoes imposed on China. This created some problems for Vickers because there were many items of American equipment on the Viscount, none of which could be installed on the Chinese aircraft due to the embargo. This effected hydraulic, navigational and electronic equipment, all of which had to be replaced by entirely British designed and manufactured items.

Little is known about CAAC's operation of the Viscounts expect that they remained in service until 1983 when two were transferred to the Chinese Air Force and the others were sold to Indonesian operator Bouraq. Of greater importance was the fact that CAAC's Viscount order opened the door for future sales of Western airliners to China, starting in the 1970s with the Hawker Siddeley Trident.

Military Viscounts

Several air forces purchased new Viscounts from Vickers, the Indian Air Force the first of them, ordering a V.723 in November 1953 and a V.730 a year later. The aircraft were delivered in late 1955 and early 1956 and both were fitted with VIP interiors. Despite the different designations, the aircraft were mechanically identical, differing only in the interior specification. They served until 1967 when they were purchased by Indian Airlines.

The Pakistan Air Force was the next military customer for the Viscount, taking delivery of a single VIP V.734 in March 1956 and operating it until 1970 when it was sold to the Chinese Air Force. China operated it until 1983 when it was replaced by two former CAAC V.843s.

The first of Brazil's two VIP equipped Viscounts (a V.742D) was originally intended for Norway's Fred Olsen Transport but not taken up. It was delivered to the *Forca Aerea Brasilia* in February 1957 and was joined by a second new aircraft (a V.789D) in October 1958. The first aircraft was damaged beyond repair in a heavy landing at Rio de Janeiro in 1967 (with the Brazilian President aboard) and the second was retired in 1970.

The South African Air Force acquired a new V.781D for VIP duties in 1958, this aircraft remaining in service until 1991, the aircraft's 33 year career making it the longest any Viscount stayed with a single operator.

Second hand Viscounts were used by several air forces including Turkey (three ex THY V.794s 1971-92), Oman (an assortment of five V.808s, V.814s and V.836s 1971-79) and the Royal Australian Air Force which operated two VIP aircraft (a V.836 and V.839) between 1964 and 1969.

These aircraft found their way into Australian service via a roundabout route. Originally laid down as V.816s for Trans-Australia Airlines but not taken up, they were both completed as VIP transports, one for the Union Carbide Corporation and one for the Iranian government. Both became available in 1964 and were purchased for the RAAF but they remained in service only until 1969 when they were replaced by BAC One Elevens.

A government Viscount operator was Canada's Department of the Interior, which took delivery of a new V.737 in March 1955, while the Canadian Ministry of Transport received a V.797D in October 1958. The second aircraft was VIP equipped and used to transport the Canadian Prime Minister and other senior government figures.

The South African Air Force's sole Viscount, a V781D delivered in 1958 and operated continuously by the SAAF for the next 33 years.

Corporate Viscounts

Several corporate buyers purchased new Viscounts and many other second hand aircraft were converted to usually luxurious configurations, mainly for operation in the USA. The operators of new aircraft were the US Steel Corporation (three V.764Ds), Standard Oil (one V.765D), Kuwait Oil (one V.776D), the Royal Bank of Canada (one V.793D), the Tennessee Gas Transmission Corporation (one V.835) and Union Carbide (one V.836).

Howard Hughes ordered a new VIP Viscount 700D in 1955 for his Hughes Tool Corporation. Perhaps predictably, a period of intrigue, mystery and strange instructions followed, including orders that the aircraft be stored in a remote corner of the Weybridge factory and it was not to be approached or inspected by Vickers personnel! After more than a year of eccentric idiocy on Hughes' behalf, the aircraft was released and subsequently sold to El Salvador's TACA International.

The release of second hand Viscounts – particularly the former Capital V.745s – created the opportunity to convert many aircraft to corporate specifications, usually with comfort-able and well equipped interiors and long range fuel tanks in the belly.

The list of users of converted corporate Viscounts is long and varied and includes US college basketball teams, travel clubs, the Oral Roberts religious organisation, the Cathedral of Tomorrow and soul musician Ray Charles. Viscounts have often been associated with touring rock bands, including the Rolling Stones and Paul McCartney, both of whom have used Viscounts during concert tours of the USA. Speaking of the Beatles – the aircraft noise which opens the track *Back In The USSR* is instantly recognisable (to any aviation buff over 40) as being that of a Vickers Viscount!

Viscount Today

By late 1995, only 14 Viscounts were still listed as being in airline service: one each with Guila Air, TAB Zaire, LEGA, Trans Service Airlift, Zairean Airlines, Bouraq Indonesia and eight with British World Airlines (BWA).

Known as British Air Ferries until 1993, BWA is to the Viscount what Dan-Air was to the Comet, collecting Viscounts from various sources, modifying them, keeping them airworthy and operating them. As BAF,

China's CAAC was the last Viscount customer, ordering six V.843s in 1961 for delivery in 1963-64. B-402 is illustrated here in company with other CAAC aircraft including a Boeing 707, three Hawker Siddeley Tridents and an Ilyushin Il-62.

Royal Australian Air Force Viscount A6-436, one of two used in the VIP transport role between 1964 and 1969. They were replaced by BAC One Elevens. (RAAF)

the charter and freight operator procured its first Viscount in 1981 and steadily built up its fleet throughout the remainder of the 1980s, more than 30 aircraft passing through its hands over the years with 800 and 810 series aircraft being concentrated on. The maximum number in service at any one time was 18 in the mid 1980s.

The company also developed a Viscount life extension programme in conjunction with British Aerospace, designed to increase an aircraft's life by 15 years or up to 75,000 flights.

In addition to the Viscounts, BWA's 1995 fleet included BAC One Elevens and BAe 146s, with the remaining Viscounts set to soldier on for a while yet, three of the aircraft in passenger configuration working on a North Sea Contract for Shell Oil. The other five have been converted to full freighters, mostly carrying overnight parcels for British mail operator Parcelforce.

In early 1996 it was announced that the three passenger Viscounts would be replaced by ATR 72-210s later in the same year after 15 years of carrying Shell workers between Aberdeen and Sumburgh. These Viscounts will then be converted to freighters.

(right) British Air Ferries (now British World Airlines) remains the world's major Viscount operator in the mid 1990s with eight aircraft on strength. Since 1981 it has had more than 30 Viscounts in its fleet at various times including (top) V.808C freighter G-BBDK and (bottom) V.806 G-AOYN, photographed on landing at Gatwick in May 1987. (Bruce Malcolm/D Fraser)

BWA faces several problems with its Viscounts, not the least of which is the cost of maintaining them. As is usually the case with older aircraft, the capital investment in them is next to nothing but the day to day maintenance costs can be high. Each engine costs about £100,000 to overhaul and each propeller about £20,000. Despite this, BWA's Viscounts are profitable.

The other problem is finding a replacement for the freighters when that time comes, as there little else in the 8 tonne payload class which BWA

regards as economically viable. Some of BWA's Viscounts still have 2,500-3,000 hours life remaining. The freighter aircraft fly about 500 hours annually, while those involved in passenger operations have been logging about 1,500 hours each year.

The bottom line of all this is that there still should be some Viscounts flying into the early part of the 21st century, by which time Vickers' remarkable pioneering turboprop airliner will be well past its 50th birthday.

VISCOUNT PRODUCTION

Important Note: This table makes no attempt to chronicle the full careers of the Viscounts. It is intended only to list the aircrafts' places of manufacture, first flights and delivery dates and their initial operator and registration plus any other points of interest. For information on the Viscounts' subsequent careers and fates, specialist publications such as The Aviation Hobby Shop's *Turboprop Airliner Production List* are recommended.

Abbreviations: BEA – British European Airways; TAA – Trans Australia Airlines; TCA – Trans Canada Air Lines; BWIA – British West Indian Airways; LAV – Linea Aeropostal Venezolanas; MEA – Middle East Airlines; PAL – Philippine Air Lines; THY – Turk Hava Yollari; BUA – British United Airways; NZNAC – New Zealand National Airways Corporation; PLUNA – Primeras Lineas Uraquayas de Navegacion Aerea; LANICA – Lineas Aereos de Nicaragua; SAA – South African Airways; VASP – Viacao Aerea Sao Paulo; CAAC – Civil Aviation Administration of China; lsd – leased; F/flight – first flight; C/No – constructor's number; Regist – registration; Deliv – delivery (date); w/o – written off; ntu – not taken up.

C/No	Type	F/flight	Customer	Regist	Deliv	Factory/Notes
1	630	16/07/48	Min of Supply	G-AHRF	–	Wisley, also VX211
2	663	15/03/50	Min of Supply	VX217	–	Wisley, G-AHRG ntu
3	700	28/08/50	Vickers	G-AMAV	–	Weybridge
4	701	20/08/52	BEA	G-ALWE	01/53	Weybridge
5	701	03/12/52	BEA	G-ALWF	02/53	Weybridge
6	701	07/01/53	BEA	G-AMNY	02/53	Weybridge
7	701	11/02/53	BEA	G-AMOG	03/53	Weybridge
8	708	11/03/53	Air France	F-BGNK	05/53	Weybridge
9	701	27/03/53	BEA	G-AMOA	04/53	Weybridge
10	708	27/05/53	Air France	F-BGNL	08/53	Weybridge
11	701	10/04/53	BEA	G-AMOB	04/53	Weybridge
12	708	03/07/53	Air France	F-BGNM	09/53	Weybridge
13	701	14/05/53	BEA	G-AMOC	06/53	Weybridge
14	708	26/08/53	Air France	F-BGNN	10/53	Weybridge
15	701	17/06/53	BEA	G-AMOD	06/53	Weybridge
16	708	19/09/53	Air France	F-BGNO	12/53	Weybridge
17	701	26/06/53	BEA	G-AMOE	07/53	Weybridge
18	708	13/10/53	Air France	F-BGNP	12/53	Weybridge
19	701	23/07/53	BEA	G-AMOF	08/53	Weybridge
20	701	03/09/53	BEA	G-AMNZ	10/53	Weybridge
21	701	01/10/53	BEA	G-AMOH	10/53	Weybridge
22	701	20/10/53	BEA	G-AMOI	11/53	Weybridge
23	701	04/11/53	BEA	G-AMOJ	11/53	Weybridge
24	701	21/11/53	BEA	G-AMOK	12/53	Weybridge
25	701	08/12/53	BEA	G-AMOL	01/54	Weybridge
26	701	22/12/53	BEA	G-AMOM	01/54	Weybridge
27	701	16/01/54	BEA	G-AMON	03/54	Weybridge
28	701	01/12/53	BEA	G-AMOO	12/53	Hurn
29	701	08/01/54	BEA	G-AMOP	03/54	Hurn
30	707	30/01/54	Aer Lingus	EI-AFV	03/54	Hurn
31	707	16/02/54	Aer Lingus	EI-AFW	03/54	Hurn
32	707	12/03/54	Aer Lingus	EI-AFY	03/54	Hurn
33	708	14/04/54	Air France	F-BGNQ	05/54	Hurn
34	707	14/03/54	Aer Lingus	EI-AGI	04/54	Hurn
35	708	06/05/54	Air France	F-BGNR	06/54	Hurn
36	708	30/05/54	Air France	F-BGNS	06/54	Hurn
37	708	16/06/54	Air France	F-BGNT	07/54	Hurn
38	708	05/07/54	Air France	F-BGNU	07/54	Hurn
39	708	29/07/54	Air France	F-BGNV	08/54	Hurn
40	724	12/10/54	TCA	CF-TGI	12/54	Weybridge
41	724	24/12/54	TCA	CF-TGJ	01/55	Weybridge
42	724	14/02/55	TCA	CF-TGK	02/55	Weybridge
43	724	13/02/55	TCA	CF-TGL	03/55	Hurn
44	720	29/08/54	TAA	VH-TVA	10/54	Hurn
45	720	20/10/54	TAA	VH-TVB	11/54	Hurn
46	720	17/11/54	TAA	VH-TVC	12/54	Hurn
47	720	01/12/54	TAA	VH-TVD	12/54	Hurn
48	720	23/12/54	TAA	VH-TVE	01/55	Hurn
49	720	30/01/55	TAA	VH-TVF	04/55	Hurn
50	724	15/03/55	TCA	CF-TGM	03/55	Hurn
51	724	31/03/55	TCA	CF-TGN	04/55	Hurn
52	724	20/04/55	TCA	CF-TGO	05/55	Hurn
53	724	10/05/55	TCA	CF-TGP	05/55	Hurn
54	724	27/05/55	TCA	CF-TGQ	06/55	Hurn
55	724	21/06/55	TCA	CF-TGR	06/55	Hurn
56	724	02/07/55	TCA	CF-TGS	07/55	Hurn
57	724	21/07/55	TCA	CF-TGT	08/55	Hurn
58	724	10/08/55	TCA	CF-TGU	08/55	Hurn
59	724	31/08/55	TCA	CF-TGV	09/55	Hurn
60	724	07/02/56	TCA	CF-TGW	02/56	Weybridge
61	701	07/10/54	BEA	G-ANHA	10/54	Hurn
62	701	02/11/54	BEA	G-ANHB	11/54	Hurn
63	701	01/12/54	BEA	G-ANHC	12/54	Hurn
64	701	24/04/55	BEA	G-ANHD	05/55	Hurn
65	701	22/06/55	BEA	G-ANHE	06/55	Hurn
66	701	04/07/55	BEA	G-ANFH	07/55	Hurn
67	735	23/09/55	Iraqi Airways	YI-ACK	10/55	Hurn
68	735	14/10/55	Iraqi Airways	YI-ACL	11/55	Hurn
69	735	08/11/55	Iraqi Airways	YI-ACM	12/55	Hurn
70	737	15/03/55	Canadian DoT	CF-CXK	03/55	Weybridge
71	702	17/06/55	BWIA	VP-TBK	07/55	Hurn
72	702	06/08/55	BWIA	VP-TBL	08/55	Hurn
73	702	06/08/55	BWIA	VP-TBM	09/55	Hurn
74	732	26/04/55	Hunting Clan	G-ANRR	05/55	Weybridge
75	732	07/06/55	Hunting Clan	G-ANRS	06/55	Weybridge
76	732	05/07/55	Hunting Clan	G-ANRT	07/55	Weybridge
77	736	20/10/55	Fred Olsen	LN-FOF	11/55	Hurn
78	736	08/11/55	Fred Olsen	LN-FOL	12/55	Hurn
79	723	08/11/55	Indian A F	IU683	12/55	Weybridge
80	730	14/12/55	Indian A F	IU684	01/56	Weybridge
81	702	05/10/55	BWIA	VP-TBN	11/55	Hurn
82	763D	07/10/58	TACA	YS-09C	10/58	Weybridge, stored 1955-58
83	734	29/02/56	Pakistan A F	J751	03/56	Weybridge
84	720	08/01/56	TAA	VH-TVG	01/56	Hurn
85	739	01/12/55	Misrair	SU-AIC	07/55	Hurn
86	739	21/12/55	Misrair	SU-AID	02/56	Hurn
87	739	12/01/56	Misrair	SU-AIE	01/56	Hurn
88	744	14/05/55	Capital	N7402	06/55	Hurn
89	744	30/06/55	Capital	N7403	07/55	Hurn
90	744	14/07/55	Capital	N7404	07/55	Hurn
91	755D	26/04/56	Cubana	CU-T603	05/56	Weybridge
92	755D	24/05/56	Cubana	CU-T604	06/56	Weybridge
93	755D	16/06/56	Cubana	CU-T605	06/56	Weybridge
94	749	19/01/56	LAV	YV-C-AMV	02/56	Hurn
95	749	08/02/56	LAV	YV-C-AMX	03/56	Hurn
96	749	10/02/56	LAV	YV-C-AMY	03/56	Hurn
97	747	15/09/55	Butler	VH-BAT	09/58	Weybridge
98	748D	28/03/56	Central African	YP-YNA	05/56	Hurn
99	748D	05/05/56	Central African	YP-YNB	05/56	Hurn
100	748D	24/05/56	Central African	YP-YNC	06/56	Hurn
101	748D	14/06/56	Central African	YP-YND	07/56	Hurn
102	748D	07/07/56	Central African	YP-YNE	07/56	Hurn
103	745D	03/11/55	Capital	N7405	11/55	Hurn
104	745D	19/11/55	Capital	N7406	11/55	Hurn
105	745D	01/12/55	Capital	N7407	12/55	Hurn
106	745D	19/11/55	Capital	N7408	12/55	Hurn
107	745D	20/12/55	Capital	N7409	12/55	Hurn
108	745D	06/01/56	Capital	N7410	01/56	Hurn
109	745D	20/01/56	Capital	N7411	03/56	Hurn
110	745D	02/02/56	Capital	N7412	02/56	Hurn
111	745D	13/02/56	Capital	N7413	02/56	Hurn
112	745D	22/02/56	Capital	N7414	03/56	Hurn
113	745D	02/03/56	Capital	N7415	03/56	Hurn
114	745D	10/03/56	Capital	N7416	03/56	Hurn
115	745D	21/03/56	Capital	N7417	03/56	Hurn
116	745D	27/03/56	Capital	N7418	03/56	Hurn
117	745D	10/04/56	Capital	N7419	04/56	Hurn
118	745D	17/04/56	Capital	N7420	04/56	Hurn
119	745D	24/04/56	Capital	N7421	05/56	Hurn
120	745D	01/05/56	Capital	N7422	05/56	Hurn
121	745D	08/05/56	Capital	N7423	05/56	Hurn
122	745D	15/05/56	Capital	N7424	05/56	Hurn
123	745D	23/05/56	Capital	N7425	05/56	Hurn
124	745D	29/05/56	Capital	N7426	05/56	Hurn
125	745D	05/06/56	Capital	N7427	06/56	Hurn
126	745D	12/06/56	Capital	N7428	06/56	Hurn
127	745D	19/06/56	Capital	N7429	06/56	Hurn
128	745D	22/06/56	Capital	N7430	07/56	Hurn
129	745D	06/07/56	Capital	N7431	07/56	Hurn

C/No	Type	F/flight	Customer	Regist	Deliv	Factory/Notes	C/No	Type	F/flight	Customer	Regist	Deliv	Factory/Notes
130	745D	16/07/56	Capital	N7432	07/56	Hurn	203	745D	22/10/56	Capital	N7447	10/56	Hurn
131	745D	22/07/56	Capital	N7433	07/56	Hurn	204	745D	28/10/56	Capital	N7448	11/56	Hurn
132	745D	30/07/56	Capital	N7434	08/56	Hurn	205	745D	30/10/56	Capital	N7449	11/56	Hurn
133	745D	10/08/56	Capital	N7435	08/56	Hurn	206	745D	09/11/56	Capital	N7450	11/56	Hurn
134	745D	12/08/56	Capital	N7436	08/56	Hurn	207	745D	14/11/56	Capital	N7451	11/56	Hurn
135	745D	24/08/56	Capital	N7437	08/56	Hurn	208	745D	19/11/56	Capital	N7452	11/56	Hurn
136	745D	01/09/56	Capital	N7438	09/56	Hurn	209	745D	26/11/56	Capital	N7454	12/56	Hurn
137	745D	08/09/56	Capital	N7439	09/56	Hurn	210	745D	02/12/56	Capital	N7455	12/56	Hurn
138	745D	14/09/56	Capital	N7440	09/56	Hurn	211	745D	06/12/56	Capital	N7456	12/56	Hurn
139	745D	17/09/56	Capital	N7441	09/56	Hurn	212	745D	15/12/56	Capital	N7457	12/56	Hurn
140	759D	02/11/56	Hunting Clan	G-AOGG	11/56	Weybridge	213	745D	27/12/56	Capital	N7458	01/57	Hurn
141	742D	24/07/56	Brazilian A F	FAB2100	02/57	Hurn	214	745D	28/12/56	Capital	N7459	01/57	Hurn
142	757	18/03/56	TCA	CF-TGX	03/56	Weybridge	215	745D	03/01/57	Capital	N7460	01/57	Hurn
143	757	22/03/56	TCA	CF-TGY	03/56	Hurn	216	745D	24/01/57	Capital	N7461	02/57	Hurn
144	757	14/04/56	TCA	CF-TGZ	05/56	Hurn	217	745D	02/02/57	Capital	N7462	03/57	Hurn
145	747	27/08/56	Butler	VH-BUT	09/56	Weybridge	218	757	14/01/57	TCA	CF-THA	02/57	Hurn
146	756D	03/05/56	TAA	VH-TVH	06/56	Hurn	219	757	18/01/57	TCA	CF-THB	02/57	Hurn
147	756D	26/05/56	TAA	VH-TVI	06/56	Hurn	220	757	11/02/57	TCA	CF-THC	02/57	Hurn
148	756D	15/06/56	TAA	VH-TVJ	06/56	Hurn	221	757	16/02/57	TCA	CF-THD	02/57	Hurn
149	759D	07/12/56	Hunting Clan	G-AOGH	12/56	Weybridge	222	757	24/02/57	TCA	CF-THE	03/57	Hurn
150	802	27/07/56	BEA	G-AOJA	02/57	Weybridge, 1st V.800	223	757	10/03/57	TCA	CF-THF	03/57	Hurn
151	802	29/09/56	BEA	G-AOJB	02/57	Weybridge	224	757	20/03/47	TCA	CF-THG	03/57	Hurn
152	802	07/11/56	BEA	G-AOJC	01/57	Weybridge	225	776D	26/02/57	British Int'l	G-APNP	10/58	Hurn, ex 745D
153	802	29/11/56	BEA	G-AOJD	01/57	Weybridge	226	798D	22/03/57	Northeast	N6599C	02/59	Hurn, ex 745D, ex 770D demonstrator
154	802	10/01/57	BEA	G-AOJE	01/57	Weybridge							
155	802	18/01/57	BEA	G-AOJF	02/57	Weybridge	227	784D	10/04/57	PAL	PI-C772	12/59	Hurn, ex 745D
156	802	04/02/57	BEA	G-AOHG	02/57	Weybridge	228	793D	23/04/57	Bank of Canada	CF-RBC	04/59	Hurn, ex 745D
157	802	15/02/57	BEA	G-AOHH	03/57	Weybridge	229	797D	28/04/57	Canadian DoT	CF-DTA	10/58	Hurn, ex 745D
158	802	26/02/57	BEA	G-AOHI	03/57	Weybridge	230	798D	07/06/57	Northeast	N6595C	10/58	Hurn, ex 745D
159	802	07/03/57	BEA	G-AOHJ	03/57	Weybridge	231	745D	18/06/57	Capital	N7465	06/58	Hurn
160	802	20/03/57	BEA	G-AOHK	04/57	Weybridge	232	798D	28/06/57	Northeast	N6590C	08/58	Hurn, ex 745D
161	802	29/03/57	BEA	G-AOHL	04/57	Weybridge	233	798D	27/06/57	Northeast	N6591C	08/58	Hurn, ex 745D
162	802	30/05/57	BEA	G-AOHM	06/57	Weybridge	234	798D	05/07/57	Northeast	N6592C	08/58	Hurn, ex 745D
163	802	13/04/57	BEA	G-AOHN	05/57	Weybridge	235	772	06/10/57	BWIA	VP-TBS	10/57	Hurn
164	802	26/04/57	BEA	G-AOHO	05/57	Weybridge	236	772	30/10/57	BWIA	VP-TBT	11/57	Hurn
165	802	04/05/57	BEA	G-AOHP	05/57	Weybridge	237	772	20/11/57	BWIA	VP-TBU	12/57	Hurn
166	802	22/05/57	BEA	G-AOHR	06/57	Weybridge	238	772	08/12/57	BWIA	VP-TBX	01/58	Hurn
167	802	07/06/57	BEA	G-AOHS	06/67	Weybridge	239	754D	17/07/57	MEA	OD-ACT	07/57	Hurn
168	802	20/06/57	BEA	G-AOHT	07/57	Weybridge	240	754D	29/08/57	MEA	OD-ACU	09/57	Hurn
169	802	28/06/57	BEA	G-AOHU	07/57	Weybridge	241	754D	19/09/57	MEA	OD-ACV	09/57	Hurn
170	802	10/07/57	BEA	G-AOHV	07/57	Weybridge	242	754D	02/10/57	MEA	OD-ACW	10/57	Hurn
171	802	22/08/57	BEA	G-AOHW	09/57	Weybridge	243	754D	22/10/57	MEA	OD-ADD	11/57	Hurn
172	803	05/04/57	KLM Royal Dutch	PH-VIA	06/57	Weybridge	244	754D	24/11/57	MEA	OD-ADE	12/57	Hurn
173	803	24/06/57	KLM Royal Dutch	PH-VIB	07/57	Weybridge	245	754D	21/12/57	MEA	OD-ACX	01/58	Hurn
174	803	19/07/57	KLM Royal Dutch	PH-VIC	08/57	Weybridge	246	794D	09/01/58	THY	TC-SEC	01/58	Hurn
175	803	24/08/57	KLM Royal Dutch	PH-VID	10/57	Weybridge	247	779D	11/03/57	Fred Olsen	LN-FOM	04/57	Hurn
176	803	11/09/57	KLM Royal Dutch	PH-VIE	10/57	Weybridge	248	804	31/08/57	Transair (BUA)	G-AOXU	09/57	Weybridge
177	803	28/09/57	KLM Royal Dutch	PH-VIF	10/57	Weybridge	249	804	18/09/57	Transair (BUA)	G-AOXV	09/57	Weybridge
178	803	18/10/57	KLM Royal Dutch	PH-VIG	11/57	Weybridge	250	779D	13/04/57	Fred Olsen	LN-FOH	04/57	Hurn
179	803	01/11/57	KLM Royal Dutch	PH-VIH	11/57	Weybridge	251	779D	07/05/57	Fred Olsen	LN-FOI	05/57	Hurn
180	803	22/11/57	KLM Royal Dutch	PH-VII	12/57	Weybridge	252	779D	23/07/57	Fred Olsen	LN-FOK	08/57	Hurn
181	756D	10/01/57	TAA	VH-TVK	01/57	Hurn	253	802	18/07/57	BEA	G-AOHW	08/57	Weybridge
182	701	16/07/56	BEA	G-AOFX	07/56	Weybridge	254	802	29/07/57	BEA	G-AORC	08/57	Weybridge
183	764D	02/10/56	US Steel Corp	N905	12/56	Hurn	255	806	09/08/57	Vickers	G-AOYF	–	Weybridge, demonstrator w/o Jo-hannesburg 10/57
184	764D	26/10/56	US Steel Corp	N906	11/56	Hurn							
185	764D	30/11/56	US Steel Corp	N907	12/56	Hurn							
186	760D	13/12/56	Hong Kong A/W	VR-HFI	01/57	Hurn							
187	760D	14/02/57	Hong Kong A/W	VR-HFJ	02/57	Hurn	256	806	04/10/57	BEA	G-AOYG	03/58	Weybridge
188	761D	26/06/57	Union of Burma	XY-ADF	07/57	Hurn	257	806	14/11/57	BEA	G-AOYI	01/58	Weybridge
189	761D	27/08/57	Union of Burma	XY-ADG	09/57	Hurn	258	806	02/12/57	BEA	G-APDW	12/57	Weybridge
190	761D	26/09/57	Union of Burma	XY-ADH	10/57	Hurn	259	806	09/12/57	BEA	G-AOYJ	01/58	Weybridge
191	765D	24/01/57	Standard Oil	N306	02/57	Hurn	260	806	13/01/58	BEA	G-AOYK	02/58	Weybridge
192	768D	30/07/57	Indian Airlines	VT-DIO	08/57	Hurn	261	806	23/01/58	BEA	G-AOYL	02/58	Weybridge
193	768D	12/09/57	Indian Airlines	VT-DIF	09/57	Hurn	262	806	26/02/58	BEA	G-AOYM	03/58	Weybridge
194	768D	11/10/57	Indian Airlines	VT-DIG	10/57	Hurn	263	806	07/03/58	BEA	G-AOYN	03/58	Weybridge
195	768D	30/10/57	Indian Airines	VT-DIH	11/57	Hurn	264	806	18/03/58	BEA	G-AOYO	04/58	Weybridge
196	768D	06/11/57	Indian Airlines	VT-DII	11/57	Hurn	265	806	01/05/58	BEA	G-AOYP	05/58	Weybridge
197	756D	22/02/57	TAA	VH-TVL	03/57	Hurn	266	806	21/03/58	BEA	G-AOYR	04/58	Weybridge
198	745D	24/09/56	Capital	N7442	09/56	Hurn	267	806	23/05/58	BEA	G-AOYS	06/58	Weybridge
199	745D	02/10/56	Capital	N7443	10/56	Hurn	268	806	21/04/58	BEA	G-AOYT	05/58	Weybridge
200	745D	07/10/56	Capital	N7444	10/56	Hurn	269	757	12/05/57	TCA	CF-THH	05/57	Hurn
201	745D	11/10/56	Capital	N7445	10/56	Hurn	270	757	19/05/57	TCA	CF-THI	05/57	Hurn
202	745D	16/10/56	Capital	N7446	10/56	Hurn	271	757	28/05/57	TCA	CF-THK	06/57	Hurn

C/No	Type	F/flight	Customer	Regist	Deliv	Factory/Notes	C/No	Type	F/flight	Customer	Regist	Deliv	Factory/Notes
272	757	29/11/57	TCA	CF-THL	12/57	Hurn	347	813	14/10/58	SAA	ZS-CDU	10/58	Hurn
273	757	08/12/57	TCA	CF-THM	12/57	Hurn	348	813	07/11/58	SAA	ZS-CDV	11/58	Hurn
274	757	18/12/57	TCA	CF-THN	01/58	Hurn	349	813	26/11/58	SAA	ZS-CDW	12/58	Hurn
275	757	18/01/58	TCA	CF-THO	01/58	Hurn	350	813	07/12/58	SAA	ZS-CDX	12/58	Hurn
276	757	22/01/58	TCA	CF-THP	01/58	Hurn	351	813	22/12/58	SAA	ZS-CDY	01/59	Hurn
277	757	02/02/58	TCA	CF-THQ	02/58	Hurn	352	813	15/01/59	SAA	ZS-CDZ	01/59	Hurn
278	757	17/02/58	TCA	CF-THR	02/58	Hurn	353	812	14/02/58	Continental	N240V	05/58	Weybridge
279	757	27/01/58	TCA	CF-THS	02/58	Hurn	354	812	31/05/58	Continental	N243V	06/58	Weybridge
280	781D	18/05/58	Sth African A F	150	06/58	Hurn	355	812	01/04/58	Continental	N241V	05/58	Weybridge
281	807	11/12/57	NZNAC	ZK-BRD	12/57	Weybridge	356	812	06/05/58	Continental	N242V	05/58	Weybridge
282	807	17/01/59	NZNAC	ZK-BRE	01/59	Weybridge	357	812	19/06/58	Continental	N244V	06/58	Weybridge
283	807	24/02/59	NZNAC	ZK-BRF	03/59	Weybridge	358	812	01/07/58	Continental	N245V	07/58	Weybridge
284	798D	31/07/57	Northeast	N6594C	09/58	Hurn, ex 745D	359	812	12/07/58	Continental	N246V	08/58	Weybridge
285	745D	21/08/57	Capital	N7464	02/58	Hurn	360	812	20/08/58	Continental	N248V	09/58	Weybridge
286	798D	26/08/57	Northeast	N6593C	09/58	Hurn, ex 745D	361	812	10/09/58	Continental	N249V	10/58	Weybridge
287	745D	06/12/57	Capital	N7463	01/58	Hurn	362	812	01/10/58	Continental	N250V	10/58	Weybridge
288	798D	21/10/58	Northeast	N6596C	10/58	Hurn	363	812	13/10/58	Continental	N251V	11/58	Weybridge
289	808	13/05/57	Aer Lingus	EI-AJI	05/57	Weybridge	364	812	25/10/58	Continental	N252V	03/59	Weybridge
290	808	24/12/57	Aer Lingus	EI-AJJ	01/58	Weybridge	365	812	06/12/58	Continental	N253V	03/59	Weybridge
291	808	13/02/58	Aer Lingus	EI-AJK	02/58	Weybridge	366	812	02/04/59	Continental	N254V	04/59	Weybridge
292	768D	12/02/58	Indian Airlines	VT-DIX	03/58	Hurn	367	not allocated					
293	768D	06/03/58	Indian Airlines	VT-DIZ	03/58	Hurn	368	814	08/04/59	Lufthansa	D-ANAM	04/59	Weybridge
294	768D	08/04/58	Indian Airlines	VT-DJA	04/58	Hurn	369	814	16/04/59	Lufthansa	D-ANAB	04/59	Weybridge
295	768D	17/05/58	Indian Airlines	VT-DJB	05/58	Hurn	370	814	18/07/61	Lufthansa	D-ANAC	07/61	Hurn
296	768D	30/05/58	Indian Airlines	VT-DJC	06/58	Hurn	371	838	06/09/61	Ghana Airways	9G-AAV	10/61	Hurn
297	782D	04/03/58	Iranian A/L	EP-AHA	03/58	Weybridge	372	838	07/10/61	Ghana Airways	9G-AAW	10/61	Hurn
298	782D	28/03/58	Iranian A/L	EP-AHB	04/58	Weybridge	373	756D	14/06/58	TAA	VH-TVM	07/58	Hurn
299	782D	30/04/58	Iranian A/L	EP-AHB	05/58	Weybridge	374	756D	02/07/58	TAA	VH-TVN	07/58	Hurn
300	784D	01/05/57	PAL	PI-C770	05/57	Hurn	375	815	14/08/59	Pakistan Int'l	AP-AJF	08/59	Weybridge
301	757	23/05/57	TCA	CF-THJ	05/57	Hurn	376	815	18/09/59	Pakistan Int'l	AP-AJG	09/59	Weybridge
302	757	23/02/58	TCA	CF-THT	03/58	Hurn	377	785D	11/03/58	Alitalia	I-LIRS	03/58	Hurn
303	757	03/03/58	TCA	CF-THU	03/58	Hurn	378	785D	30/03/58	Alitalia	I-LIZT	04/58	Hurn
304	757	13/03/58	TCA	CF-THV	03/58	Hurn	379	785D	23/04/58	Alitalia	I-LIRP	04/58	Hurn
305	757	25/03/58	TCA	CF-THW	04/58	Hurn	380	785D	08/05/58	Alitalia	I-LIZO	04/58	Hurn
306	757	13/04/58	TCA	CF-THX	04/58	Hurn	381	806	13/06/58	BEA	G-APEX	06/58	Weybridge
307	757	23/04/58	TCA	CF-THY	05/58	Hurn	382	806	07/07/58	BEA	G-APEY	07/58	Weybridge
308	757	09/05/58	TCA	CF-THZ	05/58	Hurn	383	757	23/06/58	TCA	CF-TIC	06/58	Hurn
309	757	07/05/58	TCA	CF-TIA	05/58	Hurn	384	757	25/02/58	TCA	CF-TID	03/59	Hurn
310	757	05/06/58	TCA	CF-TIB	06/58	Hurn	385	757	10/03/59	TCA	CF-TIE	03/59	Hurn
311	806	25/10/57	BEA	G-AOYH	12/57	Weybridge	386	757	23/03/59	TCA	CF-TIF	03/59	Hurn
312	805	03/02/58	Eagle Aviation	G-APDX	03/58	Weybridge	387	757	16/04/59	TCA	CF-TIG	05/59	Hurn
313-315		not built, Eagle Aviation order cancelled (V.821)					388	825		not built, Black Lion Aviation order cancelled			
316	810	23/12/57	Vickers	G-AOYV	–	Weybridge, V.810 prototype	389	812	23/07/58	Continental	N247V	08/58	Weybridge
							390		not allocated				
317	818	03/11/58	Cubana	CU-T621	11/58	Weybridge	391	798D	30/11/58	Northeast	N6597C	12/58	Hurn
318	818	19/11/58	Cubana	CU-T622	04/59	Weybridge	392	798D	21/12/58	Northeast	N6598C	01/58	Hurn
319	818	25/06/59	Cubana	CU-T623	08/59	Weybridge	393	739	03/07/58	Misrair	SU-AKN	07/58	Hurn
320	835	04/09/59	Tennessee Gas	N500T	09/59	Weybridge	394	739	15/07/58	Misrair	SU-AKO	07/58	Hurn
321	769D	20/01/58	PLUNA	CX-AQN	05/58	Weybridge	395	804	15/04/58	Transair (BUA)	G-APKG	04/58	Weybridge
322	769D	03/02/58	PLUNA	CX-AQO	05/58	Weybridge	396	806	02/07/58	BEA	G-APKF	07/58	Weybridge
323	769D	15/02/58	PLUNA	CX-AQP	05/58	Weybridge	397	827	30/09/58	VASP	PP-SRC	10/58	Hurn
324	784D	05/09/57	PAL	PI-C771	09/57	Hurn	398	827	23/10/58	VASP	PP-SRD	11/58	Hurn
325	785D	12/03/57	Alitalia	I-LIFE	03/57	Hurn	399	827	13/11/58	VASP	PP-SRE	12/58	Hurn
326	785D	11/04/57	Alitalia	I-LIFT	04/57	Hurn	400	827	06/12/58	VASP	PP-SRF	12/58	Hurn
327	785D	18/05/57	Alitalia	I-LILI	05/57	Hurn	401	827	20/01/59	VASP	PP-SRG	01/59	Hurn
328	785D	18/08/57	Alitalia	I-LAKE	08/57	Hurn	402	831	04/02/59	Airwork (BUA)	G-APND	02/59	Hurn
329	785D	23/06/57	Alitalia	I-LARK	06/57	Hurn	403	831	09/03/59	Airwork (BUA)	G-APNE	03/59	Hurn
330	785D	19/07/57	Alitalia	I-LOTT	07/57	Hurn	404-411		not built, California Eastern Airways order cancelled (V.823)				
331	773	30/10/57	Iraqi Airways	YI-ACU	11/57	Hurn	412	806	04/06/58	BEA	G-APIM	06/58	Weybridge
332	786D	05/07/97	Lloyd Aero Col	HK-943	08/57	Hurn	413	806	21/07/58	BEA	G-APJU	08/58	Weybridge
333	786D	23/12/57	LANICA	AN-AKP	01/58	Hurn	414	832	23/02/59	Ansett-ANA	VH-RMG	03/59	Hurn
334	786D	19/01/58	LANICA	AN-AKQ	02/58	Hurn	415	832	19/03/59	Ansett-ANA	VH-RMH	04/59	Hurn
335	815	17/12/58	Pakistan Int'l	AP-AJC	01/59	Hurn	416	832	09/04/59	Ansett-ANA	VH-RMI	04/59	Hurn
336	815	27/01/59	Pakistan Int'l	AP-AJD	02/59	Hurn	417	832	06/05/59	Ansett-ANA	VH-RMJ	05/59	Hurn
337	815	15/02/59	Pakistan Int'l	AP-AJE	02/59	Hurn	418	806	24/03/59	BEA	G-APOX	04/59	Weybridge
338	814	22/09/58	Lufthansa	D-ANUN	10/58	Weybridge	419	831	30/05/59	Airwork	ST-AAN	06/59	Hurn, for lease to Sudan Airways
339	814	01/12/58	Lufthansa	D-ANOL	12/58	Weybridge							
340	814	15/12/58	Lufthansa	D-ANAD	01/59	Weybridge	420	790		not built, planned local service variant			
341	814	31/01/59	Lufthansa	D-ANIP	02/59	Weybridge	421	808	21/12/58	Aer Lingus	EI-AKJ	01/59	Weybridge
342	814	16/02/59	Lufthansa	D-ANUR	03/59	Weybridge	422	808	19/01/59	Aer Lingus	EI-AKK	01/59	Weybridge
343	814	10/03/59	Lufthansa	D-ANEF	03/59	Weybridge	423	808	11/03/59	Aer Lingus	EI-AKL	03/59	Weybridge
344	814	20/03/59	Lufthansa	D-ANIZ	03/59	Weybridge	424	833	13/05/59	Hunting Clan	G-APTB	06/59	Weybridge
345	789D	01/12/57	Brazilian A F	FAB2101	10/58	Hurn	425	833	09/06/59	Hunting Clan	G-APTC	06/59	Weybridge
346	813	17/09/58	SAA	ZS-CDT	10/58	Hurn	426	833	01/07/59	Hunting Clan	G-APTD	07/59	Weybridge

VISCOUNT PRODUCTION (cont)

C/No	Type	F/flight	Customer	Regist	Deliv	Factory/Notes	C/No	Type	F/flight	Customer	Regist	Deliv	Factory/Notes
427	739	21/03/60	Misrair	SU-AKW	04/60	Hurn, last 700 series to fly	444	828	08/07/61	All Nippon	JA8202	07/61	Hurn
428	807	10/05/61	NZNAC	ZK-BWO	05/61	Hurn	445	828	24/08/61	All Nippon	JA8203	09/61	Hurn
429	794D	16/07/58	THY	TC-SEV	08/58	Hurn	446	838	07/03/62	Ghana Airways	9G-AAU	11/61	Hurn
430	794D	01/09/58	THY	TC-SEL	09/58	Hurn	447	814	09/12/61	Lufthansa	D-ANAF	01/62	Hurn
431	794D	12/10/58	THY	TC-SES	10/58	Hurn	448	828	07/03/62	All Nippon	JA8205	04/62	Hurn
432	794D	08/11/58	THY	TC-SET	12/58	Hurn	449	828	25/04/62	All Nippon	JA8206	05/62	Hurn
433	816	08/05/59	TAA	VH-TVP	05/59	Hurn	450	828	28/05/62	All Nippon	JA8207	06/62	Hurn
434	816	08/06/59	TAA	VH-TVQ	06/59	Hurn	451	843	14/03/63	CAAC	402	07/63	Hurn
435	836	24/08/59	Union Carbide	N40N	05/61	Hurn, ex V.816	452	843	20/03/63	CAAC	404	08/63	Hurn
436	839	../09/59	Iranian Govt	EP-MRS	05/61	Hurn, ex V.816	453	843	08/08/63	CAAC	406	09/63	Hurn
437	837	10/02/60	Austrian A/L	OE-LAF	02/60	Weybridge	454	843	01/10/63	CAAC	408	12/63	Hurn
438	837	17/02/60	Austrian A/L	OE-LAG	02/60	Weybridge	455	843	12/11/63	CAAC	410	02/64	Hurn
439	837	25/02/60	Austrian A/L	OE-LAH	03/60	Weybridge	456	843	02/01/64	CAAC	412	04/64	Hurn, last Viscount to fly
440	837	04/03/60	Austrian A/L	OE-LAK	03/60	Weybridge							
441	837	02/05/60	Austrian A/L	OE-LAL	05/60	Weybridge	457	828	18/09/62	All Nippon	JA8208	10/62	Hurn
442	837	22/07/60	Austrian A/L	OE-LAM	08/60	Weybridge	458	828	22/10/62	All Nippon	JA8209	11/62	Hurn
443	828	07/06/61	All Nippon	JA8201	06/61	Hurn	459	828	19/12/62	All Nippon	JA8210	12/62	Hurn

Queen's Building at London Heathrow in the late 1950s with several BEA Viscounts visible. This terminal housed airline operations and staff plus facilities for the public including a terraced roof garden, exhibition hall, news cinema, children's playroom, post office and grille room and buffet.

DE HAVILLAND
COMET

The first Comet 4, BOAC's G-APDA, over Hatfield House, a sacred site for anyone who loves the words 'de Havilland'. (BAe)

Nearly five decades on, it is difficult to appreciate just what an enormous advance in civil aviation technology was represented by the world's first jet airliner, the de Havilland Comet.

In these days of routine jet services ranging from short regional flights with 50 passengers to international routes in airliners carrying 500 passengers and capable of flying between any two points on the globe with only one stop and within a 24 hour period, the modestly performing Comet seems insignificant. But in its time, this pioneering airliner was as advanced as was possible in civil aviation and looked as if it (in combination with the Vickers Viscount turboprop) would give Britain an insurmountable lead in the field of airliner design and production.

The first prototype Comet was flown on 27 July 1949 and British Overseas Airways Corporation (BOAC) inaugurated the world's first commercial jet airliner service between London Heathrow and Johannesburg on 2 May 1952. Other airlines seemed to be queuing up to order this truly revolutionary aircraft, but within a short time the dreams of de Havilland, Britain and BOAC were in tatters.

In late 1952 and early 1953 two Comets were lost in takeoff accidents (one of them on delivery to Canadian Pacific Airlines) due to over-rotation while still on the ground, resulting in the wing stalling and the aircraft failing to leave the ground. Another aircraft was lost in mid 1953 when it broke up after entering severe turbulence on departure from Calcutta.

These accidents could not be directly attributed to the Comet itself,

but two other losses in 1954 marked the end of the Comet – at least in its original form – as a viable project for both the manufacturer and airlines. As is discussed in a later chapter of this book, the two 1954 crashes were the result of structural failure due to metal fatigue. This was in many ways the price of progress into a not yet completely understood area, particularly when the relatively new art and science of cabin pressurisation (to the then very high differential of 8.25lb/sq in) was involved. The necessary incorporation of pressurisation in the Comet – it was designed to cruise at up to 40,000 feet (12,190m) – had induced metal fatigue in certain areas at a rate which could not have been anticipated at the time, with disastrous results.

Considerable time and effort was expended in identifying the cause of the crashes and finding solutions. The information gained was shared with the world's aviation industry, to everyone's benefit in the years ahead.

The accidents and subsequent investigations effectively ended the Comet programme for four years until the larger and extensively revised Comet 4 family came along in 1958. A safe and economical aircraft, the Comet 4 coincided with the arrival of the Boeing 707 and Douglas DC-8, unfortunately for de Havilland and the British aircraft industry generally. The lead which had been established by the early Comets was therefore swept way by the delays caused by the accidents, leaving the door open for the American manufacturers to move in and dominate the market.

Total Comet production – in terms

of aircraft actually flown – amounted to just 112 aircraft, of which 74 were of the later Comet 4 family. Two additional airframes served as prototypes for the Nimrod maritime reconnaissance/anti submarine warfare aircraft.

Some 40 of the earlier aircraft had their construction abandoned when the crash investigations were underway. Despite all this, the small number of Comet 4s proved themselves in service with several operators, and after 22 years, the last of them was retired from airline service with Dan-Air in November 1980.

Pioneer Days

The aircraft manufacturing company which bore the much loved de Havilland name and which was responsible for the Comet and many other classic aircraft designs over the years had – as did most other now famous manufacturers – most humble beginnings.

Geoffrey (later Sir Geoffrey) de Havilland was one of the pioneers of aviation and like so many of his contemporaries had been bitten by the flying bug following the exploits of the Wright brothers and others. But de Havilland did have one significant difference from others of his era; when he decided to go into the business of building aeroplanes in 1909 at the age of 27 he had never actually seen one fly, let alone experienced the sensations of flight.

An accident of birth helped the draughtsman at the Motor Omnibus Construction Company of Walthamstow, London, become one of the most revered names in aviation. Unable to finance his plans himself and

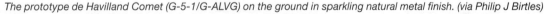

The prototype de Havilland Comet (G-5-1/G-ALVG) on the ground in sparkling natural metal finish. (via Philip J Birtles)

An early de Havilland classic, the DH.9 day bomber of 1917. More than 5,500 were built.

with a poor rector father who was unable to help, the young de Havilland's maternal grandfather Jason Saunders, an Oxford businessman, invested the then significant sum of £1,000 in de Havilland's dreams, money he'd intended leaving in his will anyway.

Armed with the £1,000 and joined by his friend Frank Hearle (a mechanic with the Vanguard Omnibus Co and later his brother in law) de Havilland set up shop in Fulham, London and began designing not only his first aeroplane but also the four cylinder, water cooled 45hp (35kW) engine which would power it. This engine was built for de Havilland by the Iris Motor Company for £250.

In November 1909 de Havilland's Aircraft Number One, a canard biplane with the single engine driving two propellers through bevel gears, was ready for flight. First attempts proved fruitless due to a lack of wind but finally, in December, the aircraft, the powerplant and Geoffrey de Havilland all lurched into the air for the first time. The result was a broken main spar due to the pilot's mishandling of the controls just after take off, a crumpled pile of wreckage and a bruised tyro pilot.

Aircraft Number Two was rather more successful, de Havilland getting this aeroplane – a modified and stronger development of the original – off the ground for its first hop in

September 1910. Shortly afterwards, de Havilland took his son Geoffrey Jnr up for a ride. At eight weeks of age, little Geoffrey was probably the youngest person to fly by that stage.

With money running short and Aircraft Number Two gradually proving itself, representations were made to sell the aircraft to the British government. These were successful and the aircraft went to the Government Balloon Factory at Farnborough, an organisation keen to get into heavier than air flight. This was the British Government's first aircraft purchase and de Havilland went with it to Farnborough to supervise its development and to design new aircraft under the auspices of what would be known as the Royal Aircraft Factory.

De Havilland remained at Farnborough until just before the outbreak of World War I, his designs including the B.E.2 reconnaissance scout which first flew in 1912 and served the Royal Flying Corps in the early stages of the war. The B.E.2 was de Havilland's first mass produced design with some 4,000 built and de Havilland himself flew one to a world altitude record of 10,560ft (3,219m) over Salisbury Plain in August 1912.

Due to the design and manufacture of aircraft being allocated to pri-

In many ways the aeroplane which 'made' de Havilland, the Moth. In the foreground is a DH.60M Metal Moth with a pair of DH.60G Gipsy Moths behind. (SW Media)

The aircraft which trained a generation of pilots during World War II and beyond, the DH.82 Tiger Moth. (SW Media)

vate companies, de Havilland's time at Farnborough came to an end in 1914 and after a short stint as Inspector of Aircraft in the Aeronautical Inspection Directorate, he returned to designing and flying by joining the Aircraft Manufacturing Company (Airco) where his designs had their source acknowledged by the 'DH' prefix being attached to the model number of each type.

De Havilland's Airco period witnessed the building of the legend that would grow around the de Havilland name in years to come thanks to some genuine classics of the era including the DH.4 two seat single engined bomber (of which 1,449 were built in Great Britain and no fewer than 4,846 under licence in the USA – the US Army withdrew its last example in 1932) and its heavily modified and ultimately much more powerful derivative the DH.9. Production of the DH.9/9A series amounted to more than 5,500 and like the DH.4 the type served with numerous air forces and was extensively used by pioneer airlines for commercial operations.

Of note is the fact that the world's first international air service (between London and Paris) was flown on 25 August 1919 by an Air Travel and Transport DH.4A.

The de Havilland Aircraft Company

Unfortunately for Airco, its days were numbered with the end of World War I and the wholesale cancellation of military orders which accompanied it. By 1920 the company was in serious financial trouble as the anticipated expansion in civil aviation did not take place. Airco was taken over by the Birmingham Small Arms Company (BSA) which wanted not the

aviation activities but merely the plant and equipment which went with it.

As a result, Geoffrey de Havilland was released from his contract with the new owners but took with him – at a modest price – the aviation assets including the prototype DH.18 eight passenger airliner, a pair of incomplete DH.14 day bomber prototypes and some DH.9A repair contracts. With some of his own capital and other money provided by Airco's founder, Holt Thomas, the de Havilland Aircraft Company was formed on 25 September 1920 at the Stag Lane airfield in north-west London.

With de Havilland went some 60 ex-Airco employees (more would soon follow), among them Arthur Hagg as chief designer, the man who would later be responsible for aircraft of elegant design such as the de Havilland Albatross and Airspeed Ambassador. Later on, the company's administration and production would move to Hatfield, north of London, a location steeped in de Havilland history, the birthplace of many classic aircraft and until its closure as a production site in 1994, a centre of British Aerospace's commercial aircraft activities and the location of the BAe 146 airliner production line.

De Havilland's activities in its early days included not only the design and manufacture of numerous types of aircraft ranging from ultralights to airliners and military types but also charter flying, crop dusting and other flying tasks designed to keep the cash flow going. The real breakthrough came in 1925 with the introduction of the first DH.60 Moth two seat light biplane, an aircraft which set the scene for the large numbers of de Havilland light aircraft to follow,

brought fame and prosperity to the company and revolutionised private flying in Britain and elsewhere.

DHs Diverse

The various Moth models provided de Havilland's bread and butter throughout the latter half of the 1920s and the '30s and allowed the company to develop a wide range of biplane and monoplane light aircraft during the period, among them the DH.83 Fox Moth, DH.85 Leopard Moth and DH.87 Hornet Moth. The ultimate expression of the Moth biplane family was the DH.82 Tiger Moth, used as the standard *ab initio* trainer of the Royal Air Force and other Commonwealth air forces during World War II and manufactured in large quantities in Britain, Canada, Australia and New Zealand.

Light aircraft weren't de Havilland's only activities during the 1930s. In a decade of intense activity, de Havilland put no fewer than 15 new designs into the air including the twin engined biplane DH.84 Dragon, DH.89A Dragon Rapide and DH.90 Dragonfly (one of the first aircraft intended for executive use) plus the four engined DH.86 airliner, the twin engined DH.88 Comet long range racer (winner of the 1934 England to Australia air race) and the four engined DH.91 Albatross, an elegant airliner capable of carrying up to 23 passengers. All of these aircraft were of basically timber construction, but in late 1938 the company first flew its DH.95 Flamingo twin engined 12 to 18 seat all metal airliner.

Further illustration of de Havilland's diversity and internal depth of expertise is provided by the fact that throughout that period and for many

The remarkably efficient DH.83 Fox Moth which could carry a pilot and four passengers on only 130 horsepower.

Another of de Havilland's extensive range of light aircraft of the 1930s, the DH.87A Hornet Moth. (Ray Verhoeven)

Simply efficiency: the DH.84 Dragon, first flown in 1932. (Stewart Wilson)

The DH.89 Dragon Rapide eight seater served not only as civil transport but also as a military navigation and wireless trainer. Many remained in service well into the 1960s. (SW Media)

years after the company was not only building aircraft but in most cases powering them with one or another of the numerous Gipsy inline engine variants which had been developed over the years. On top of that, the company was also producing propellers for its own and other makes of aircraft. Throughout World War II a de Havilland propeller of some sort would provide the thrust for most British aircraft.

Mossies and Jets

De Havilland's main activity during World War II was developing and manufacturing the Mosquito, arguably the company's most famous aircraft and the most versatile combat aircraft of its era. Developed under the design leadership of R E Bishop (who died only in 1989 and led the design of several important de Havilland types including the Hornet, Vampire, Comet, Dove, Heron and DH.110/Sea Vixen), the Mosquito was produced in bomber, night fighter, fighter bomber/interdictor, photographic reconnaissance, trainer and even naval variants, total production amounting to 7,781 aircraft in Britain, Canada and Australia.

Wartime also saw the company venturing into the jet age with the development and first flight (in September 1943) of the Vampire twin boom design. The Vampire was also extensively developed into fighter, night fighter, fighter-bomber and trainer variants and remained in production until the late 1950s after having been built in several countries.

Not surprisingly, Vampires were in the main powered by de Havilland jet engines and inseparable from the development of the Vampire is the pioneering work on its powerplant, what in production form would be known as the de Havilland Goblin. A centrifugal flow turbojet, the Goblin provided 2,700lb (12kN) thrust in its early production forms and 3,500lb (15.7kN) thrust by the end of its development. The more powerful Ghost engine (as fitted to the Venom and early model Comets) was of similar design but enlarged.

The man responsible for the development of the Goblin was Major Frank Halford, who had began designing a jet engine for de Havilland's engine division in early 1941 following a visit (with Sir Geoffrey de Havilland) to RAF Cranwell to examine Frank Whittle's work on jets and to witness a flight by the Gloster E.28/29, Britain's first jet aircraft.

With approval given to go ahead with the project, de Havilland became the first British company to develop a jet engine for production and second only on the world scene to activities in Germany.

Great secrecy surrounded the Halford H.1 jet engine project, which was code named 'Supercharger'. The first drawings were issued in August 1941 and the prototype engine was run on Hatfield's test bed for the first time just eight months later, on 13 April 1942. One month later, the British Government gave permission for development of the aircraft which would be powered by the new engine to go ahead – the Vampire.

The security surrounding the project continued, with armed guards posted around the test bed when the new engine was on it and the strange noises coming from the building being put down to a new electrical plant.

Tests continued with the engine's speed being progressively increased until full thrust was recorded in June 1942, about 1,700lb (7.6kN) at that stage. There had been a bit of a hiccup on the way when the engine seized as a result of the intakes being sucked flat, but damage was minimal.

By the beginning of 1943 the Halford H.1 was ready for flight testing. By this stage the Vampire was still six months away, so the opportunity was taken to install two of the engines in a prototype Gloster Meteor as the Frank Whittle designed Rover/Power Jets engine intended for that aircraft was not ready.

Therefore, the first Meteor to fly (DG206) was actually the fifth airframe and when this historic aircraft took to the air for the first time on 5 March 1943 from Cranwell, it was powered by the Halford H.1/de Havilland Goblin jet engine.

Halford's and de Havilland's achievement was a truly remarkable one when looked back on. The time between the H.1 project being given the go ahead and its first flight was a little over two years: during that time Frank Halford's team had taken on pioneering work in an entirely new area of technology including thermodynamics, metallurgy and manufacturing and testing techniques; they had developed their new engine to produce the required power and they had developed it to run reliably.

The first Vampire flew in September 1943 but in the meantime the Americans were naturally being kept fully informed on the progress of not only the Goblin but also the other jet engines being developed in Great Britain. In October 1943 an engine was sent to Lockheed for installation in the prototype XP-80 Shooting Star, this aircraft flying for the first time in January 1944.

Thus both Britain's and the USA's first production jet fighters made their initial flights powered by Major Frank Halford's de Havilland engine, a notable achievement.

The sleek DH.91 Albatross airliner of wooden construction.

Perhaps the most famous de Havilland of them all, the DH.98 Mosquito. This is an NF.II night fighter.

DH.115 Vampire Trainer, one expression of the original Vampire theme. At one stage, a 'large Vampire' design was considered to meet the Brabazon Committee's Type 4 requirement for a jet mailplane.

De Havilland was producing an extremely diverse range of aircraft in the late 1940s and well into the 1950s, ranging from jet fighters and jet airliners to more basic commercial types such as the Dove and (illustrated here) DH.114 Heron feederliner. The company also built the engines for most of them. (Bruce Malcolm)

Postwar Expansion

The postwar 'De Havilland Enterprise' was an extraordinary company designing and manufacturing a wide range of aircraft. If developing the world's first jet airliner wasn't enough, the list of other DH types emerging from the factories in the decade following the end of the war is quite remarkable: the DH.100 Vampire, DH.103 Hornet and Sea Hornet (first flown 1944), DH.104 Dove light transport (1945), DH.108 tailless jet research aircraft (1946), DH.110 all weather fighter (1951, later developed into the Sea Vixen naval fighter), DH.112 Venom fighter-bomber (1949) and Sea Venom all weather naval fighter (1952), DH.113 Vampire night fighter (1949), DH.114 Heron feederliner (1950), and DH.115 Vampire Trainer (1950).

In addition, the company was also building the Chipmunk trainer which had been designed by De Havilland Canada (the Canadian subsidiary also designed and built large numbers of Beaver and Otter STOL utility aircraft during this period), while in Australia De Havilland Aircraft was manufacturing Mosquitos and then Vampires under licence as well as a few examples of its own Drover three engined light transport.

On top of all this was the company's range of jet and piston engines, propellers, rocket engines and the design and development of air-to-air missiles such as Blue Jay (later Firestreak) and the Blue Streak long range ballistic missile.

A 'Jet Mailplane'

The Brabazon Committee's Type 4 specification for a pressurised "jet propelled mailplane for the North At-

R E Bishop, de Havilland's Design Director and leader of the team responsible for conceiving the Comet.

lantic" carrying a ton (1,015kg) of cargo at a speed of over 400mph (644km/h) represented an extremely advanced concept for the day, a time when the notion of jet propulsion was very new and in fact only two jet aircraft had been flown in Britain – the Gloster E.28/39 prototypes. The fact that the original proposal with its small payload bore little resemblance to the DH.106 Comet as it eventually emerged results from an early ignorance of what a jet powered commercial aircraft might be capable of, what power might be available from the engines and what form airframe development might take.

As the bank of knowledge grew,

so did the requirements of the specification. The first specification was issued in 1943. By July 1944 the Committee had justifiable doubts about a jet aircraft having the range to fly the Atlantic even with one stop and instead moved towards an aircraft for European and Empire services powered by two or more turbojets with subsequent development including a re-engined version for Atlantic services. By that stage the jet airliner was looked at being a 14 seater with a range of 700 to 800 miles (1,126 to 1,287km), a cruising speed of 450mph (724km/h) and a maximum weight of around 30,000lb (13,600kg) including a 3,000lb (1,360kg) payload.

Early Investigations

De Havilland had in the meantime been looking at several unorthodox layouts for a jet transport, with sanction from the Brabazon Committee from mid 1943 with a view to building an aircraft capable of filling the Type 4 requirement. Even before that, in 1941, the company had examined the possibility of a jet powered version of the prewar Flamingo airliner powered by two Halford H.1 engines. A 'Jet Mosquito' had also been looked at.

Among the jet airliner ideas examined was a 1943 twin boom design with three Halford H.1 or H.2 (later DH Goblin and Ghost, respectively) engines grouped in the rear of the fuselage pod with air intakes in the wing roots, as on the Vampire. In fact this design would have looked much like an enlarged Vampire had it been built. This concept (within an all metal design of about 80 feet/24.4m wing span) encompassed several variations, one carrying just six passengers between London and New York

VM703, one of two Avro Lancastrians fitted with DH Ghost engines in the outer positions from 1947. These testbeds logged 425 hours testing the Ghost before it flew on the first Comets. (via Philip J Birtles)

at 500mph (805km/h) or 12 passengers over 1,400 mile (2,253km) stage lengths; another carrying up to 20 passengers over half that range.

This basic 'large Vampire' format was studied in several size variations in 1943-44 using three Ghosts as the powerplant until it was replaced with another radical design retaining the three engines grouped together in the rear fuselage but dispensing with the twin boom idea and replacing it with a canard layout with small foreplanes on the nose working in conjunction with mainplanes at the rear. This is considered to be the first planned application of the canard layout to a jet aircraft.

An ongoing concern was that a turbojet powered airliner would have insufficient range for economical trans-Atlantic operations, or that if sufficient fuel was carried, the payload would be small and impractical. With this in mind, much discussion was carried out during 1944 on the relative merits of pure jet and turboprop aircraft to fill the Type 4 requirement. De Havilland was convinced that pure jet was the way to go for long haul operations and important support was forthcoming from BOAC, which encouraged finding sufficient range to fly the North Atlantic. BOAC reasoned that offering a speed of 500mph for a mail carrier would encourage customers to pay higher fares and thus make the project viable for the operator.

By late 1944 BOAC had indicated it would need 25 of these new jet transports, a bold decision when the fact that the form and specification of the aircraft was still far from settled. The government (mainly through the Ministry of Aviation – later Ministry of Supply) was closely involved in the evolution of the Type 4 requirement into what would emerge as the Comet. It is important to note that this involvement was a positive one which pushed the point that it did not want to waste money on an experimental type which would have no production future, but rather an aircraft which would have appeal to operators.

In late 1944, Specification 20/44 for a jet transport was issued and shortly afterwards de Havilland allocated the company designation DH.106 to the project, the design of which continued to evolve and grow throughout 1945 under the direction of chief designer R E Bishop. Bishop was a man of firm beliefs; he was almost obsessive about controlling weight, looked for mechanical simplicity (his rejection of electrical devices when mechanical ones would do earned him the nickname 'Bishop Bellcrank and Lever') and he dis-

Vampire TG278 was part of the pre Comet testing of the Ghost engine. Fitted with extended wingtips, John Cunningham took this aircraft to a new world's altitude record of 59,446 feet (18,119m) in March 1948

trusted theorists and academics. In this he was later proved to have some justification for his opinions, for it was the metallurgists who had promoted the high strength zinc based aluminium alloys which would later suffer tragic fatigue failures in the Comet.

Ghost Development

By now, the powerplant was established as four H.2/Ghost centrifugal flow turbojets each rated at 5,000lb (22.4kN) thrust. Basically an enlarged and more powerful development of the H.1/Goblin, the Ghost had a single stage centrifugal compressor, a single stage turbine and 16 combustion chambers. Intended originally for the de Havilland Venom fighter-bomber, the engine had to be considerably modified for civil application with about 80 per cent of the components being redesigned.

As applied to the Comet, the intake system had to be revamped as air was introduced directly into the engine through front intakes while the Venom had bifurcated intakes situated in the wing roots. A large amount of bleed air was also required to provide cabin pressurisation and other services. These challenges were overcome and in June 1948 the Ghost became the first jet engine approved for commercial operations after passing the very stringent civil type approval requirements.

The first 'civil' Ghost for the Comet was bench tested in September 1945 and flight testing started in July 1947 in Avro Lancastrian VM703 in which

the outer Rolls-Royce Merlin piston engines were replaced with Ghosts. A second Lancastrian (VM729) was subsequently converted and between them the two aircraft logged 425 hours in this configuration, providing much useful information about intakes, fuel systems, jetpipe cooling, inflight relighting and other aspects.

The Lancastrians were limited to an altitude of 25,000 feet (7,620m), so a Ghost engined Vampire with extended wingtips was used for high altitude testing. This Vampire (TG278) set a new world's altitude record of 59,446 feet (18,119m) in March 1948 with de Havilland test pilot John Cunningham at the controls.

Tailless Diversions

Considerable effort was expended on wind tunnel and general aerodynamic research throughout 1944 and 1945, without the benefit of captured German data which would be made available to Britain, the USA and the Soviet Union after the war.

It was realised at an early stage that a practical aircraft was needed and this evolved as the bank of knowledge on all aspects of its design improved. Also realised was the fact that the technological challenge was massive, whether it be in the areas of powerplant and airframe development, systems, pressurisation or structure.

Less obvious factors also had to be taken into account as a result of the fact that this aircraft would be travelling faster and higher than any airliner before it. How could a cabin

One of the DH.106 concepts was a tailless aircraft with highly swept wings. To test the concept, three DH.108 'Swallows' were built using the Vampire's fuselage as the basis. The first of them flew in May 1946 and all three crashed. This is the third DH.108 which in April 1948 became the first British aircraft to exceed the speed of sound.

environment suitable for safe and comfortable travel be evolved? What effects would sustained high altitude flight have on passengers and crew? What effects would speed, height and altitude have on the structure of the aircraft? Would navigation and air traffic control systems be able to cope with an airliner travelling at better than eight miles per minute? And so on.

De Havilland moved away from the 'Large Vampire' and canard concepts in 1945 and towards an equally radical one – a tailless aircraft with highly swept (40deg) wings. Powered by four Ghost engines partially recessed under the wing roots, this design could accommodate 24 passengers three abreast in a fuselage of 8ft (2.44m) diameter and have a maximum takeoff weight of 82,000lb (37,195kg). It was estimated that a trans-Atlantic operations with a single stop at Gander, Newfoundland, were possible if the passenger load was reduced to 18. Allowing for a 30 minute stop at Gander and the prevailing westerly winds, elapsed times were estimated at 8.5 hours London-New York and 6.75 hours return.

A range of 2,200 miles (3,540km) was possible with the full complement of passengers enabling operations on the Empire routes from Britain allowing flights to Cape Town in 15 hours elapsed time with three stops *en route* or to Sydney in 24 hours with five stops.

This tailless configuration demanded further information as to its behaviour on a real aircraft, with the result that three Vampires were modified in 1946-47 as the DH.108. Built to Specification E.18/45, the DH.108 (unofficially called the 'Swallow') was created by combining a modified wooden Vampire fuselage pod with an extended rear section and a swept (43deg) metal wing and single fin and rudder. Two examples were initially ordered, the first of them – for low speed research – flying in May 1946 and the second – for high speed flying – the following August. A third DH.108 was also built for high speed research, flying in July 1947.

The thought of attempting to break the world air speed record was also in the back of the designers' minds, a mark at that stage set at 616mph (991km/h) by a Gloster Meteor. All three DH.108s crashed, one of the accidents claiming the life of Geoffrey de Havilland Jnr in September 1946 when the second aircraft broke up over the Thames estuary during a test run for an attempt on the record. The third aircraft set a new 100 kilometres closed circuit record of 605.2mph (974km/h) in April 1948 in the hands of John Derry while five months later the same pilot and aircraft became the first British combination to exceed the speed of sound, in a dive.

The 108's contribution to the DH.106 airliner design was limited as the decision to abandon a tailless configuration had been taken even before the research aircraft had flown. Regardless, the aircraft did contribute to the general bank of aerodynamic knowledge at the time.

The DH.108 was a remarkable aircraft nevertheless, John Cunningham (who became DH's chief test pilot on the death of Geoffrey de Havilland Jnr) later pointing out its capability of cruising at Mach 0.88 at 35,000 feet on the extremely modest power of a 2,800lb (12.5kN) thrust Goblin. "Phenomenal! What does that today?", he quite rightly pointed out. Cunningham also noted the 108's tendency to pitch oscillation and general instability, characteristics which were less than desirable in any aircraft, let alone one intended to fly passengers around the world.

Conventional Moves

The decision to remove the tailless airliner from the equation was as a result of the conclusion that it involved unnecessary technical risk and probable weight penalties. The next revision to the evolution of concept which eventually led to the Comet was the return to a design with conventional horizontal tail surfaces but still with the fuselage and highly swept wing of the tailless design.

This proposal was published in the first full brochure to be issued on the DH.106 in May 1946 and showed a trans-Atlantic aircraft with a maximum weight of 93,000lb (42,185kg) but a still modest payload of 5,000lb (2,268kg). Clearly, a more efficient design had to be evolved and this was found during the course of 1946 by reverting to less radical concepts. By the end of the year the DH.106 design was very close to the Comet configuration with wings swept back at a modest 20 degrees, unswept vertical and horizontal tail surfaces, four Ghost engines buried in the wing roots, a longer fuselage of 9ft 9in (2.97m) diameter allowing seating for a maximum of 32 passengers seated

Testing the Comet's nosewheel undercarriage in a special rig constructed for the purpose using a truck chassis and Mosquito mainwheel outriggers. The photograph is dated February 1948. (via Philip J Birtles)

A mock-up Comet nose fitted to a Horsa II glider (TL348) to test crew visibility and the effects of rain at low speeds. The Horsa was towed by a Handley Page Halifax. (via Philip J Birtles)

four abreast and a maximum weight of 100,000lb (45,360kg) including a 7,000lb (3,175kg) payload. This fuselage diameter would later prove adequate for five abreast seating when high density economy class configurations became common.

Payload range figures for this design included the capability to carry a 7,000lb (3,175kg) payload (24 passengers plus freight) from London to Gander (and then on to New York) against a 100mph (161km/h) headwind with reserves for diversions. The 'Empire routes' version would carry 32 passengers over a range of 2,200 miles (3,540km).

The decision to reduce the DH.106's wing sweepback cost about 30mph (48km/h) in cruising speed, reducing it to an estimated 505mph (813km/h) but brought with it considerable benefits including much better economics and reduced technical risk. The decision to stick with the Ghost centrifugal flow turbojet was also taken in the interests of less risk as it was further developed than axial flow types such as the Rolls-Royce AJ.65, later Avon. By the end of 1946 the installation of axial flow engines in the DH.106 was considered to be inevitable further down the line due to their greater growth potential and inherently better specific fuel consumption. But for now, early Comets would be powered by Ghosts.

In January 1947 the British Ministry of Supply issued an "Intention to Proceed" to de Havilland covering eight DH.106s for BOAC, the first production order to be placed by any airline for a turbine powered airliner.

British South American Airlines ordered six aircraft shortly afterwards and after its subsequent merger with BOAC the overall order settled on 16 including two prototypes for the Ministry of Supply. The contracts were on a fixed price basis of £250,000 plus £45,000 for the engines per aircraft, a figure which was increased slightly when the decision to replace the large single wheel main undercarriages of the prototypes with the four wheel bogies which were fitted to production aircraft.

These orders left the DH.106 programme some distance away from breakeven, but de Havilland decided it was a justifiable commercial risk as other orders would surely follow.

In late 1947, the DH.106 was formally given the name 'Comet'.

Preflight Testing

An extensive testing programme was carried out during 1947-49 while the first Comets were being constructed at de Havilland's Hatfield facility. A feature of this period was the extreme security surrounding the project, a marked contrast to today's approach, where the development of a new airliner is given as much publicity as possible before (and after) its first flight.

In the case of the Comet it was only in April 1949 – three months before the prototype first took to the air – that some preliminary information about the new airliner was published in the bimonthly *de Havilland Gazette* house magazine. The necessity to keep design details away from possible competitors while "leeway lost in

the war years" was made up was proffered as the explanation, as was the wish to avoid a lengthy publicity campaign during the type's development which might create the impression that difficulties were being experienced. This was due to the Comet having what could have been considered a lengthy gestation period, although considering the amount of new technology involved, it was quite reasonable and shorter than de Havilland had estimated.

Testing of the Ghost engine under the wings of a pair of Avro Lancastrians has already been mentioned; other airborne testing which preceded the Comet's first flight included the fitting of a mockup nose and cockpit section to the forward fuselage of a wartime Airspeed Horsa transport glider so as to investigate crew visibility and the effects of rain at low speeds.

The glider was flown by John Cunningham, towed by a Handley Page Halifax. Cunningham himself had to undergo some testing in preparation for his forthcoming role as the Comet's first pilot. Perhaps surprisingly, the wartime night fighter ace they nicknamed 'Cat's Eyes' had no large aeroplane experience so in 1948 he completed a conversion course on BOAC's newly delivered Lockheed Constellations, put on the airline's uniform and 'flew the line' for a period. A few hundred hours were logged and with them came not only invaluable time in a large, pressurised airliner, but also first hand knowledge into the workings of an airline, and in particular the Comet's first customer.

The high level of innovation in the design of the Comet made a great deal of static testing necessary. The 'firsts' incorporated in the design included high pressure underwing refuelling, hydraulically powered controls with no manual reversion (with duplicated systems for ailerons, elevator and rudder driven by three independent sources of hydraulic power) and in the case of production aircraft, four wheel bogie main undercarriage units.

Another recent innovation was the extensive use of Redux metal to metal bonding in the structure. De Havilland had some experience with the process in the manufacture of the Dove and it would go on to be used in many other aircraft.

Structural Testing

Proving the integrity of the Comet's structure took up a great deal of the development effort in the two years before first flight. All sorts of new problems had to be considered stemming from the fact that the aircraft would be carrying 40 or so passengers at up to 40,000 feet (12,200m) at 500mph (805km/h). To achieve this, the cabin pressure differential of 8.25lb/sq in was twice that of previous pressurised aircraft and the effects of sustained flight at high altitude and very low temperatures on items of hardware such as flexible hoses and the bag fuel tanks which were integral with the wing structure had to be examined.

Creating a suitable cabin environment was one of the major problems confronting the Comet's designers, requiring not only an effective pressurisation system but also air conditioning, dehumidifiers, cooling, heating and the ability to completely change the cabin air every three minutes.

De Havilland installed a decompression chamber capable of accommodating large sections of a Comet fuselage so as to test the structure, pressurisation and air conditioning systems and to simulate flight at up to 70,000 feet (21,330m) and temperatures as low as minus 70degC. The fuselage was designed to a safety factor of 2.5 or 20.6lb/sq in pressure differential, while actual testing subjected the fuselage sections to twice the normal figure, or 16.5lb/sq in. A full size fuselage section failed early in the testing process, emphasising the dangers inherent in an explosive situation.

This, and the fact that the source of the failure was difficult to trace, prompted de Havilland to undertake future testing in a water tank, a first for Britain. This ensured that any failure of the structure would not involve a catastrophic explosive destruction of it, allowing proper examination of the damage afterwards.

More traditional structural testing was also undertaken on the wing structure using hydraulic rams to bend and stretch the wings so as to simulate flying hours well beyond that which the Comet would be expected to log during its lifetime. The result of all this was a pressure hull which had been successfully tested to over 16,000 flights but as later events were to tragically prove, actual flights in the real world would substantially reduce this figure.

The inadequacies of the Comet's structural testing procedures were not the result of any incompetence on the part of the designers and engineers, but due to the lack of knowledge which by definition must accompany any pioneering venture.

Final Design

The detail design of the Comet changed little between late 1946 and rollout of the first prototype in July 1949. While the overall length remained 93ft 0in (28.35m), the wing span was increased from 111ft 0in (33.83m) to 115ft 0in (35.05m) and the maximum takeoff weight was raised to 105,000lb (47,628kg).

The four de Havilland Ghost 50 Mk.1 turbojets were each rated at 5,050lb (22.6kN) thrust for takeoff and 4,320lb (19.4kN) thrust maximum continuous. Total fuel capacity was 6,050imp gal (27,503 litres) in integral wing tanks.

The engines were mounted close together and buried in the wing roots. This configuration brought with it several advantages including reduced asymmetric control problems due to the engines being close together and reduced drag, but also several disadvantages such as structural complexity in the wing due to the need for cutouts for intakes, exhausts and the engines themselves, the need for greater protection against engine disintegration (and the weight penalty that goes with it), the danger of acoustic damage to the structure around the exhaust and the tendency for the cabin to be noisier than other engine configurations.

The Comet was the only Western production jet airliner to have its engines in this layout – although early

The first DH.106 Comet under construction in the de Havilland Experimental Shop at Hatfield, probably in early 1949.

Soviet designs such as those produced by Tupolev adopted it widely – and the Americans tended towards underwing podded engines as on the Boeing 707 and Douglas DC-8. The rear mounted engine configuration appeared later and was pioneered by France's Caravelle, the first short haul jet airliner to achieve production and an aircraft which used the Comet's nose/cockpit area in its design.

Britain persisted with engines buried in the wing roots for some of its military designs, particularly in bombers such as the Valiant, Vulcan and Victor.

The Comet's structural design was basically conventional although the extensive use of Redux bonding in many places instead of rivets was certainly not. The wing was of two spar design with 20 degrees of sweep and a thickness/chord ratio of a relatively thin 11 per cent.

The de Havilland designed undercarriage (initially with a single large wheel and then a four wheel bogie) retracted outwards to wells in the wings while the twin wheel nose leg assembly retracted rearwards into a bay below the cockpit floor. The undercarriage was hydraulically operated as were the flying controls, nosewheel steering, brakes and the large plain flaps outboard of the engines and split flaps inboard. Control surfaces consisted of ailerons, elevators, rudder and upper and lower slotted plate airbrakes on each wing. As mentioned above, the powered flight controls had no manual reversion but considerable systems redundancy.

Accommodation was provided for a flight crew of four (two pilots, navigator and flight engineer) and up to 44 passengers, four abreast in a small forward cabin/smoking room with eight seats and the main cabin with up to 36. The split cabin was made necessary by structural members carrying air conditioning ducting. These members were in line with the forward wing spar and remained a feature of the Comet throughout its life.

Cabin doors were of the inwards opening 'plug' type to help maintain pressurisation seal and integrity. The main passenger door was at the rear of the port side of the aircraft and the crew entry door was on the forward starboard side behind the cockpit and opening into the area occupied by the main luggage and freight hold of 200cu ft (5.66m^3) capacity. A second hold (185cu ft/5.24m^3) was located under the rear cabin floor.

By July 1949 all was in readiness for the maiden flight of this, the world's first purpose built jet airliner.

The first Comet makes a short 'hop' from Hatfield's runway during high speed taxying trials on 27 July 1949. Later in the same day the aircraft would record its official first flight.

One of Mexicana's three Comet 4Cs (top) immediately after takeoff; and a stately portrait of Comet 1XB XM823 (the former Air France Comet 1A F-BGNZ) while being used by De Havilland Propellers. (Philip J Birtles)

Extremes of climate: BOAC Comet 4 G-APDK (top) in the warm at Melbourne's Essendon Airport in April 1963; and G-APDF in the snow at London (bottom) in January 1963. (Eric Allen)

Ex BOAC Comet 4s: Malaysian Airways' Singapore registered 9V-BAS (top) at Singapore in February 1966; and Dan-Air's G-APDJ (bottom), one of more than 40 Comets the airline purchased second hand over the years. (Eric Allen)

A poor quality but very rare colour shot of the prototype Comet G-ALVG (top). Photographed in Sydney in March 1967 (bottom) is RAF Comet C.4 XR395. (BAe/Eric Allen)

BOAC Comet 4 leases: East African Airways' 5Y-AMT (top) leased 1971-72; and Kuwait Airways' G-APDN (bottom), leased 1965-66 and remaining in basic BOAC colours. They were photographed at Nairobi and Heathrow, respectively. (Eric Allen)

Testbed Comets: The A&AEE's XW626 (top – the former BOAC Comet 4 G-APDS) with radar for the AEW Nimrod in the nose and Nimrod vertical tail surfaces. Comet 4C XS235 delivered new to the A&AEE in 1963 (bottom) was the last Comet still flying in 1996. (BAe/Paul Merritt)

COMET DEVELOPMENT

COMET PROTOTYPES

The press embargo which had surrounded the Comet during its development period was finally lifted on 27 July 1949, the day of the new airliner's first flight and coincidentally, chief test pilot John Cunningham's 32nd birthday.

The aircraft had been rolled out of Hatfield's Experimental hangar two days earlier in overall natural metal finish and carrying the Class B registration G-5-1. Upon delivery to the Ministry of Supply in September 1949 it would be given the normal civil registration G-ALVG and would also soon be painted in full BOAC livery.

On 27 July, the press was invited to Hatfield to witness the Comet taxying and making high speed runs along the runway, during which it became briefly airborne. The maiden flight was conducted later in the same day once the press had departed, the crew comprising Cunningham, second pilot John Wilson, flight engineer Frank Reynolds, electrics man Harry Waters and observer Tony Fairbrother.

Cunningham took the aircraft to 10,000 feet (3,000m) on this first outing, checking low and medium speed handling before returning to Hatfield 31 minutes later with no problems recorded.

Unfortunately for de Havilland, the fact that the press missed out on witnessing the historic occasion caused considerable ill feeling. The decision to go ahead with the flight at the time chosen was not planned, it was simply that when he was informed the aircraft was ready, Cunningham made the decision to go then rather than

wait as conditions were suitable. Some important Fleet Street and specialist press noses were put severely out of joint by this, accusing the company of all sorts of deceit, arrogance and just about everything else except high treason. One senior aviation journalist said he would never write the name de Havilland again, and he didn't!

The remainder of the press corps quickly forgave de Havilland, of course, as they knew they couldn't afford to be left out of reporting an event as significant as the world's first jet airliner.

Flight Testing

The prototype Comet carried the responsibility for flight testing on its own for a year before being joined by the second aircraft (G-ALZK) on 27 July 1950, the first anniversary of the maiden flight.

G-ALVG recorded 32 flying hours in the three weeks after its first flight, 200 hours were flown in the first five months and by mid June 1950 the tally had increased to over 320 hours.

Various milestones were reached along the way: its first public appearance was at the SBAC Display at Farnborough in September 1949, the first overseas trip (to Castle Benito, Libya for initial high temperature trials) was recorded the following month and full tropical trials were conducted at Nairobi in Kenya during April and May 1950.

The trip to Libya gave first indications of the Comet's capabilities. On the outbound flight the journey was covered in 3hr 23min, an average speed of 440mph (708km/h), cruising

at 35,000 feet (10,668m). The Kenya journey was flown from Hatfield to Cairo and then Cairo to Nairobi, both stages of just under 2,200 miles (3,540km). Flight times were within six minutes of each other (5hr 09min and 5hr 15min) and average speeds were around 420mph (676km/h). These were astonishing numbers for the time and could not be matched by any other aircraft.

Performance testing revealed the Comet's overall capabilities which included a maximum cruising speed of 490mph (788km/h) at up to 40,000 feet (12,190m) and a range (with full reserves) of 2,650 miles (4,265km) carrying a capacity payload of 12,000lb (5,443kg). With the payload reduced to 8,850lb (4,014kg) – still enough for a maximum passenger load but without extra freight or mail – the range could be extended to 2,920 miles (4,700km) with reserves.

In terms of trans-Atlantic flying, these figures permitted the Comet to fly from Prestwick to Gander and then onto New York with an 8,500lb payload, most of the time. The Prestwick-Gander stage with a length of 2,116 miles (3,405km) was the most demanding as strong headwinds were the norm and there would be times when they were too much if the required fuel reserves (including a 400 miles/644km diversion to Goose Bay) were to be preserved. The return journey was not a problem thanks to tailwinds.

For passengers travelling from London to New York, even refuelling stops at Prestwick and Gander did little to interfere with a substantial time saving compared to piston en-

The Comet prototype during an early test flight and still carrying the Class B registration G-5-1. (via Philip J Birtles)

First flight of the prototype Comet at Hatfield on 27 July 1949. As is discussed in the text, this event caused some ructions among the gentlemen of the British press! (via Philip J Birtles)

gined airliners. Elapsed time for the outbound leg would come down from 18 to 12 hours, and from over 12 to nine hours in the reverse direction.

The Comet prototype achieved enviable levels of reliability from the start of its testing. Few modifications were incorporated between first flight and certification, wing fences to control spanwise airflow being the only obvious addition to the aircraft's lines.

Other ideas were also tested. Concern had been shown during the Comet's design and development period about possible shortcomings in its takeoff performance from hot and high airfields in Africa. The use of rocket assisted takeoff (RATO) gear was considered then and put to the test during May 1951 on the first prototype courtesy a Sprite liquid fuel rocket engine under each wing. The result was some spectacularly noisy and smoky departures from Hatfield but the idea was not developed.

The prototype was also the first to receive the four wheel bogie main undercarriage which would be fitted to production Comets. The new units were installed in December 1950 for initial trials, and remained fixed down as they could not be retracted into the wells designed for a single large wheel without extensive and unnecessary modification.

This aircraft was also fitted with a drooped wing leading edge in late 1952 following a ground stall accident suffered by a BOAC Comet 1 at Rome resulting from over-rotation during the takeoff run. A similar accident also occurred at Karachi in March 1953 to Canadian Pacific Airlines' first Comet 1 during its delivery flight, this time with fatal results. The new leading edge profile was subsequently adopted as standard.

Another idea was also partially tested on the prototype – flight refuelling. A dummy probe was fitted in May 1951 and the aircraft flown with a Lancaster tanker. Several linkups were performed (with no fuel transferred, naturally) but it was decided the idea was impractical for civil operations and was quickly dropped.

Proving Flights

The second prototype Comet (G-ALZK) was used mainly for route proving and operational technique trials and was delivered to BOAC on loan in March 1951. Over the next seven months, 'ZK undertook 12 overseas tours during which time it flew to Egypt, India, South Africa and other parts of Africa, Pakistan and elsewhere, logging 460 flying hours, 91,000 miles (146,400km) and 91 landings at 31 foreign airports in the process. Much valuable information was gathered and delays due to technical problems were minimal. The flights proved the viability of the Comet neatly fitting into BOAC's route structure and did much to encourage other airlines to look closely at the aircraft and in several cases, to order it.

The first four production Comet 1s were in the air by the end of 1951 and contributed to the certification process. By early 1952 the various Comets had between them logged over 2,000 flight hours.

The prototype Comet displays its clean lines for the camera. In the late 1940s and early '50s the Comet's shape was regarded by many as futuristic.

Early Comets in production at Hatfield with the fuselages of the second prototype (06002) and first production aircraft (06003) visible. (via Philip J Birtles)

The first three Comets in formation and in BOAC livery. From the top: the second prototype (G-ALZK), first prototype (G-ALVG) and first production aircraft (G-ALYP). (via Philip J Birtles)

The Comet first prototype (G-ALVG) in BOAC colours showing the perforated air brakes under the wing and the single wheel main undercarriage which appeared only on the two prototypes. (via Philip J Birtles)

On 22 January 1952, Comet 1 G-ALYS (c/n 06005) officially became the world's first jet airliner when it was awarded its Certificate of Airworthiness by the Ministry of Civil Aviation. Commercial services could now begin.

The two prototypes had relatively brief lives after this milestone had been achieved. Both were broken up, G-ALVG at Farnborough in 1953 and G-ALZK at Hatfield in 1957.

COMET 1

The production Comet 1 differed from the prototypes in only one significant way and that was the incorporation of the four wheel bogie main undercarriage. The maximum takeoff weight was initially the same as the prototypes at 105,000lb (47,628kg) but this was subsequently increased to 107,000lb (48,535kg).

The first of nine Comet 1s for BOAC (G-ALYP) took to the air for the first time on 9 January 1951 and was used in the certification test programme until being formally delivered to its customer in April 1952. BOAC had received its first Comet two months earlier and by the end of July 1951 it had seven in service with the remaining two following in September.

BOAC's aircraft were fitted with only 36 passenger seats – 'slumber-seats' as they were called – offering a very high degree of comfort. The historic occasion of the world's first commercial jet passenger service was recorded on 2 May 1952 when

G-ALYP departed London Heathrow for Johannesburg via Rome, Cairo, Khartoum, Entebbe and Livingstone. Thirty passengers were aboard the Comet for its journey of 23hr 37min and the aircraft was commanded by Captain A M Majendie.

This was time of great promise for the British aircraft industry and the British people, both of which saw the Comet as a symbol of great things ahead for the nation. Viscount Swindon, speaking in the House of Lords in July 1952 summed it up by saying: "I feel that we have such a lead in civil jet aircraft, and these machines have established such a reputation for themselves, that we may not only get orders from all the world but possibly collar the market for a generation".

Some good underside detail in this shot of the second prototype Comet, first flown on 27 July 1950. (via Philip J Birtles).

The first production Comet 1 for BOAC (G-ALYP), first flown on 9 January 1951 and delivered to the airline three months later. Note the four wheel bogie main undercarriage fitted to all production Comets. (via Philip J Birtles)

M.C.A. Form No. 958

UNITED KINGDOM

MINISTRY OF CIVIL AVIATION

CERTIFICATE OF AIRWORTHINESS

No. A.3215

NATIONALITY AND REGISTRATION MARKS	CONSTRUCTOR AND CONSTRUCTOR'S DESIGNATION OF AIRCRAFT	AIRCRAFT SERIAL No. (CONSTRUCTOR'S No.)
G-ALYS	The de Havilland Aircraft Co. Ltd. Comet D.H.106 Series 1.	06005

CATEGORY :	Normal
SUBDIVISION :	(a) Public transport for passengers (b) Public transport for mails (c) Public transport for goods (d) Private (e) Aerial work (h) Demonstration (i) Crew familiarisation

This Certificate of Airworthiness is issued pursuant to the Convention on International Civil Aviation dated 7th December, 1944, and the Air Navigation Order, 1949, the Air Navigation (General) Regulations, 1949, and the Air Navigation (Radio) Regulations, 1949, in respect of the above-mentioned aircraft, which is considered to be airworthy when maintained and operated in accordance with the requirements of the above-mentioned Order and Regulations, and the pertinent Flight Manual.

John S Maclay

Minister of Civil Aviation.

Date 22nd January, 1952.

This certificate is valid for the period(s) shewn below

Signature, Official Stamp and Date

From	22nd January, 1952	to	21st January, 1953.
From		to	
From		to	
From		to	
From		to	

No entries or endorsements may be made on this Certificate except in the manner and by the persons authorised for the purpose by the Minister of Civil Aviation.

If this Certificate is lost, the Secretary, Ministry of Civil Aviation (R.L.2) should be informed at once, the Certificate Number being quoted.

Any person finding this Certificate should forward it immediately to the Secretary, Ministry of Civil Aviation, (R.L.2), Ariel House, Strand, London, W.C.2.

(9158) Wt. 9786-J938 900 4 49 C.& Co. 745(8)

This optimistic view was typical, but there were also balancing opinions. Gilbert Perier, the president of Belgian flag carrier Sabena said (also in 1952): "In ten years time the US aircraft builders will be the major suppliers of all jet commercial air fleets encircling the world". Unfortunately for Britain he was absolutely correct.

Following the withdrawal of the Comet's Certificate of Airworthiness in 1954 following a series of crashes (see next chapter), BOAC's five surviving Comet 1s were allocated to various static test tasks as part of the investigations into the accidents. None flew again and all were eventually broken up.

Comet 1A

The initial triumphs recorded by the Comet resulted in sales to several airlines for a Comet 1 variant, the 1A. This differed from the original by incorporating minor structural changes which allowed an increase in maximum takeoff weight to initially 110,000lb (49,896kg) and then 115,000lb (52,164kg). Provision was made for extra fuel to be carried in the wing centre section, increasing maximum capacity to 6,906imp gal (31,395 l). Ghost 50-2 engines with water-methanol injection for improved airfield performance in hot/high/heavy conditions were also fitted.

All export sales for the first series of Comets were to Mk.1A standard and the first order was placed by Canadian Pacific Airlines in December 1949 when it ordered two. Subsequent orders were placed in 1951 by Union Aero-Maritime de Transport – UAT (2 plus another later on), Air France (3) and the Royal Canadian Air Force (2).

A historic document – the first full certificate of airworthiness issued to a commercial jet transport on 22 January 1952. (via Philip J Birtles)

DE HAVILLAND COMET VARIANTS

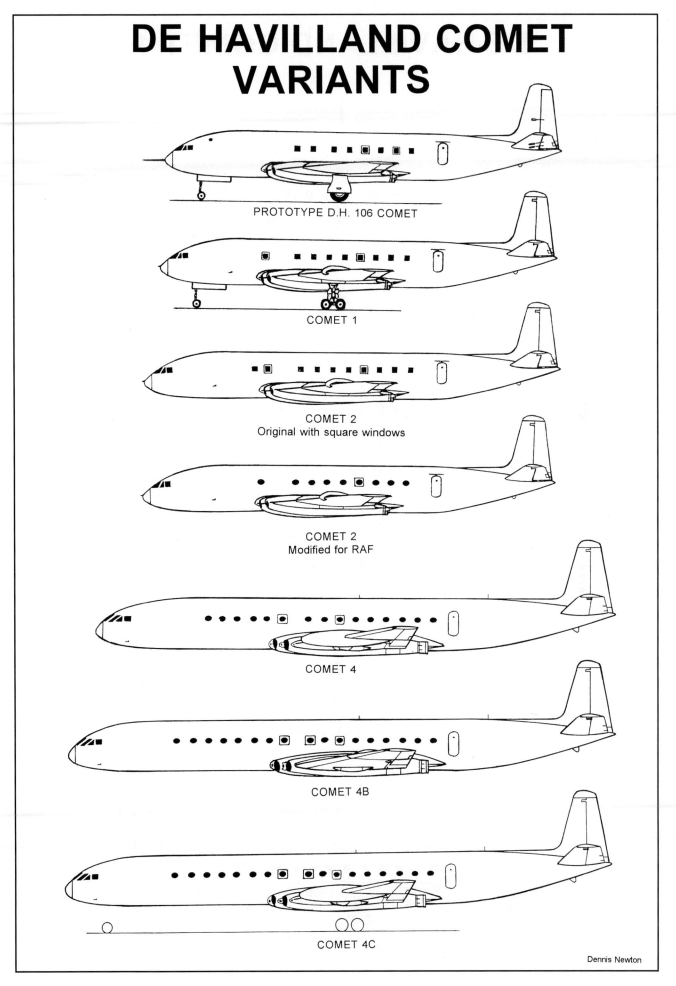

PROTOTYPE D.H. 106 COMET

COMET 1

COMET 2
Original with square windows

COMET 2
Modified for RAF

COMET 4

COMET 4B

COMET 4C

Dennis Newton

DE HAVILLAND COMET 1

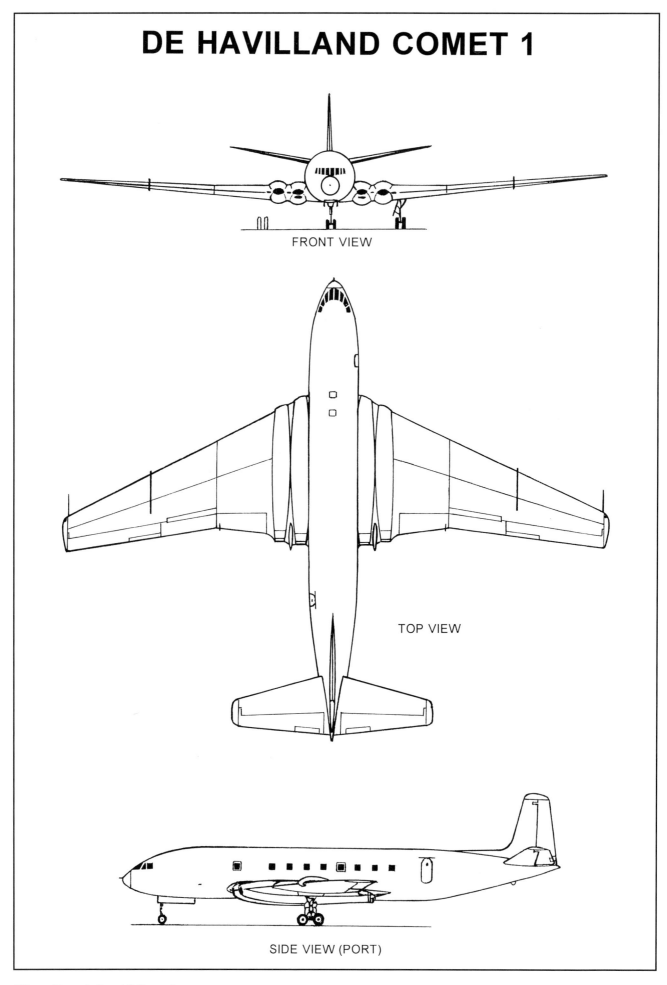

FRONT VIEW

TOP VIEW

SIDE VIEW (PORT)

DE HAVILLAND COMET 4

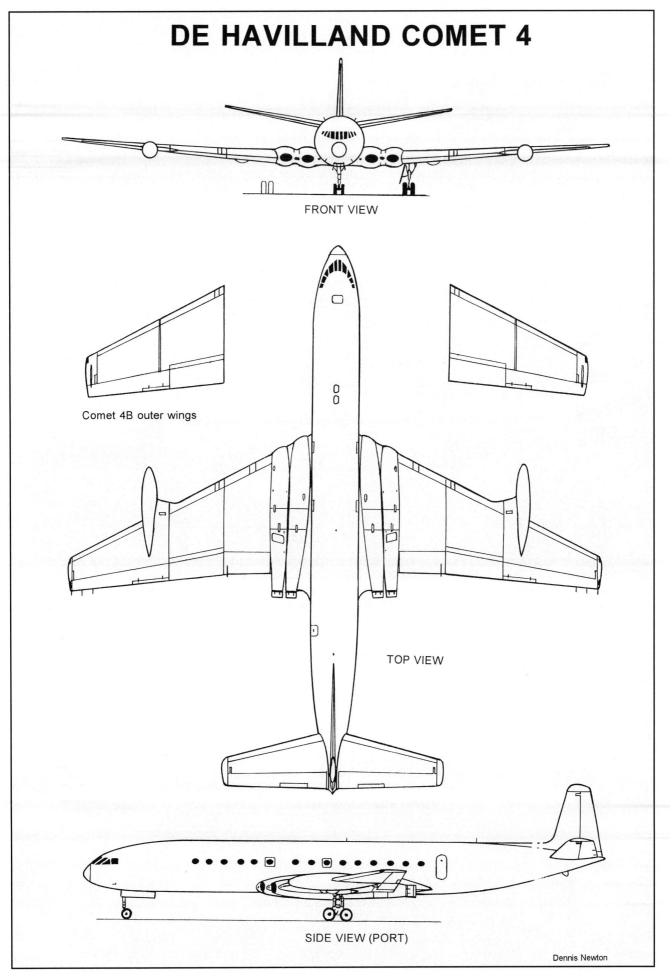

FRONT VIEW

Comet 4B outer wings

TOP VIEW

SIDE VIEW (PORT)

Dennis Newton

An fascinating shot taken at the 1952 SBAC show at Farnborough with Comet 1 G-ALYS sharing the ramp with a Hawker Sea Hawk, Avro 707, Supermarine Attacker, Percival Prince, Airspeed Ambassador, what could be the second prototype Miles Marathon's twin fins (the others had triple fins), Vickers Varsity, Bristol Freighter and Gloster Meteor. In front of the Meteor is what appears to be an example of the rarely seen RFD Winged Target. (via Mike Kerr)

One of three Comet IAs delivered to France's UAT in 1952-53. UAT became the first foreign airline to put the Comet into service when it began flying them on the Paris-Casablanca-Dakar route in February 1953. (via Philip J Birtles)

The Royal Canadian Air Force received two Comet 1As in 1953. Grounded the following year, they were subsequently modified and redelivered in 1957. (via Philip J Birtles)

Former Air France Comet 1A in Series 1XB form with structural modifications including the fitting of oval rather than square windows. This aircraft (XM823) was used as a flying laboratory between 1957 and 1968 and was the last airworthy Ghost powered Comet. It is photographed during its final flight on 8 April 1968. (Philip J Birtles)

The first Comet 1A to fly was CPA's CF-CUM (c/n 06013) in August 1952, although this aircraft was never delivered to the Canadian operator and diverted to BOAC instead after the airline's second aircraft (CF-CUN c/n 06014) ground stalled during its takeoff run at Karachi in March 1953 while on its delivery flight. The aircraft crashed off the runway, killing all 14 on board.

The other eight Comet 1As went to their intended customers and UAT became the first foreign airline to put the Comet into service when it began operating them on the Paris-Casablanca-Dakar route in February 1953. Air France began Comet services between Paris, Rome and Beirut in August 1953 and the RCAF received its two aircraft in March and April of the same year. UAT lost one of its Comets at Dakar in June 1953 when it overshot the runway during landing, fortunately without casualty.

After the Comet groundings UAT's aircraft never flew again and were later scrapped. Both the RCAF Comets and two of Air France's machines were returned to the manufacturer where they were eventually converted to Comet 1XB configuration incorporating a strengthened structure, 5,500lb thrust Ghost 50-4 engines and an increased maximum weight of 117,000lb (53,071kg). They were redelivered to the RCAF in 1957 and served with 412 Squadron until 1964 when they were retired.

The two Air France Comet 1As were also converted to 1XB standards in 1957, by which time they had been acquired by British Ministry of Supply. One flew with Aircraft and Armament Experimental Establishment (A&AEE) at Boscombe Down for Decca trials until February 1964 and the other was used by de Havilland as an equipment testbed by its Propeller Division (later Hawker Siddeley Dynamics) until April 1968 when it recorded the last flight by any Comet 1 variant.

COMET 1

Powerplants: *Four de Havilland Ghost Mk.50-1 turbojets each rated at 5,050lb (22.6kN) thrust for takeoff and 4,320lb (19.4kN) thrust max continuous. Fuel capacity 6,050imp gal (27,503 l) in wing tanks; additional 856imp gal (3,891 l) centre section tank on Comet 1A.*

Dimensions: *Wing span 115ft 0in (35.05m); length 93ft 0in (28.35m); height 28ft 4.5in (8.65m); wing area 2,015sq ft (187.2m²), undercarriage track 28ft 5.5in (8.68m); wheelbase 31ft 11in (9.73m).*

Weights: *Max takeoff 107,000lb (48,535kg); capacity payload 12,500lb (5,670kg).*

Accommodation: *(BOAC) 36 passengers four abreast in forward and main cabins; maximum 44 passengers; total baggage capacity 385cu ft (10.90m³) in forward and underfloor holds.*

Performance: *Max cruise 426kt (788km/h); normal cruise 392kt (724km/h); range with max payload 1,522nm (2,816km); max range (no reserves) 3,358nm (6,211km)*

Comet 1/1A production: *prototypes 2, BOAC 9, UAT 3, CPA 2, Air France 3, RCAF 2; total 21.*

COMET 2

During the early stages of Comet development, de Havilland had considered installing axial flow turbojets in the aircraft, mindful of their growth potential and specific fuel consumption advantages over the centrifugal flow engines. Specifically, the Rolls-Royce AJ.65 (later Avon) was considered but the decision to go ahead with the Ghost centrifugal flow powerplant was made as the Avon was then in the early stages of its development whereas as the Ghost was more of a known quantity.

Regardless, de Havilland continued to study an Avon powered Comet and the decision to build a prototype was taken even before the first Ghost powered aircraft had flown. The Comet with Avon engines was designated the Series 2 and the

sixth Comet 1 airframe (the intended fourth for BOAC) was set aside to become the prototype.

Dubbed the Comet 2X, this aircraft (G-ALYT) was simply a Comet 1 airframe fitted with four Avon Mk.501 engines each rated at 6,500lb (29.1kN) thrust or 30 per cent more than the power offered by the Comet 1's Ghosts. Being slimmer than the Ghost, the Avon (diameter 41.5in/105cm versus 53.0in/135cm) fitted into the engine bay areas easily with only minimal structural modifications required, although the intakes had to be enlarged to allow for the Avon's greater appetite for air, as did the jet pipes.

The Comet 2X flew for the first time from Hatfield on 16 February 1952, three months before BOAC inaugurated Comet 1 scheduled services.

Airline interest was strong, BOAC opening the orderbook with a requirement for 11 aircraft, followed by Canadian Pacific (3), UAT (3), Air France (6), British Commonwealth Pacific Airlines (3), Japan Air Lines (2), Venezuela's LAV (2) and Panair do Brasil (4), a total of 34 aircraft. In order to cope with the expected demand, de Havilland and Short Bros and Harland established an agreement whereby a second Comet production line would be established at Belfast in Northern Ireland, initially to build the Comet 2.

Circumstances dictated that this plan would come to nought following the crashes and groundings which followed in 1954. A third production facility at Chester was also planned, and this did eventually come on line.

Comet 2 Production

The production version from the Comet 2 differed from the 2X prototype in having more powerful 7,300lb (32.7kN) thrust Avon 503 or 504 engines and a fuselage stretch of 3ft 0in (0.91m). The wings incorporated the modified leading edge profile which

The prototype Comet 2X (G-ALYT) during an early test flight in 1952. This was the first Comet fitted with Rolls-Royce Avon engines. (via Philip J Birtles)

had been developed following the loss of the two Comet 1s which had suffered ground stalls during their takeoff runs due to over-rotation.

Maximum weight was initially set at 120,000lb (54,432kg) and the aircraft was capable of carrying its full 13,500lb (6,123kg) payload over a range of about 2,200 miles (3,540km). Basic passenger capacity remained at 44, four abreast.

The first production Comet 2 (BOAC's G-AMXA) was flown from Hatfield by John Cunningham on 29 August 1953 and by the end of the year three were in the air and about 20 more were in various stages of construction. It all ground to a halt in April 1954 with the loss of a second BOAC Comet 1 within the space of three months under mysterious circumstances, forcing the grounding of the entire fleet and in effect the suspension of production for over three years.

No Comet 2s were flown operationally by any of the airlines which had ordered them, although certification trials indicated some useful performance and payload/range improvements over the original model and various point to point records were set during them.

In the end, 16 Comet 2s were completed including the prototype, most of them recording their first flights in 1956-57 after incorporating modifications deemed necessary by the investigations into the earlier accidents. The construction of some 30 Comet 2s was abandoned, most of them at Chester. This factory would later produce various of the Comet 4 family and completed only one Comet 2, the last of its type, flown in May 1957. Shorts at Belfast built some fuselages, but no complete Comets would ever come from that source.

Like the Comet 1, the Series 2 could be modified to new structural standards in the wake of the crash investigations, but this would add substantially to their empty weights and therefore seriously effect their operating economics. Additionally, the cost of modification would be prohibitive to commercial operators.

As a result, all of the 15 'production' Comet 2s flew in British military colours, different standards of modification and build standards resulting in several subvariants:

Comet 2X: The original prototype remained structurally unmodified after the crash investigations but flew on in unpressurised form as an engine testbed for the more powerful Avon variants which would power the sole Comet 3 and later Comet 4 models. It was retired in 1959.

Comet C.2: Eight aircraft incorporating fully modified structures (including replacing the original square cabin windows with oval ones), full passenger carrying certification, four 7,300lb (32.7kN) thrust Avon 117/118s, reinforced cabin floor for mixed passenger/freight operations, maximum weight 127,600lb (57,880kg), accommodation for 36-48 passengers in standard RAF aft-facing configuration.

No 216 Squadron Royal Air Force began to receive its Comet C.2s in August 1956 and in doing so became the world's first military jet transport squadron. The aircraft remained in service until March 1967.

Comet T.2: Similar to the C.2 but without the reinforced floor. Two examples delivered to 216 Squadron RAF in June 1956 as trainers. They were subsequently upgraded to C.2 standards.

Comet 2R: Three aircraft which retained unmodified fuselages and square cabin windows and therefore flew without pressurisation. Power

A production Comet C.2 (XK669) of RAF Transport Command, originally built as a T.2 trainer. Note the oval shaped cabin windows, incorporated – along with other structural modifications – in the wake of the crash investigations. (via Philip J Birtles)

An unpressurised Comet 2R with unmodified structure and square cabin windows. This is XK655 of 51 Squadron RAF. (Philip J Birtles)

Comet 2E G-AMXD (foreground) in company with the sole Comet 3, G-ANLO. Before the disasters of 1953-54 it was planed to offer airlines these two Comet marks as a complementary pair. (via Philip J Birtles)

Comet 2E XN453 of the Royal Aircraft Establishment with which it served between 1959 and 1973. (Philip J Birtles)

Shorts built some Comet 2 fuselages at its Belfast factory but no complete aircraft came from that source. This is the first fuselage built by the Northern Ireland manufacturer.

was provided by Avon 117s. Delivered to 51 Squadron in February, April and July 1957, these aircraft performed electronic intelligence gathering duties in and around Eastern Europe and the Soviet Union until the two survivors were replaced by Nimrods. After the loss of one Comet 2R in a 1959 hangar fire, a Comet C.2 (XK695) was converted to 2R standards and therefore was the only one of its type with full structural modifications and oval windows incorporated and pressurisation system functional.

Comet 2E: Structurally similar to the C.2 but with Avon 118s in the inner positions and more powerful 10,500lb (47.0kN) thrust Avon RA.29 Mk.524 engines outboard. These new generation 'large bore' Avons would power the later Comet 4 family, and as such the two Comet 2Es provided much useful data for those aircraft and helped speed certification.

The 2Es (G-AMXD and G-AMXK) emerged in 1956-57 with fully modified structures and oval windows and were operated by BOAC on various of its routes to build up operating experience with the new Avon engine.

G-AMXD was allocated to the RAE Farnborough in 1959 (as XN453) for use in the development of long range radio aids while G-AMXK was used by Smith's Industries for automatic landing system development work and subsequently as XV144 for use by the Blind Landing Experimental Unit.

The cockpit of a Comet 2. (via Philip J Birtles)

COMET 3

Announced at the SBAC show at Farnborough in September 1952, the Comet 3 represented the first true growth version of the basic design, offering a substantial improvement in carrying capacity and payload/range capability. By comparison with the Comet 1, the 3 featured a fuselage stretch of 18ft 6in (5.64m) to an produce an overall length of 111ft 6in (33.98m), a modified wing of greater area, oval cabin windows, increased weights and fuel capacity and installation of RA.16 Avons rated at 9,000lb (40.3kN) thrust with their jet pipes angled slightly away from the fuselage to reduce cabin noise and the chance of damage.

Capable of carrying 58 first class or 78 tourist class passengers (or combinations thereof) four and five abreast, the Comet 3 featured pinion fuel tanks on the wing leading edges which increased total capacity to 8,308imp gal (37,768 l). Maximum takeoff weight was 145,000lb (65,772kg). Estimated performance included a cruising speed of better than 500mph (805km/h) and a range with 17,450lb (7,915kg) capacity payload of 2,700 miles (4,345km).

A prototype was ordered by the Ministry of Supply with early 1954 as the scheduled first flight date followed by first deliveries in late 1956. Airline interest was high and by the first half of 1954 orders had been placed by BOAC (11), Air India (2) and Pan American (3). The latter order – which included options on a further seven aircraft – was obviously of great significance to the Comet programme as it was claimed to be the first by an American airline for a British airliner. When PanAm placed its order, BOAC agreed release three of its aircraft to ensure early delivery to the important customer across the Atlantic.

Part of the Comet 3's attraction was the substantially improved operating economics it displayed over the earlier models, and more importantly, the piston engined transports it was intended to replace. De Havilland figures showed that compared to these aircraft and despite much higher fuel consumption, lower payload and substantially greater purchase price, the Comet 3 had considerably better revenue earning potential and overall would be about 10 per cent more economically efficient.

The company also pointed the Comet's superior productivity due to its higher speed, its lower maintenance costs and that although its fuel consumption was about three times greater than the pistons, the cost of jet fuel was only two-thirds as much. That, in combination with higher speeds meant that one cancelled out the other. Then there was the matter of passenger appeal and the time which would be saved on any route.

De Havilland's marketing plan was to offer the Comet 2 and 3 side by side as complementary products with different range and capacity characteristics.

A One-Off

All this conspired to make the Comet 3 look like it was going to be a winner in the marketplace, but by the time the first (and only, as it turned out) example – G-ANLO – recorded its maiden flight 19 July 1954 – again in the hands of John Cunningham – the Comet fleet had been grounded, production had in effect halted and the whole programme looked as if it might be over. To add to de Havilland's troubles, Boeing had flown its Model 367-80 (the prototype for the 707 jet transport series) just four days earlier. A new and potentially powerful force had arrived on the scene at a time when the Comet's prospects looked bleak.

This was undoubtedly the lowest point of the Comet venture but development flying with the Comet 2 and 3 continued regardless, the latter in particular contributing greatly to the effort which would result in the rejuvenated Comet 4 four years hence and the partial redemption of the entire programme. In the meantime, plans to put the Comet 3 into series production were scrapped and the construction of ten aircraft at Hatfield was abandoned.

As the Comet 3 was dimensionally and aerodynamically identical to the Comet 4, its input to that programme was substantial and that in conjunction with the subsequent fitting of Avon RA29 engines of similar specification and power to that which would be fitted to the later aircraft, meant that by the time the Comet 4 came along, more than 80 per cent of its Certificate of Airworthiness testing had already been performed.

The one and only Comet 3 shortly before its first flight in July 1954. In the background is a Comet 3 fuselage later used as a customer mock-up for the Comet 4 and finally for Nimrod trial installations, (via Philip J Birtles)

The suitably decorated Comet 3 photographed at Honolulu during its December 1955 world tour. (via Philip J Birtles)

The Comet 3 was converted to 3B specifications in 1958, flying for the first time in this new configuration on 21 August of that year. The aircraft was in effect turned into a 'flying mock up' of the Comet 4B which had been ordered by British European Airways for some of its medium range routes, swapping fuel capacity for payload. G-ANLO appeared in BEA colours as the Comet 3B, complete with pinion tanks removed.

Around The World

By mid 1955 the investigations into the Comet crashes had been completed, the reasons found, the solutions applied and the Comet was able to fly again. BOAC had kept its faith in the project by ordering 19 Comet 4s and now was the time to show the world that the aircraft was alive and well and in its new forms available for sale to the world's airlines.

John Cunningham, his deputy Peter Bugge and BOAC's Captain Peter Cane took the Comet 3 on an around the world flight starting at Hatfield in early December 1955. Flying in BOAC colours, the aircraft flew to Sydney via Cairo, Bombay, Singapore and Darwin. After visiting Perth and Melbourne before returning to Sydney, the Comet then travelled across the Tasman Sea to Auckland followed by a trans-Pacific journey to Vancouver via Fiji and Honolulu. It then visited Toronto and Montreal before tackling the 3,340 miles (5,375km) from there to London non stop.

A new London-Sydney record was set during the tour, the flying time of 24hr 24min contrasting with the previous mark of 44hr 28min set by a Qantas Constellation in 1953. The arrival in Sydney was greeted by a crowd of 25,000 which surged onto the runway forcing John Cunningham to perform a missed approach.

The 26 day journey covered 30,384 miles (48,897km), and although its of-

The Comet 3 photographed at Stockholm during one of its demonstration flights. It was dimensionally and aerodynamically identical to the forthcoming Comet 4 and as such was an important marketing tool for that aircraft. (via Philip J Birtles)

The Comet 3 was converted to 3B configuration in 1958 with pinion tanks removed. It became in effect a 'flying mock-up' of the Comet 4B which had been ordered by British European Airways. (via Philip J Birtles)

ficial purpose was to examine the operational performance of the aircraft by adhering to airline procedures (which was done, with excellent results), there is no doubt that there was a fair degree of 'flag waving' involved as well. About 600 passengers flew in the Comet during the trip, most of whom were experiencing the smoothness and speed of jet airliner travel for the first time. The effect was positive, but as one writer later noted, how many of the airline executives involved were so impressed they subsequently rushed out to buy Boeing 707s?!

The Comet 3 displayed pleasing reliability during the trip, the only technical hitch encountered being a

problem with the attachment of the starboard inner jetpipe.

G-ANLO's flying career ended as XP915 with firstly the Blind Landing Experimental Unit and finally the Royal Aircraft Establishment at Farnborough. Its final task was as a test rig for the Nimrod.

COMET 4

Work on Comet development had continued during the four year period when it was in effect out of production, culminating with a new and heavily revised family of models based on the interim Comet 3.

There is no doubt the Comet's image had suffered a battering during that period and as an image restoring

exercise a different name was briefly considered. The name 'New Comet' was in the equation for a time before the Comet 4 was finally selected as a logical continuation of the sequence. Dimensionally and aerodynamically similar to the Comet 3, the new variant received an order for 19 aircraft from BOAC in March 1955 for use on its routes to Africa and the Far East.

The Comet 4 differed from the earlier aircraft in several significant ways as far as its structure was concerned following the lessons learned from the crash investigations. It was built from stronger copper rather than potentially brittle zinc based aluminium alloys and the original thin 22 gauge sheeting used on the fuselage shell

The first Comet 4, BOAC's G-APDA, photographed taking off on its maiden flight from Hatfield on 27 April 1958. (via Philip J Birtles)

BOAC Comet 4 G-APDA in flight. Britain's international airline ordered 19 aircraft for use on its African and Far East routes.

had been logged by the Comet 3. The RA.29 Avon powerplants, too, had recorded many flight hours in various Comets before the new models appeared.

De Havilland commissioned a new pressure test tank at Hatfield in November 1955, one which was capable of accommodating a complete fuselage with wings attached, the latter sticking out of each side of the tank through water seals, allowing them to bend and flex via hydraulic jacks. This setup allowed the full gamut of pressurisation, gust and wing bending loads to be simulated and combined with the knowledge gained from the crash investigations, allowed an accurate assessment of the structure's life to be made.

The result of all this was a safe life for the structural specimen of 180,000 flying hours and applying a safety factor six, 30,000 hours for a real aircraft in service.

was replaced with 19 gauge which was 80 per cent thicker.

Power was provided by four RA.29 Avon Mk.524s each producing 10,500lb thrust for takeoff, total fuel capacity was 8,908imp gal (40,496 l) including the pinion tanks, thrust reversers were installed on the outboard engines, the maximum cabin pressure differential was increased to 8.75lb/sq in permitting flight up to 42,000 feet (12,800m), weather radar was fitted in the nose, the brakes were of the anti skid type and the maximum loaded weight was increased to 162,000lb (73,483kg).

Passenger accommodation was either 58 first class or 76 tourist class seats, the latter five abreast, although as time went on more and more passengers were squeezed into the Comet 4, culminating in Dan-Air's 99 and then 106 seat high density layouts of the 1970s.

The Comet 4 was capable of carrying its capacity payload over a 2,720 miles (4,377km) stage length with reserves.

Extensive Testing

The Comet 4 was undoubtedly the most thoroughly tested airliner the world had seen by the time it entered service in 1958 with thousands of separate fatigue tests carried out plus the airborne experience which

Into Service

The first Comet 4 (G-APDA for BOAC) was flown at Hatfield by John Cunningham on 27 April 1958. Built on production tooling, the aircraft was taken on several overseas trips during August and September of that year including to New York (the return flight to Hatfield setting an unofficial record of 6hr 16min), Canada, Mexico, Peru, Brazil and Hong Kong, the latter as part of the celebrations marking the opening of the new runway at Kai Tak airport.

BOAC's first two Comet 4s (G-APDB and 'DC) were handed over to the airline on 30 September 1958 ('DA

The Comet 4 production line at Chester. The first aircraft from that source flew in September 1958. (BAe)

A Comet 4 in the colours of Mexicana. This particular aircraft was leased from BOAC between 1965 and 1969. Mexicana was also the launch customer for the Comet 4C. (via Philip J Birtles)

followed in February 1959) and the 19th and last was delivered in January 1960. By now, the second production line at Chester was in operation, the first Comet 4 from that source being BOAC's G-APDE first flown on 20 September 1958.

Although BOAC's Comets were ordered for service on African and Far East routes, a race developed between the British airline and Pan American to inaugurate the world's first scheduled jet services across the North Atlantic. PanAm and its new Boeing 707-120s provided the competition, and although neither aircraft were ideally suited to the London-New York route as the Comet could not fly the service non-stop and the early 707s couldn't always do it due to the prevailing headwinds, both airlines were keen to reap the publicity benefits of being the first.

BOAC won, flying G-APDC from London to New York via Gander on 4 October 1958 in a total time of 10hr 22min, while G-APDB flew the return journey nonstop in 6hr 11min. Although BOAC and the Comet were victorious in this 'battle', the 'war' was certainly won by Boeing in the longer term as by 1958 the Comet's time advantage had been lost due to the groundings and the 707 – particularly in its slightly later -320 'Intercontinental' form – was a much more attractive proposition with its greater carrying capacity and range. BOAC itself became an early 707 operator, receiving its first of many in May 1959.

Despite this, two other customers were found for the Comet 4. Aerolineas Argentinas was the first, taking delivery of the first of six in March 1959. The other was East African Airways, which operated three from July 1960.

Comet 4 production therefore reached 28 (plus one structural test specimen) of which 11 were built at Hatfield and 17 at Chester.

East African Airways ordered three Comet 4s, the first of them entering service in July 1960. (Philip J Birtles)

COMET 4

Powerplants: Four Rolls-Royce RA.29 Avon Mk.524 turbojets each rated at 10,500lb (47.0kN) thrust for takeoff. Fuel capacity 8,908imp gal (40,496 l) in wing, centre section and leading edge pinion tanks.

Dimensions: Wing span 114ft 10in (35.00m); length 111ft 6in (33.99m); height 29ft 6in; wing area 2,121sq ft (197.0m²); tailplane span 47ft 5in (14.45m); wheel track 28ft 2in (8.58m); wheelbase 46ft 8in (14.22m).

Weights: Max takeoff 162,000lb (73,483kg); operational empty 75,400lb (34,201kg); max landing 120,000lb (54,432kg); max zero fuel 99,000lb (44,906kg); capacity payload (81 seats) 20,286lb (9,202kg).

Accommodation: Typical mixed class accommodation for 74 passengers, up to 106 in high density arrangement. Cabin length 72ft 8in (22.15m); max cabin width 9ft 7in (2.92m); max height 6ft 6.5in (1.99m); volume 2,815cu ft (79.7m³); total baggage capacity 589cu ft (16.68m³) in rear fuselage, forward underfloor and aft underfloor holds.

Performance: Max cruising speed 457kt (846km/h) at 31,000ft; economical cruise 438kt (811km/h) at 28,000ft; takeoff field length 6,750ft (2,057m); landing distance from 30ft (with reverse thrust) 5,740ft (1,750m); service ceiling 42,000 feet (12,802m); range with 16,800lb (7,620kg) payload and reserves 2,366nm (4,377km); max range (no reserves) 3,823nm (7,080km) at 405kt (750km/h).

Comet 4 production: BOAC 19, Aerolineas Argentinas 6, East African Airways 3; total 28.

COMET 4A

Announced in mid 1956 but never built, the Comet 4A was intended as an airliner optimised for short-medium range routes with higher cruising speeds at lower altitudes and modest airfield requirements.

G-APMA, the first Comet 4B. This aircraft was flown from Hatfield in June 1959 and delivered to BEA six months later. (via Philip J Birtles)

Compared with the Comet 4, the 4A had a 3ft 4in (1.02m) fuselage stretch and the wing span reduced by 7ft 0in (2.13m). Up to 95 economy class passengers could be carried, maximum takeoff weight was reduced to 152,500lb (69,174kg) and more payload was provided by increasing the maximum zero fuel weight by 4,000lb (1,814kg). The Comet 4's leading edge pinion tanks were retained.

It was estimated the Comet 4A would cruise at 520 to 545mph (837 to 877km/h) at 23,500 feet (7,160m) and would be economically viable on stages as short as 500 miles (805km) while retaining the capability to fly much longer stage lengths.

It appeared the Comet had finally achieved a breakthrough into the US market in July 1956 when Capital Airlines – the operator which had launched the Vickers Viscount there – ordered four Comet 4s and ten

Comet 4As in a deal worth £19m. Deliveries of the 4s were scheduled to commence in late 1958 followed by the 4As in 1959 but by then the airline had got itself into financial difficulties and the order was cancelled. Capital was taken over by United Airlines in 1961.

Much of the work carried out by de Havilland on the Comet 4A was applied to the 4B, developed for British European Airways.

COMET 4B

An example of increasing seating capacity at the expense of range, the Comet 4B was developed for use by British European Airways which wanted to offer jet speed and comfort while retaining the operating economics of turboprops.

To achieve this, in mid 1957 de Havilland announced the Comet 4B which – compared to the Comet 4 – featured a fuselage stretched by 6ft 6in (1.98m) to accommodate 84

mixed or 99 economy class passengers (119 would be squeezed in later on), the shorter span wing designed for the aborted Comet 4A, reduced fuel capacity achieved by removing the pinion tanks, a lower maximum weight and increased maximum zero fuel weight. Powerplants were the Avon 525, similarly rated to the 524s which powered the Comet 4.

Like the Comet 4A, the 4B could cruise faster at lower altitudes and was optimised for short and medium range services. The operating economics reflected this with seat/mile costs 15 per cent less than the Comet 4 on stage lengths of between 300 and 2,000 miles (480 to 3,200km).

BEA's intention was to use the new Comets on its Mediterranean services, ordering an initial six in March 1958 and eventually acquiring 14. The only other customer was Olympic Airways which ordered four in July 1959.

The lengthened fuselage of the Comet 4B is obvious in this shot of BEA's G-APMG. Note also the lack of pinion tanks on the wings. (BAe)

The sole Comet 3 was converted to 3B specifications and in effect acted as the prototype for the 4B. It first flew in this guise on 21 August 1958 in BEA livery.

The first real Comet 4B (G-APMA for BEA) was flown on 27 June 1959 and deliveries began the following November. BEA flew its first Comet 4B service on April Fool's Day 1960, between Tel Aviv and London. Olympic's first Comet 4B was delivered in May 1960 and the Greek flag carrier's fleet was operated in close co-operation with BEA.

The 18 Comet 4Bs were built at Hatfield (16) and Chester (2), the last of them (G-ARJN for BEA) flying from Hatfield in July 1961.

COMET 4C

The ultimate Comet version was the 4C, first announced in late 1957 and created by combining the 4's wings, fuel capacity and maximum weight with the 4B's longer fuselage and higher maximum zero fuel weight. The result was the most numerous of all the Comet variants with 30 built including two which remained unsold and were subsequently converted to Nimrod prototypes. Of the 28 Comet 4Cs which were completed as such, 22 were sold to seven foreign civil operators, one was delivered to the Aircraft & Armament Experimental Establishment for use in blind landing and navaid trials and the remainder went to the Royal Air Force, which designated them Comet C Mk.4.

The Comet 4C's launch customer was Mexicana, which had an order for three announced on 30 October 1959, the day before the first example took to the air. The order had obviously been known about for some time! Mexicana took delivery of its first aircraft in January 1960 but didn't start regular services (initially

between Mexico City and Los Angeles) until the following July.

Most of the 30 Comet 4Cs were built at Chester (23 aircraft), Hatfield producing only seven including the first two and concentrating mainly on Comet 4B production. The last Comet was United Arab Airlines' 4C SU-ANI, first flown on 4 February 1964 and delivered three weeks later.

By now, Comets were no longer 'de Havillands' but 'Hawker Siddeleys' following the and rationalisation of the British aircraft industry into two major groups. De Havilland, Hawker, Armstrong Whitworth, Avro, Folland and Blackburn now operated under the Hawker Siddeley banner, while the British Aircraft Corporation (BAC) comprised the old Bristol, English Electric, Vickers and Hunting companies.

The RAF's five Comet C.4s were delivered between February and June 1962 and served with 216 Squadron until June 1975, when along with just about every other Comet 4, 4B and 4C in existence, they were sold to

Dan-Air. An interesting customer was Saudi Arabia's King Ibn Saud, who took delivery of a sumptuously appointed VIP 4C in June 1962. This aircraft had a brief life, crashing in the Alps just nine months later during a training flight, killing all on board including two de Havilland personnel.

A full list of Comet 4C deliveries is included in the data table below.

The last two Comet airframes remained in storage after completion in 1962 until they were resurrected to serve as prototypes for the HS.801 Nimrod maritime patrol and anti submarine aircraft. The first was flown for the first time in October 1965 before reappearing in July 1967 with the RAF serial XV147, Nimrod aerodynamic features and original Avon engines. The second aircraft (XV148) was similarly modified except that the Avons were replaced with Rolls-Royce Spey turbofans as would be fitted to production Nimrods. This was actually the first Nimrod conversion to fly, on 23 May 1967.

Hawker Siddeley (later British

COMET 4B

Powerplants: Four Rolls-Royce RA.29 Avon Mk.525 turbojets each rated at 10,500lb (47.0kN) thrust for takeoff. Fuel capacity 7,800imp gal (35,459 l) in wing and centre section tanks.

Dimensions: Wing span 107ft 10in (32.87m); length 118ft 0in (35.97m); height 29ft 6in (8.99m); wing area 2,059sq ft (191.3m²); wheelbase 46ft 8in (14.22m); wheel track 28ft 2in (8.58m).

Weights: Max takeoff 158,000lb (71,669kg); operational empty 78,600lb (35,652kg); max zero fuel 102,500lb (46,494kg); max landing 120,000lb (54,432kg); capacity payload (101 seats) 23,900lb (10,841kg).

Accommodation: 72 first class or 101 economy class passengers initially, later up to 119 passengers in high density arrangement. Cabin length 79ft 2in (24.13m), max width 9ft 7in (2.92m), max height 6ft 6.5in (1.99m), volume 3,160cu ft (89.48m³). Baggage/freight capacity 659cu ft (18.66m³) in rear fuselage and forward and aft underfloor holds.

Performance: Max cruising speed 482kt (891km/h) at 25,000ft; economical cruise 452kt (837km/h) at 23,500ft; long range cruise 404kt (748km/h); takeoff field length 6,600ft (2,012m); landing distance from 30ft (with reverse thrust) 5,740ft (1,750m); max payload range (at 462kt, with reserves) 1,600nm (2,960km); max range (at 404kt, no reserve) 3,240nm (6,002km).

Comet 4B production: BEA 14, Olympic Airways 4; total 18.

Classic portrait of Kuwait Airways Comet 4C 9K-ACA. The first 4C (for Mexicana) flew on 31 October 1958 and 30 were built including two unsold airframes which were later converted to prototypes for the Nimrod maritime reconnaissance aircraft. (BAe)

Chester built Comet 4C SU-ALC of United Arab Airlines, formerly known as Misrair. (Philip J Birtles)

The short-lived and sumptuously appointed Comet 4C delivered to Saudi Arabia's King Ibn Saud in June 1962. (Philip J Birtles)

XR395, one of the five Comet C.4s delivered to the RAF in 1962. (Philip J Birtles)

Aerospace) built 49 Nimrods for the RAF, with deliveries beginning in October 1969. This final expression of the basic Comet design continues in service in 1996, at which time British Aerospace was offering a re-engined (with BMW Rolls-Royce BR710 turbofans) and updated conversion of existing aircraft to meet the UK Ministry of Defence's Replacement Maritime Patrol Aircraft (RMPA) requirement.

Dubbed Nimrod 2000 by BAe, the conversion programme (if adopted) could see the Nimrod in service until 2025 or longer, meaning a 56 year service life for the aircraft, or 73 years if its forbears' careers are taken into account!

COMET 4C

Powerplants: Four Rolls-Royce Avon RA.20 Mk.525B turbojets each rated at 10,500lb (47.0kN) thrust for takeoff. Fuel capacity 8,908imp gal (40,496 l) in wing, centre section and leading edge pinion tanks.

Dimensions: Wing span 114ft 10in (35.00m); length 118ft 0in (35.97m); height 29ft 6in (8.99m); wing area 2,121sq ft (197.0m²); wheelbase 53ft 2in (16.21m); wheel track 28ft 2in (8.58m).

Weights: Max takeoff 162,000lb (73,483kg); operational empty 79,600lb (36,107kg); max zero fuel 102,500lb (46,494kg); max landing 120,000lb (54,432kg); capacity payload (101 seats) 22,900lb (10,387kg).

Accommodation: 72 first class or 101 economy class passengers; later up to 119 passengers in high density arrangement. Baggage/freight capacity 659cu ft (18.66m³) in rear fuselage and forward and aft underfloor holds.

Performance: Max cruising speed 471kt ((872km/h) at 31,000ft; typical cruising speed 411 to 438kt (760 to 809km/h). Takeoff field length 6,750ft (2,057m); landing distance from 30ft (with reverse thrust) 5,740ft (1,750m); service ceiling 39,000ft (11,887m); range with 19,630lb (8,904kg) payload and reserves 2,250nm (4,168km).

Comet 4C production: Mexicana 3, United Arab Airlines 9, Middle East Airlines 4, Sudan Airways 2, Aerolineas Argentinas 1, Saudi Government 1, Kuwait Airways 2, RAF 5, A&AEE 1, unsold 2 (later converted to Nimrod prototypes); total 30.

The last two Comet 4C airframes were stored until 1967 when they were reflown as prototypes for the Nimrod with suitable aerodynamic modifications. XV147 (top) had the original Avon engines installed, while XV148 (bottom) had the Nimrod's Rolls-Royce Spey turbofans. Unlike production Nimrods, these aircraft retained most of the Comet's original cabin windows. (Philip J Birtles)

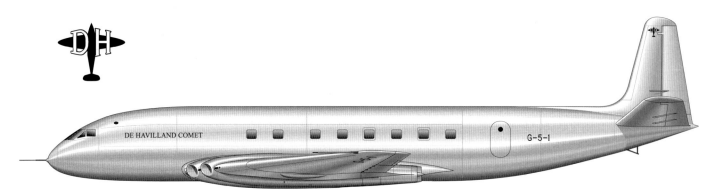

Comet 1 prototype G-5-1/G-ALVG (c/n 06001) in early markings.

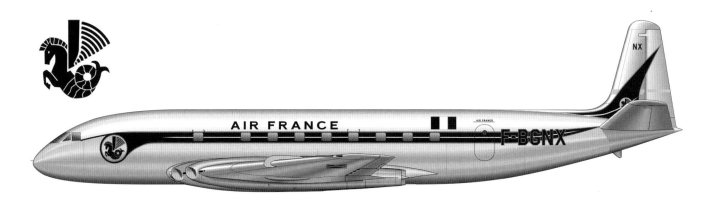

Comet 1 G-ALYP (c/n 06003) BOAC, first production aircraft delivered April 1952.

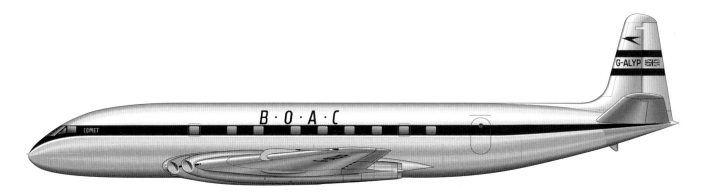

Comet 1A F-BGNX (c/n) 06020), first for Air France delivered June 1953.

Comet 1A 5301 (c/n 06017) at time of delivery to Royal Canadian Air Force March 1953.

Comet C.2 XK699 'Sagittarius' (c/n 06034) 216 Squadron RAF Transport Command 1957-67.

Comet 3 G-ANLO (c/n 6100), markings as per world tour December 1955.

Comet 4 G-APDR (c/n 6418) BOAC 1959-64.

Comet 4 G-APDB (c/n 6403) Dan-Air 1969-74. Ex BOAC, Malaysia-Singapore Airlines.

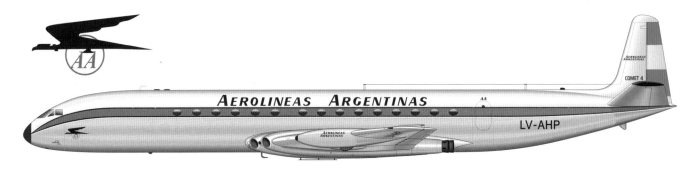

Comet 4 LV-AHP 'El Lucero del Alba' (c/n 6411) Aerolineas Argentinas May-August 1959.

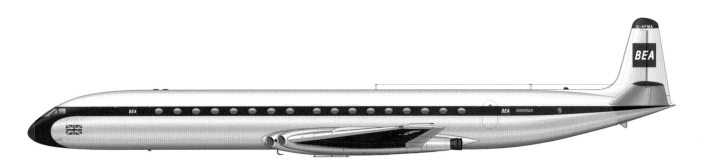

Comet 4B G-APMA (c/n 6421), first for BEA delivered December 1959.

Comet 4B G-APYC (c/n 6437) Olympic Airways at time of delivery April 1960, immediately reregistered SX-DAK 'Queen Frederica'.

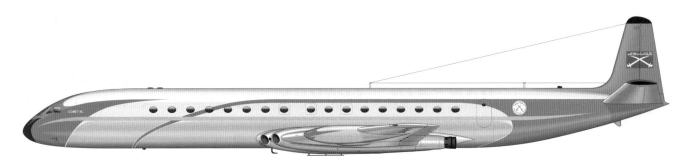

Comet 4C SA-R-7 (c/n 6461) Saudi Arabian Government 1962-63.

Comet 4C SU-ALM (c/n 6458) United Arab Airlines 1961-71. Subsequently Egyptair 1971-76.

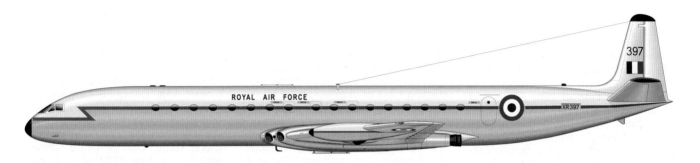

Comet C.4 XR397 (c/n 6469) 216 Squadron RAF 1962-75.

Comet 4C OD-ADR (c/n 6445) Middle East Airlines 1960-68. Destroyed in Israeli commando attack, Beirut Airport December 1968.

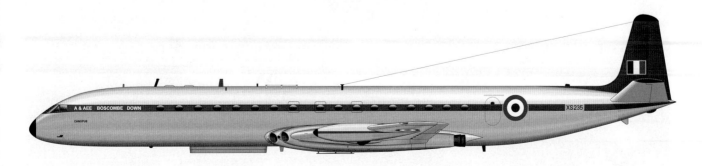

Comet 4C XS235 (c/n 6473) Aircraft & Armament Experimental Establishment Boscombe Down for avionics trials. Only Comet still flying in 1996.

EARLY OPERATIONS

When the first production Comet 1, BOAC's G-ALYP, departed London Heathrow for Johannesburg on 2 May 1952, Captain A M Majendie, his crew and passengers were fully aware of the historical nature of the occasion – the world's first commercial jet passenger service. What they would have been unaware of was the fact that within two years, the hopes and promises associated with this new order of civil aviation would lie shattered – literally – at the bottom of the sea.

That first commercial service went off without a hitch, G-ALYP travelling to Johannesburg via Rome, Cairo, Khartoum, Entebbe and Livingston in an elapsed time of 23hr 37min and returning on 5 May in 22hr 48min.

Initially, BOAC planned to operate the London-Johannesburg service once a week but strong demand resulted in this being trebled within a month. This trend continued, with the result that after a year's service, BOAC's Comets were flying 20,780 unduplicated miles (33,440km) around the world over a total network covering more than 122,000 miles (19,635km) and some 370 jet flying hours each work. That first 12 months saw the aircraft log 9,443 revenue hours and carry just under 28,000 passengers. The average load factor was a healthy 87 per cent.

An important feature of the Comet's first year of service was the high degree of mechanical reliability it displayed with mainly minor and easily fixed problems emerging. There were some early problems with the hydraulic system, it was discovered that the windscreens needed more warm air blown on them to demist them in humid conditions and more powerful windscreen wipers were needed to cope with heavier rain.

The Ghost engines also suffered relatively minor problems, the most significant one being some cracking of the centrifugal compressor due to a high frequency vibration. Cropping of the impeller blades solved the problem, this changing the frequency and therefore removed the vibration. When it entered service, the Ghost had an approved time between overhaul (TBO) of just 250 hours and by early 1953 this had increased to 600 hours. That is a minuscule figure by modern standards but in those pioneering days of commercial jet transports, a 600 hours TBO was considered high.

BOAC quickly added new services as more Comets became available, the airline's ninth and last Comet 1 being delivered in September 1952. A service to Colombo (Ceylon) was introduced the previous month (travelling from London via Beirut, Bahrein, Karachi and Bombay); in October 1952 services to Singapore began (which added Delhi, Calcutta, Rangoon and Bangkok to the network); and in April 1953 Tokyo was added to the list, the Comets flying there from Bangkok via Manila and Okinawa.

The long route to from London to Tokyo (about 10,000 miles/16,100km) well illustrates the advantage offered by the Comet over piston engined airliners, not just because of its much higher cruising speed but also because it cut out two night stops. The elapsed time between London and Tokyo by piston engined airliner was 86 hours; by Comet it was just 36 hours, a saving of more than two full days!

The first anniversary of BOAC Comet services also carried with it a note of caution as it was on that day (2 May 1953) that G-ALYV crashed near Calcutta after suffering airframe failure in severe turbulence. This was the third Comet involved in an accident during that first year of operation, more of which below ...

Other Operators

The first foreign operator to put the Comet into service was France's Union Aero-Maritime de Transport (UAT), which had ordered three Comet 1As. Delivered between December 1952 and April 1953, UAT's first service was flown on 19 February 1953 on the Paris-Casablanca-Dakar route. One of UAT's Comets was lost in June 1953 when it overshot on landing at Dakar without casualty.

UAT added more Comet services to its schedule during the course of 1953, most of them to ports in French West Africa where large numbers of French nationals were based and needed to be regularly transported between Africa and Paris. UAT was achieving an annual utilisation of about 1,700 hours for each of its Comets by mid 1953 and had established its own maintenance facilities for the aircraft and engines.

Canadian Pacific Airlines was the first export customer for the Comet, ordering two 1As as early as December 1949. Unfortunately, circumstances dictated that CPA would

Air France Comet 1A F-BGNX, one of three delivered to the airline in 1953. This aircraft's fuselage survives at the Mosquito Museum in England. (via Philip J Birtles)

never put the aircraft into service as one of the pair was written off at Karachi during its delivery flight in March 1953 as a result of over-rotation on takeoff. The second was then diverted to BOAC to help make up the capacity lost by the crashes of three of its own Comets by July of the same year.

Air France took delivery of its three Comet 1As in June and July 1953 and began operations on the Paris (Le Bourget)-Rome-Beirut service on 26 August. The previous day had seen an Air France Comet set a new London to Paris record of 51 minutes. The French flag carrier's Comets soon added Algiers, Casablanca and Cairo to their route network and continued to fly these services without major incident until all Comets were grounded in April 1954. Air France had also ordered six Comet 2s but these lapsed with the groundings.

The final Comet 1 operator was the Royal Canadian Air Force, which received its two Series 1As in March and April 1953. After the groundings, they were returned to the manufacturer and eventually modified to Comet 1XB standards with a strengthened structure, more powerful Ghost engines and increased maximum weight. Redelivered to the RCAF in 1957, the two Comets served with 412 Squadron until 1964 when they were retired.

The Royal Canadian Air Force's Comet 1A '5301' in its original guise with square windows. It and its partner were subsequently modified to Mk.1XB standards with modified structure.

THE COMET ACCIDENTS

G-ALYZ October 1952

The first major mishap involving a Comet occurred at Rome Airport on 26 October 1952 when BOAC's G-ALYZ failed to takeoff and ran off the end of the runway. The undercarriage was ripped off and the fuel tanks ruptured although there was no fire and no casualties.

The investigation was carried out by the Italian government and the official finding was pilot error due to the aircraft being over-rotated during the takeoff run and in effect stalling despite travelling at a quite high speed. The pilot error finding was questioned and even though the cause of the accident was as stated above, it resulted from a new phenomena which was peculiar to jets with their clean wings and lack of wash from the propellers helping create lift.

Another, similar accident would prove the point.

CF-CUN March 1953

Canadian Pacific Airlines Comet 1A CF-CUN *Empress of Hawaii* was the second Comet to be involved in a ground stall accident during the takeoff run, this time at night at Karachi on 3 March 1953.

The aircraft was on its delivery flight to Canada via a sales demonstration in Australia and was at the same time attempting to break the London-Sydney record. This virtual duplication of the Rome accident had more serious consequences as all 11 on board were killed when the aircraft hit a drainage culvert off the end of the runway and burst into flames.

This time the investigation was carried out by the Pakistani government and it was found the captain had raised the nose of the fully laden Comet too early and instead of lowering it again to gain airspeed, he pulled back harder in an attempt to get the aircraft off the ground, stalling the wings. The Comet's nose was eventually lowered and it did momentarily fly but too late, the starboard undercarriage hitting a low culvert and the Comet careering out of control into the empty drainage culvert.

The report into the accident mentioned that despite prior knowledge of the over-rotation problem (following the Rome accident) and subsequent demonstration of a revised technique to overcome it, the pilot kept pulling on the stick. By the time he had decided to lower the nose the Comet was already into the runway runoff area.

The investigation report also suggested that fatigue caused by time differences (jet lag in today's parlance) was a contributing factor and the record attempt put undue pressure on the crew. It was also noted that this was the first time the crew had a attempted a night takeoff in a Comet.

Ill-fated Canadian Pacific Airlines Comet 1A CF-CUN crashed at Karachi Airport during its delivery flight in March 1953. (via Philip J Birtles)

First loss: BOAC's G-ALYZ failed to become airborne at Rome in October 1952 and ran off the end of the runway.

As a result of this and the Rome accident, de Havilland developed a reprofiled wing leading edge for the Comet which made it theoretically impossible for the wing to stall during the takeoff run through to the maximum possible angle of attack.

G-ALYV May 1953

12 May 1953 was the first anniversary of BOAC Comet operations but the occasion was marked not by celebration but by the crash of the airline's Comet 1 G-ALYV near Calcutta.

This was the first Comet accident involving failure of the aircraft's structure, apparently due to the aircraft flying through a violent electrical storm shortly after leaving Calcutta bound for London via several other ports.

Climbing through 10,000 feet (3,000m), the Comet flew through heavy (and probably very turbulent) cumulo-nimbus cloud and into a severe monsoonal storm which imposed extremely heavy loads on the aircraft's structure. G-ALYV broke up as a result and 37 passengers and six crew were killed.

The Comet's wreckage was largely recovered and transported by air to Farnborough where it was 'reassembled' and thoroughly examined. It was found that the tailplane had failed due to excessive downloading "probably caused by the cumulative combination of a severe gust load and heavy manoeuvring load". The latter part of the above suggests the pilot may have pulled back too hard on the control column when heavy gusts were encountered, bearing in mind the Comet's powered and insensitive controls gave the pilots no 'feel' or indication of loads on the controls.

It was suggested that the failure of the tailplane resulted in a sudden pitch down, the rapid negative 'g' this produced resulting in the failure of the wings and then an explosive decompression of the fuselage. Subsequent investigations into the Elba and Naples Comet crashes took these conclusions one step further.

One thing which came out of the investigation into G-ALYV's crash was the suggestion that if weather radar had been fitted to the aircraft

allowing avoidance of the storm centre, there may not have been a crash to investigate. None of the early Comets had weather radar installed.

G-ALYP January 1954

On 10 January 1954, BOAC Comet I G-ALYP (the first production Comet and the aircraft which had flown the first jet service 20 months earlier) departed Rome *en route* to London after having flown from Singapore. Flying in clear air and approaching its cruising altitude, the aircraft exploded, disintegrated and fell into the sea off the Island of Elba, between Italy's west coast and the northern tip of Corsica. Six crewmembers and 29 passengers died.

BOAC immediately grounded its Comet fleet and investigations into the accident begun. Vital to these was the recovery of as much of G-ALYP's wreckage as was possible. Nobody really knew what the cause could possibly be. Although structural failure had obviously occurred was it because of a design fault? If so, what? A manufacturing or materials problem? A combination of all of

The first structural failure: BOAC Comet 1 G-ALYV broke up in severe weather near Calcutta in May 1953.

G-ALYP – the first production Comet 1 – suffered explosive decompression near the island of Elba after leaving Rome in January 1954.

these? For a time, sabotage was a popular theory among the public and press.

At the time of the accident, G-ALYP had amassed just 3,681 flying hours and 1,290 flights, only a fraction of what had been successfully achieved in static structural testing during the Comet's development.

Recovery of the wreckage was not going to be easy. It was well scattered over a body of water which was 500 feet (150m) deep and co-operation from the Italian authorities was proving difficult to obtain. Help came in the form of the Royal Navy which by using its ASDIC equipment (normally used for detecting submarines) and employing a chartered fleet of trawlers to sweep the sea bed with their nets, was able to recover about 75 per cent of the Comet which was then transported to Farnborough for reassembly and examination.

The effort which went into achieving this was monumental and the task extremely difficult but its successful conclusion was vital to the accident investigation. It took on even greater importance three months later when another BOAC Comet disintegrated in flight for no

apparent reason, and this time there was no hope of recovering any substantial remains. By the end of 1954, all that could be recovered of G-ALYP's remains had been returned Britain for examination.

The crash prompted the decision to carry out tests to destruction of a Comet 1 airframe in a new water tank at the Royal Aircraft Establishment, Farnborough. The tank was large enough to accommodate a complete Comet fuselage and was able to simulate the full gamut of loads and stresses imposed on an airframe in only a fraction of the time it takes in the real world. Additionally, if the structure failed, it would not only be safer for those involved but also it would not disintegrate, making for easier recovery and examination.

Although explosive decompression was thought to be the cause of G-ALYP's demise, by late March 1954 no definite reason for its occurrence had been established although some educated guesses resulted in about 50 modifications being incorporated in BOAC's Comets in the hope they might solve the problem. Engine fire, control surface flutter and structural fatigue were all considered

possibilities and had to remain in the equation until definitely ruled out.

On 23 March the grounding order was lifted and Comet services resumed.

G-ALYY April 1954

On 8 April 1954 – just 16 days after the Comet was allowed to fly again, another explosive decompression occurred, this time to BOAC's G-ALYY near Naples. The similarities with the previous accident were marked: the aircraft had departed Rome (this time bound for Cairo and on to South Africa) in clear weather and was climbing to cruising altitude when it exploded and disintegrated. This time 21 people were killed, seven crew and 14 passengers, and the aircraft had only 900 flights in its log book.

The wreckage fell into a very deep part of the Mediterranean making the salvage of all but a few pieces of flotsam wreckage impossible. Some bodies were also recovered. The accident resulted in the immediate grounding of all Comets and the revoking of its Certificate of Airworthiness. This affected not only BOAC but also UAT, Air France and the

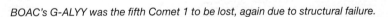

BOAC's G-ALYY was the fifth Comet 1 to be lost, again due to structural failure.

Reconstruction of G-ALYP's fuselage and tail unit at Farnborough. About 75 per cent of the wreckage was eventually recovered from the sea after a massive salvage operation.

RCAF, all of whose Comet operations stopped at that point. The fleet had accumulated about 36,000 flying hours by then.

It would be nearly three years before the Comet would again be permitted to carry fare paying passengers but at the time it looked as if the world's first jet airliner was going to have a brief, spectacular and unfortunate career.

Intensive Investigation

A Court of Enquiry was established by the British Minister of Transport and Civil Aviation to report on the findings of the investigations into the Comet crashes, concentrating on the Elba (G-ALYP) and Naples (G-ALYY) accidents.

The Comet's structural integrity was the obvious centre of attention and two key activities were used to shed some light on this: the RAE's water tank which contained the fuselage of Comet 1 G-ALYU, and the remains of the Elba Comet, which was being 'reconstructed' at Farnborough over a period of several months as parts were gradually recovered. In addition, Comet 1A G-ANAV (the surviving Canadian Pacific aircraft which had been allocated to BOAC) was test flown to check that uncontrolled flutter of some part of the airframe had not contributed to the accidents.

The water tank test specimen at Farnborough provided the breakthrough in July 1954 when the structure failed after 1,830 simulated 'flights' had been made, these in addition to the 1,239 real flights the aircraft had logged prior to its grounding. De Havilland's engineers were mortified by this as the failure occurred well before the company's own estimates of a 'safe' life, remembering that over 16,000 'flights' had been simulated during the Comet's early structural testing.

It was later realised that de Havilland's testing methods had been fatally flawed due to a lack of knowledge. The test cabins had been pressurised to more than twice their normal level in order to impose greater stresses and – or so it was thought – to provide a healthy safety margin. The effect was the opposite as the higher pressure tended to bed down component parts, change the molecular structure of the metal and actually make it more resistant to fatigue failure! Nothing was known of this phenomenon at the time.

Examination of the test fuselage in the Farnborough water tank revealed the initial failure had occurred at a rivet hole in the corner of one of the square cabin windows and spread, creating a tear in the cabin skin eight feet (2.4m) long. Hairline fatigue cracks were also found starting in the rivet holes for the square ADF antenna cutout on the top of the fuselage.

The water test tank at Farnborough with Comet 1 G-ALYU inside. Fatigue testing was carried out around the clock until the structure failed. (via Philip J Birtles)

Proof Positive

Proof that this was the cause of the mystery was provided in August 1954 when an Italian trawler dragged up a significant piece of G-ALYP's wreckage which included much of the top of the cabin. Included in this section was the part containing the cutout for the ADF aerial, revealing a substantial fatigue crack starting at one of the ADF cutout's rivet holes. At last, the mystery was solved.

This revelation allowed the path of the fatigue failure to be traced when combined with the evidence revealed by other pieces of wreckage. From the initial failure at the ADF hatch, the damage spread quickly and catastrophically under the influence of the pressurised cabin which burst open. From the ADF hatch it spread to the centre cabin which exploded, the parts hitting the wings and tail of the aircraft, the latter and the rear fuselage separating from the remainder of the airframe. Then the forward fuselage separated at the main spar followed by failure of both outer wings.

This conclusively proved that G-ALYP had suffered an explosive decompression resulting from fatigue failure, but what of the Naples aircraft, G-ALYY? There was no substantial wreckage to examine to say for sure, but there were some bodies recovered from both accidents. Pathological examination showed identical injuries in both cases and therefore an identical cause for them. This proved beyond doubt that the same thing had happened to both Comets – explosive decompression resulting from the propagation of fatigue cracks caused by constant pressurisation and depressurisation of the cabin.

These discoveries also raised doubts about what had really happened to G-ALYV, the BOAC Comet which had crashed after breaking up in a severe storm out of Calcutta in

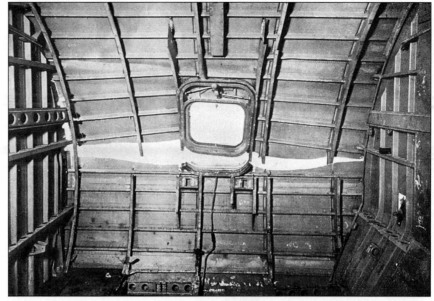

A view from inside G-ALYU's fuselage after it had failed in the water test tank. Shown is the source of the failure, the forward cabin window and escape hatch.

May 1953. Some doubts have been cast on the turbulence being the sole cause.

According to T R Nelson, a former British Accident Investigation Branch senior investigator who was directly involved in the Comet enquiries: "In retrospect, it is my personal opinion that the basic cause of the Calcutta accident was probably the same as that of the Naples and Elba accidents, namely metal fatigue of the fuselage resulting in explosive decompression. G-ALYV was just reaching cruising altitude after climbing through cumulo-nimbus cloud. It is possible that the extra stress of the violent turbulence could have precipitated the development of a fatigue crack. The stated cause of the accident, 'structural failure of the aircraft owing to overstressing in severe turbulence', was not incorrect, but – with the wisdom of hindsight – the primary failure of the tailplane is doubtful".

The Court of Enquiry published its findings in February 1955 and concluded that no-one could be blamed for the disasters. It was simply a case of pushing into the unknown, and the unknown pushing back.

THE SECOND CAREER

With the publishing of the Court of Enquiry's findings into the Comet 1 accidents in February 1955, the way was now clear for the aircraft to fly again in modified form. As related in the previous chapter, suitably modified Comet 2s (and several 1s) continued flying from 1956 but de Havilland's main efforts revolved around development of a new family of Comets, the 4, 4B and 4C. These aircraft became available from 1958 and provided the Comet with an opportunity to resurrect its career, albeit in small numbers when compared with the larger American rivals which had appeared in the meantime, the Boeing 707 and Douglas DC-8.

Classic portrait of an Olympic Airways Comet 4B carrying the British registration G-APYC. (BAe)

The first of the new generation, the Comet 4. BOAC put its new Comets into service in October 1958.

Nevertheless, 10 airlines, one private operator, one air force and one research agency ordered new Comet 4s, 4Bs and 4Cs, a total of 74 aircraft built between 1958 and 1962 when production ended. Comets delivered after that date were from factory stock.

BOAC

British Overseas Airways Corporation reaffirmed its faith in the Comet's future by placing an order for 19 Comet 4s in March 1955. Preparation for their entry to service and certification was helped by the availability of the aerodynamically similar Comet 3 and the two Comet 2Es (G-AMXD and G-AMXK) which had the Comet 4's RA.29 Avon engines installed in the outboard positions. This speeded certification of the new model and the

use of these two aircraft on some of BOAC's routes in 1957-58 helped establish operating procedures.

The first Comet 4 (G-APDA) was flown from Hatfield on 27 April 1958 and was joined by the second and third aircraft (G-APDB and 'DC) in July and September, respectively. The latter pair were the first delivered to BOAC, on 30 September.

G-APDA was in the meantime used for certification trials and for several overseas trips in August and September 1958 including to New York (Idlewild Airport, now Kennedy), Canada, South America, Central America and Hong Kong.

BOAC intended to use its Comets on African and Far East routes but the temptation to steal a march on the American competition (Pan Am and Boeing) was too great to resist,

with the result that the airline's first Comet 4 revenue flight was also the world's first trans-Atlantic jet airliner service.

A press flight between London and New York was flown on 2 October 1958, followed two days later by the real thing, performed by G-APDC. There was considerable publicity associated with this event, which beat Pan Am's first trans-Atlantic service by just three weeks. At the same time, G-APDB was flying in the opposite direction across the Atlantic. Flights to New York normally required a fuel stop at Gander thanks to the prevailing westerly wind, although return flights could be nonstop for the same reason.

The Comet's basic unsuitability to this route meant it flew the Atlantic for a comparatively brief time, the last scheduled service taking place in October 1960 after which Rolls-Royce engined Boeing 707-420s took over.

The Comet 4 was much better suited to the African and Far East routes for which it had originally been ordered. Services to Europe, the Caribbean and South America were added to the network and from 1960 Comets were also flying to Australia, the Singapore-Sydney leg of the Kangaroo Route flown in conjunction with Qantas.

Remembering what an advance the original Comet 1 had been in terms of time saved over a given route, it's worth considering the leap forward the Comet 4 was over that aircraft. Using the London-Tokyo route as an example, the Comet 1 took an elapsed 36 hours with eight stops *en route*; the Comet 4 was capable of flying to Tokyo in about 26 hours elapsed time, stopping only four times and carrying twice the payload. The piston engined time for the 10,000 miles (16,100km) route had been 86 hours!

BOAC Comets at London Heathrow, circa 1960.

One of the few second generation Comets which didn't end up with Dan-Air! BOAC Comet 4 G-APDT photographed at Heathrow in 1974 as a ground training aid. Note the engine test 'muffler'. (Philip J Birtles)

BOAC took delivery of its 19th and last Comet 4 (G-APDJ) in January 1960. The first 12 months of operations had seen the airline's North Atlantic traffic grow by 40 per cent and the Comets carried more than 76,000 passengers in 15,150 revenue flying hours.

Despite this early success, the Comet 4 was always destined to have a relatively short life with BOAC due to its limited passenger capacity and range. It became quickly obsolescent as the 1960s progressed as first the Boeing 707 and then the Vickers VC10 and Super VC10 came into service in greater numbers. The final BOAC Comet 4 revenue flight was recorded on 23-24 November 1965 when G-APDM flew from Auckland to Sydney and then on to London.

Aerolineas Argentinas

The Argentine flag carrier was the first export customer for the Comet 4, ordering six aircraft in March 1958. They were delivered between January 1959 and July 1960, the delivery flight of the first aircraft (LV-PLM) from Hatfield to Buenos Aires setting a record time for the 7,000 miles

(11,265km) journey of 18.5 hours. When services began in March 1959 they were the first commercial jet operations in Latin America.

Aerolineas Argentinas took delivery of a seventh Comet – a 4C – in April 1962. This aircraft was built in anticipation of an order from Middle East Airlines which did not materialise and went to Argentina instead as a replacement for a Comet 4 which had been lost.

Aerolineas Argentinas' Comets generated considerable traffic growth, their first three months of service seeing a 36 per cent increase between South America and Europe and no less than 84 per cent on routes to North America. The airline's surviving Comets were out of service by the end of 1971.

BEA

The Comet 4B was developed for British European Airways and the airline ordered initially six in March 1958. The number was eventually increased to 16, the first of them delivered in November 1959. All 16 had been delivered by mid 1961 although BEA's operational fleet was 14 aircraft

as two were leased to Olympic Airways immediately upon delivery. The two airlines operated their Comet 4Bs (18 between them) in close cooperation over the next eight years, their fleets in effect being combined.

BEA began to withdraw its Comet 4Bs from regular service in 1969, the last scheduled flight being recorded on 31 October 1971 when G-APMA flew from Malaga in Spain (Picasso's birthplace, incidentally) to London Heathrow. Some aircraft were sold but 10 were transferred to BEA Airtours, the airline's inclusive tour/charter subsidiary. They remained in service in this role until January 1973.

Two BEA Comet 4Bs were lost while in service, the first (G-AJRM) in December 1961 when it crashed after takeoff from Ankara, and then G-ARCO in October 1967 when it was destroyed by a terrorist bomb over the Mediterranean.

Olympic Airways

The Greek flag carrier purchased two Comet 4Bs in its own right (delivered in April and May 1960) and operated two more leased upon delivery from BEA. As mentioned above, BEA

Aerolineas Argentinas was the first export customer for the Comet 4, ordering an initial six in March 1958. LV-AHN was the first, delivered in January 1959. (Philip J Birtles)

The Comet 4B was developed for BEA, the airline ordering 16 with deliveries starting in November 1959. (BAe)

BEA began withdrawing its Comet 4Bs from regular service in 1969 and transferred some of them to its Airtours charter and inclusive tour subsidiary. G-APMC is illustrated at London Gatwick in November 1973. (Philip J Birtles)

Olympic Airways operated its four Comet 4Bs in close co-operation with BEA. Two of the Comets were leased from the British airline. SX-DAO was one of those and is photographed on short finals at Heathrow in September 1968. (Philip J Birtles)

Eygptair was known as Misrair when it first ordered Comets and then as United Arab Airlines. The airline received nine Comet 4Cs in from June 1960 of which SU-ALM was the sixth, delivered in July 1961. (Philip J Birtles)

Middle East Airlines ordered four Comet 4Cs in early 1960 of which three were destroyed in an Israeli commando attack on Beirut Airport in December 1968. OD-ADQ was among the victims. (Philip J Birtles)

and Olympic operated their Comets in close co-operation until the second half of 1969 when the two leased aircraft were returned to BEA for resale and the other pair was purchased by the British operator, also for resale.

From Athens, Olympic flew its Comets to numerous destinations including London, Amsterdam, Cairo and Beirut.

Mexicana

Mexicana operated a total of five Comets between 1960 and 1970, starting with a trio of 4Cs ordered new. These were delivered from January 1960 and were supplemented in 1964 and 1965 by a pair of ex BOAC Comet 4s. Mexicana's main claim to fame with the Comet is that it was the first to order the 4C and its first aircraft (XA-NAR, flown 31 October 1959) was in effect the prototype of this Comet variant.

Mexicana flew an extensive domestic network plus international services to the central and west USA and Cuba. It was on these routes that the Comets were mainly used. They were retired in 1970.

United Arab Airlines

UAA (originally Misrair, then United Arab Airlines from 1960 and finally Egyptair from October 1971) was the largest foreign customer for the Comet, taking delivery of nine 4Cs from June 1960. The final aircraft was also the last Comet built (excluding the two converted to Nimrod prototypes) and was delivered in February 1964. The first delivery took place only five months after the order was placed.

UAA operated its Comets over a wide variety of routes encompassing the extremes of stage lengths from the relatively short Cairo to Beirut hop of about 350 miles (560km) where it replaced Viscounts to the 2,200 miles (3,540km) Cairo-London sector.

UAA had a very high accident rate with its Comets, five of the nine coming to sticky ends during the aircraft's career with the airline. The survivors were withdrawn from use in 1976.

Middle East Airways

MEA ordered four Comet 4Cs in January 1960 and took an option on

a fifth. This was not taken up and the aircraft sold to Aerolineas Argentinas instead. The first MEA Comet was delivered in December 1960 and all four were operational by March 1961. A BOAC Comet 4 was leased for a few months before the first delivery in order to gain experience on the type.

Services were flown throughout the Middle East, to Cairo, Pakistan, Turkey and various points in Europe including London, Frankfurt and Athens. Unfortunately, three of the four Comets didn't survive beyond December 1968 when they were destroyed in an Israeli commando attack on Beirut Airport. This sudden loss of capacity forced MEA to lease two Comet 4Cs from Kuwait Airways for six months after the attack. The surviving MEA Comet was sold in 1973.

Sudan Airways

Sudan Airways took delivery of two Comet 4Cs in November and December 1962. Originally intended for Mexicana but not delivered, the Comets remained with Sudan Airways until 1973 and were operated

Sudan Airways Comet 4C ST-AAW, one of two delivered in late 1962. Its stablemate (ST-AAX) was the final Hatfield built Comet. (via Philip J Birtles)

Kuwait Airways was the final customer for the Comet. 9K-ACA was the first of two delivered in 1963 and 1964. (via Philip J Birtles)

VP-KPJ, the first of three new Comet 4s delivered to East African Airways in 1960 and 1962. (via Philip J Birtles)

Malaysia-Singapore Airlines (originally Malaysian Airways) purchased several ex BOAC Comet 4s in 1965. 9V-BAT is the former G-APDC, the Comet with which BOAC inaugurated trans-Atlantic services in October 1958. (Philip J Birtles)

Channel Airways operated five second hand Comet 4Bs between 1970 and 1972. G-APMB was a former BEA aircraft and its basic livery is retained with 'Channel Airways' titles painted onto the upper fuselage. It was photographed at Manchester (Ringway) Airport in November 1971. (Philip J Birtles)

mainly on routes to the Middle East and the Gulf region. Sudan Airways' second aircraft (ST-AAX, c/n 6463) was the final Hatfield built Comet, flying for the first time on 8 December 1962.

Kuwait Airways

Kuwait Airways was the final customer for the Comet, ordering two 4Cs which were delivered in January 1963 and February 1964. An additional three Comet 4s were leased from BOAC in 1965-66. The arrival of Trident 1Es meant that Kuwaiti Comet 4Cs were operated only until late 1968 when they were leased to Middle East Airlines before being sold to Dan-Air.

Saudi Arabian Airlines

As discussed previously, a single Comet 4C was ordered by the Saudi Government for operation by Saudi Arabian Airlines on behalf of King Ibn Saud. The luxuriously appointed aircraft was delivered in June 1962 but survived only until March the following year when it crashed at night in the Italian Alps during a training flight. American Saudi Arabian Airlines pilots were flying the Comet at the time

and all on board were killed including de Havilland test pilot John Hanslip and flight engineer Ken Rouse.

East African Airways

EAA was the last Comet 4 customer, taking delivery of two new aircraft in July and August 1960 and a third (the last Comet 4 built) in April 1962. The airline also leased an ex BOAC Comet 4 between 1965 and 1967 and two others (by then owned by Dan-Air) in 1970.

EAA used its Comets on international services between its Kenyan headquarters at Nairobi to London, Bombay, Aden, Durban, Salisbury and Johannesburg. The last of them was withdrawn from service in early 1971 and sold.

Channel Airways

This British operator purchased three former BEA and two ex Olympic Airways Comet 4Bs in 1970 along with an ex BOAC Comet 4 for spares the following year. The airline operated inclusive tour flights but went into bankruptcy in February 1972, the Comets – along with most others still in existence at around that time – being sold to Dan-Air.

Malaysian Airways

Malaysian Airways (Malaysia-Singapore Airlines/MSA 1966-71) purchased BOAC's first five Comet 4s in 1965 to form the backbone of its international services fleet. The airline had previously leased a Comet 4 from BOAC in late 1963 but this was damaged beyond repair on landing at Singapore a few months later. Another BOAC Comet 4 was leased from BOAC between late 1967 and early 1969 before being sold to Dan-Air. At the time the Comets were acquired, BOAC and Qantas each had a one-third interest in the airline.

MSA kept its Comets only until 1969 when they were sold to Dan-Air.

Other Operators

Two other airlines briefly operated Comets. Air Ceylon was the first, leasing a single Comet 4 from BOAC in 1965 and Ecuador's AEREA (Aerovias Ecutorianas) leased one BOAC aircraft for two years from March 1966. The Air Ceylon Comet (G-APDS) later gained some fame as the Aircraft & Armaments Experimental Establishment's XW626 when it was converted to a testbed for the aborted Nimrod AEW project.

Dan-Air had no fewer than 48 second hand Comet 4s, 4Bs and 4Cs on its books over the years. This is G-ARJN, a former BEA aircraft acquired by Dan-Air in 1973. (Philip J Birtles)

Dan-Air Comet 4 G-APDB, the former BOAC aircraft which flew the first New York to London jet service in October 1958. It was retired in November 1973 after having logged 36,268 hours, the most of any Comet 4. (Philip J Birtles)

Dan-Air Services

Dan-Air became the largest and last commercial operator of the Comet, acquiring large numbers of aircraft from 1966 as other operators retired them. The surviving fleets of East African Airways, Egyptair, Malaysia-Singapore Airlines, Kuwait Airways, Channel Airways, Olympic Airways, BEA Airtours, Sudan Airways, the Royal Air Force all ended up in Dan-Air's hands.

The total of Dan-Air Comet 4, 4B and 4C acquisitions reached no fewer than 48 aircraft between 1966 and 1975, or nearly two-thirds of the production total. Some aircraft – notably Comet 4s – were purchased only for spare parts and the others were put to work on Dan-Air's inclusive tour charter operations or leased out to other operators from time to time.

The airline's mode of operation – high passenger loads over relatively short distances – resulted in the Comet being subjected to different kinds of stresses than it had been before due to the carriage of less fuel in the wings and the concentration of weight in the fuselage. Passenger ac-

commodation was increased to as many as 119 in the long fuselage Comet 4B and 4C, necessitating a strengthened cabin floor, some modification of the wing structure and re-evaluation of the aircraft's fatigue spectrum.

This work was performed with help of Hawker Siddeley at Hatfield and new 'safe' lives calculated. As originally delivered to BOAC, the Comet 4 had a safe life of 12,000 flights, an extension to this requiring modifications to be performed on the aircraft's front spar top and bottom booms, the rear spar top boom and the skinning near the wheel well cutout.

Flying from London Gatwick, Dan-Air's Comets averaged about 1,500 hours annual utilisation, although this figure is coloured by the extremely high utilisation achieved during the summer peak season (about 360 hours per month per aircraft) and the very low utilisation during the cooler months.

By early 1977 Dan-Air had 15 Comets in active service but the number gradually diminished after that as the aircraft began to run out

of flying hours and the cost of fuel and maintenance became prohibitive compared with more modern types.

The last Comet revenue flight was flown by Dan-Air's G-BDIW (a former RAF C.4) on 9 November 1980 when 119 enthusiasts flew from Gatwick to Dusseldorf.

RAF Comets

The Royal Air Force operated a total of 18 Comets over the years, comprising eight C.2 transports, two T.2 trainers (later modified to C.2 standards), three unpressurised 2Rs used for intelligence gathering operations and five C.4s, similar to the civil Comet 4C.

With the exception of the trio of Comet 2Rs, the RAF's earlier aircraft were all structurally upgraded following the BOAC accidents and the investigation which followed. Their characteristics are described in the previous chapter.

The ten Comet C.2/T.2s were delivered in 1956-57 and operated by No 216 Squadron at Lyneham. With the delivery of these aircraft, 216 became the first jet transport squadron

RAF Comet C.2 XK692 of 216 Squadron RAF. The aircraft were often used as flying ambulances. (via Philip J Birtles)

Comet C.2 XK716 photographed in 1970, three years after retirement. This was the last Comet 2 built and the only one to be completed at Chester, built up from main assemblies produced by Short Brothers at Belfast. (Philip J Birtles)

RAF Comet C.4 XR397, one of five delivered in 1962 for use by 216 Squadron. They remained in service until 1975. (BAe)

The sole Comet 3 ended its operational days as XP915 with the Blind Landing Experimental Unit at Bedford. Note the long nose probe, known as 'The Spike'. (Philip J Birtles)

Former BOAC Comet 4 G-APDF as the RAE's XV814. It was extensively used for radio, radar and avionics development work at Farnborough and flew until 1993. Note the Nimrod vertical tail surfaces. (via Philip J Birtles)

in the world. The Comets were used for general transport and support duties around the world, flying as far afield as the Weapons Research Establishment at Woomera, Australia, the USA and various parts of the Far East. VIPs were also carried and the Comets were often used to support V-bomber deployments around the world as well as general troop carrying.

Casualty evacuation was an important role, the Comet C.2 capable of transporting up to 36 patients, six in stretchers and the remainder seated, along with the necessary medical crew.

The Comet C.2 remained in RAF service until 1967, by which time five examples of the larger and longer ranging C.4 had been in service with 216 Squadron for five years. Ordered in September 1960, these aircraft were among the last Comets built and were delivered between February and June 1962. They continued the work the earlier mark had been carrying out until June 1975 when 216 Squadron was disbanded and the Comets sold to Dan-Air.

As noted above, it was a former RAF Comet C.4 (XR398/G-BDIW)

which performed the type's last commercial flight in November 1980.

The Comet 2Rs were operated by 192 Squadron at Watton (subsequently renumbered 51 Squadron based at Wyton) from April 1957 officially on long range calibration duties, but actually heavily involved in intelligence gathering missions around allies of the Soviet Union in Eastern Europe. The two survivors (one was destroyed in a hangar fire in September 1957) and the C.2 replacement were finally withdrawn from service in 1974, replaced by especially equipped Nimrods.

Testbed Comets

Apart from its airline career, various Comets have enjoyed distinguished careers in research and development roles at the Royal Aircraft Establishment (RAE), the Blind Landing Experimental Unit (BLEU), Aircraft and Armaments Experimental Establishment (A&AEE) and other units.

Among them are the RAE's Comet 4 XV814 (the former BOAC G-APDF) which from 1967 was extensively used for radio, radar and avionics de-

velopment work at Farnborough and was retired as late as 1993 as the second last flying Comet. Fitted with a large 'baggage pannier' shaped radome under its forward fuselage, XV814 also acquired a Nimrod style enlarged fin fillet to compensate and in its later years the entire vertical tail assembly from a Nimrod was fitted, including the fairing on top housing satellite communications equipment.

The sole Comet 3 (G-ANLO) also served in an experimental capacity as XP915 with the BLEU at Bedford from 1961 and later as a test rig for the Nimrod. Several Comet 1s were used for both static and flying tests associated with the fatigue problems of the mid 1950s; former BOAC Comet 4 G-APDS was transferred to the A&AEE in early 1969 (after completing leases with Air Ceylon and Kuwait Airways) as XW626 where it was used for the development of the radar for the aborted Nimrod AEW.3 programme, complete with oversize radome; and the two Comet 2Es (G-AMXD/XN453 and G-AMXK/XV144) were used for testing the RA.29 Avon as fitted to the Comet 4, BOAC route proving and experience flying, the

XW626 – the former BOAC G-APDS – was used by the A&AEE for trials of the aborted Nimrod AEW variant's radar. It was photographed at the Farnborough Air Show in September 1977. (Philip J Birtles)

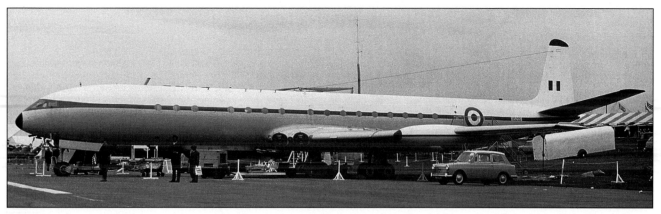

The world's last flying Comet as she was in 1968. Comet 4C XS235 'Canopus' was delivered new to the A&AEE as a flying radio and avionics laboratory. (Philip J Birtles)

testing of long range navigation aids (XN453) and blind and automatic landing equipment (XV144).

The only Comet ordered specifically for experimental and testing purposes was the 4C XS235 which was delivered to the A&AEE in December 1963, the third last Comet to fly. Named *Canopus*, this aircraft was put to work as a flying laboratory on behalf of the Radio and Navigation Division of Boscombe Down fitted with various avionics, navigation equipment, radio altimeters and associated equipment. The cabin is full of recording and analysis equipment which was continually updated over the years as new technology became available.

As these words were written in early 1996, *Canopus* was still flying from Boscombe Down and as such is the last remaining airworthy Comet in the world. This historic aircraft is expected to continue flying until around 1998 and there are tentative plans to keep it in the air for a time after that. It would certainly be wonderful to see this aircraft in the air on 27 July 1999, the 50th anniversary of the prototype Comet's first flight. Anybody reading this book after that date will know whether this thought came true or not!

After it is finally retired, it is planned that *Canopus* will be included in a proposed de Havilland Heritage Centre on Hatfield Aerodrome.

At the time of writing in 1996, XS235 'Canopus' was the last Comet still flying. There is hope that this aircraft will still be in the air in July 1999 to celebrate the 50th anniversary of the Comet's first flight. (Paul Merritt)

COMET PRODUCTION

Abbreviations: BOAC – British Overseas Airways Corporation; BEA – British European Airways; RAF – Royal Air Force; MoS – Ministry of Supply; RAE – Royal Aircraft Establishment; BLEU – Blind landing Experimental Unit; UAT – Union Aeromaritime de Transport; RCAF – Royal Canadian Air Force; CPA – Canadian Pacific Airlines; A&AEE – Aircraft and Armaments Experimental Establishment; DH – de Havilland; AA – Aerolineas Argentinas; MEA – Middle East Airways; EAA – East African Airways; UAA – United Arab Airlines; MSA – Malaysia-Singapore Airlines; MoD – Ministry of Defence; cr – crashed; t-o – takeoff; w/o – written off; ret – retired; F/flight – first flight; deliv – delivered; dbr – damaged beyond repair; lsd – leased; ntu – not taken up; cvtd – converted.

C/No	Mark	F/flight	Customer	Deliv	Regist	Notes
06001	1	27/07/49	MoS	–	G-ALVG	orig G-5-1, scrapped 07/53
06002	1	27/07/50	MoS	07/50	G-ALZK	scrapped 07/57
06003	1	09/01/51	BOAC	04/52	G-ALYP	cr into sea near Elba 01/54
06004	1	28/05/51	BOAC	05/52	G-ALYR	dbr Calcutta 07/53
06005	1	08/09/51	BOAC	02/52	G-ALYS	scrapped 1955
06006	2X	16/02/52	MoS	03/52	G-ALYT	lsd BOAC 07/53, scrapped 1967
06007	1	13/12/51	BOAC	03/52	G-ALYU	RAE water tank testing 04/54
06008	1	09/04/52	BOAC	04/52	G-ALYV	cr near Calcutta 05/53
06009	1	25/05/52	BOAC	06/52	G-ALYW	RAE structural testing 1955
06010	1	09/07/52	BOAC	07/52	G-ALYX	scrapped 06/55
06011	1	10/09/52	BOAC	09/52	G-ALYY	cr Tyrrhenian Sea 04/54
06012	1	23/09/52	BOAC	09/52	G-ALYZ	cr on t-o Rome 10/52
06013	1A	11/08/52	CPA/BOAC	08/53	G-ANAV	CPA ntu, scrapped 1955
06014	1A	24/12/52	CPA	03/53	CF-CUN	cr on t-o Karachi 03/53
06015	1A	13/11/52	UAT	12/52	F-BGSA	wfu 04/54, scrapped 1961
06016	1A	21/01/53	UAT	02/53	F-BGSB	wfu 04/54, scrapped 1961
06017	1A	21/02/53	RCAF	03/53	5301	cvtd 1XB 09/57, wfu and scrapped 10/64
06018	1A	25/03/53	RCAF	04/53	5302	cvtd 1XB 09/57, wfu 10/64, scrapped 1975
06019	1A	15/04/53	UAT	04/53	F-BGSC	dbr Dakar 06/53
06020	1A	06/05/53	Air France	06/53	F-BGNX	wfu 04/54, scrapped 08/56, fuselage at Mosquito Museum
06021	1A	22/05/53	Air France	07/53	F-BGNY	cvtd 1XB 02/57, MoS G-AOJU 04/57, RAF XM829 10/58, A&AEE 06/61, fire dump Stanstead 02/64
06022	1A	16/03/53	Air France	07/53	F-BGNZ	DH G-5-23 06/56, cvtd 1XB 03/57, MoS G-APAS 05/57, DH Propellers XM823 10/58, Cosford Aerospace Museum 09/78
06023	2R	29/08/53	RAF	02/58	XK655	ex Mk.2 G-AMXA, Stathallan Collection 08/74
06024	T.2	03/11/53	RAF	06/56	XK669	ex Mk.2 G-AMXB, scrapped 04/67
06025	2R	25/11/53	RAF	07/57	XK659	ex Mk.2 G-AMXC, wfu 05/74
06026	2E	20/08/54	MoS	08/57	G-AMXD	lsd BOAC 08/57-03/58, RAE 05/59 XN453, wfu 02/73
06027	2R	18/07/55	RAF	04/57	XK663	ex Mk.2 G-AMXE, w/o in hangar fire 09/57
06028	T.2	12/03/56	RAF	06/56	XK670	wfu 1966
06029	C.2	16/07/56	RAF	08/56	XK671	wfu 11/66
06030	C.2	21/08/56	RAF	09/56	XK695	cvtd 2R 06/60, wfu 12/74, donated Imperial War Museum Duxford
06031	C.2	29/09/56	RAF	11/56	XK696	wfu 10/66
06032	C.2	17/11/56	RAF	12/56	XK697	wfu 12/72
06033	2E	10/07/57	BOAC	08/57	G-AMXK	DH 01/58, MoS 10/60, RAE XV144 11/66, wfu 1974
06034	C.2	13/12/56	RAF	01/57	XK698	wfu 1967
06035	C.2	02/02/57	RAF	02/57	XK699	wfu 06/67
06036	2	–	–	–	–	structural test specimen for Ministry of Aviation
06037	C.2	26/04/57	RAF	05/57	XK715	wfu 03/66
06038-06044	–	–	–	–	–	Comet 2 airframes not completed
06045	C.2	06/05/57	RAF	05/57	XK716	wfu 06/67
06046-06070	–	–	–	–	–	Comet 2 airframes not completed
06100	3	19/07/54	MoS	08/54	G-ANLO	cvtd 3B 08/58, BLEU XP915 06/61, RAE, later Nimrod test rig
06101	3	–	–	–	–	structural test specimen for MoS
06102-06110	–	–	–	–	–	Comet 3 airframes not completed
6401	4	27/04/58	BOAC	02/59	G-APDA	Malaysian 9M-AOA 12/65, MSA 9V-BAS 12/66, Dan-Air G-APDA 11/69, wfu 11/69
6402	4	–	–	–	–	structural test airframe
6403	4	27/07/58	BOAC	09/58	G-APDB	Malaysian 9M-AOB 09/65, MSA 12/66, Dan-Air G-APDB 10/69, wfu 02/74, preserved Duxford
6404	4	23/09/58	BOAC	09/58	G-APDC	Malaysian 9M-AOC 10/65, MSA 9V-BAT 12/66, Dan-Air G-APDC 08/69, wfu 04/73
6405	4	05/11/58	BOAC	11/58	G-APDD	Malaysian 9M-AOD 11/65, MSA 12/66, Dan-Air G-APDD 10/69, lsd EAA 5Y-AMT 12/70-02/72, wfu 08/72
6406	4	20/09/58	BOAC	10/58	G-APDE	Malaysian 9M-AOE 10/65, MSA 9V-BAU 12/66, Dan-Air G-APDE 11/69, lsd EAA 5Y-ALF 02-11/70, wfu 05/72
6407	4	11/12/58	BOAC	12/58	G-APDF	RAE XV814 03/67
6408	4	27/01/59	AA	01/59	LV-PLM	rereg LV-AHN, Dan-Air 12/71 for spares
6409	4	21/11/58	BOAC	12/58	G-APDH	lsd Malaysian 10/63, dbr on landing Singapore 03/64
6410	4	25/02/59	AA	03/59	LV-PLO	rereg LV-AHO, dbr on landing Buenos Aires 02/60
6411	4	24/03/59	AA	05/59	LV-PLP	rereg LV-AHP, cr Asuncion 08/59
6412	4	02/01/59	BOAC	02/59	G-APDK	Dan-Air 05/66, lsd EAA 5Y-ALD 01-03/70, wfu 05/73
6413	4	27/04/59	BOAC	05/59	G-APDL	lsd EAA 5Y-ADD 10/65-03/67, Dan-Air 01/69, dbr on landing Newcastle 10/70
6414	4	21/03/59	BOAC	04/59	G-APDM	lsd MEA OD-AEV 03-06/67, lsd MSA 9V-BBJ 01/68-01/69, Dan-Air 01/69, catering training 05/74

6415	4	29/05/59	BOAC	06/59	G-APDN	lsd Kuwait A/W 11/65-02/66, Dan-Air 10/67, cr near Barcelona 07/70
6416	4	29/04/59	BOAC	05/59	G-APDO	Dan-Air 05/66, wfu 06/73
6417	4	29/05/59	BOAC	06/59	G-APDP	lsd MSA 9V-BBH 11/67-01/69, Dan-Air G-APDP 02/69, RAE XX944 07/73, wfu 04/75
6418	4	09/07/59	BOAC	07/59	G-APDR	Mexicana XA-NAZ 12/64, rereg XA-NAP, Channel Airways for spares 06/71
6419	4	06/08/59	BOAC	08/59	G-APDS	lsd Air Ceylon 1965, lsd Kuwait A/W 10/65-02/66, A&AEE XW626 01/69, cvtd Nimrod AEW testbed 06/77
6420	4	02/10/59	BOAC	10/59	G-APDT	lsd Mexicana XA-POW/NAB 11/65-12/69, wfu 12/69
6421	4B	27/06/59	BEA	12/59	G-APMA	sold for scrap 07/72
6422	4B	17/08/59	BEA	11/59	G-APMB	Channel A/W 06/70, Dan-Air 04/72, wfu 12/78
6423	4B	01/10/59	BEA	11/59	G-APMC	lsd Olympic 05-09/69, BEA Airtours 03/70, Dan-Air 11/73 and stored, scrapped 04/75
6424	4C	31/10/59	Mexicana	06/60	XA-NAR	wfu 12/70, Westernair N888WA 07/73, Redmond Air 11/79 wfu, Museum of Flight (Seattle) 1994
6425	4C	03/12/59	Mexicana	01/60	XA-NAS	wfu 12/70, Westernair N999WA 06/74, Onyx Avn 12/76, Redmond Air 05/79 wfu, scrapped
6426	4B	05/01/60	BEA	01/60	G-APMF	BEA Airtours 04/70, Dan-Air 01/73, wfu 11/74
6427	4	12/11/59	BOAC	11/59	G-APDG	lsd MEA 11/60, Kuwait A/W 9K-ACI 12/66, lsd MEA 12/68-05/69, Dan-Air 09/70, wfu 05/73
6428	4	07/12/59	BOAC	12/59	G-APDI	AEREA Ecuador HC-ALT 03/66, wfu 03/68
6429	4	23/12/59	BOAC	01/60	G-APDJ	Dan-Air 05/72, wfu 11/72
6430	4	15/02/60	AA	03/60	LV-AHR	cr after t-o Sao Paulo 11/61
6431	4	14/07/60	EAA	07/60	VP-KPJ	rereg 5X-AAO 04/64, Dan-Air 11/70 and wfu
6432	4	18/02/60	AA	03/60	LV-AHS	Dan-Air 11/71 and wfu
6433	4	28/07/60	EAA	09/60	VP-KPK	rereg 5X-AAF 04/64, Dan-Air 01/71 and wfu
6434	4	02/07/60	AA	07/60	LV-AHU	Dan-Air 11/71 and wfu
6435	4B	17/03/60	BEA	03/60	G-APMD	BEA Airtours 03/70, Dan-Air 09/72, wfu 01/75
6436	4B	26/04/60	BEA	05/60	G-APME	BEA Airtours 08/70, Dan-Air 02/72, wfu 05/78
6437	4B	07/04/60	Olympic	04/60	SX-DAK	BEA G-APYC 08/69, Channel A/W 01/70, Dan-Air 04/72, MoD 12/78 and wfu
6438	4B	03/05/60	Olympic	05/60	SX-DAL	BEA G-APYD 09/69, Channel A/W 01/70, Dan-Air 04/72, Science Museum 10/79
6439	4C	21/05/60	Utd Arab	06/60	SU-ALC	cr near Tripoli 01/71
6440	4B	30/06/60	BEA	07/60	G-APZM	lsd Olympic SX-DAN 07/60-03/70, Channel A/W G-APZM 05/70, Dan-Air 04/72, wfu 11/78
6441	4C	15/06/60	Utd Arab	06/60	SU-ALD	cr in sea near Bombay 07/63
6442	4B	25/07/60	BEA	07/60	G-APMG	BEA Airtours 03/70, Dan-Air 01/73, wfu 11/77
6443	4C	07/10/60	Mexicana	11/60	XA-NAT	wfu 12/70, Westernair N777WA 05/73, derelict Mexico City
6444	4C	22/11/60	Utd Arab	12/60	SU-ALE	cr after t-o Munich 02/70
6445	4C	03/12/60	MEA	12/60	OD-ADR	w/o Israeli commando attack Beirut 12/68
6446	4C	04/02/61	MEA	02/61	OD-ADQ	w/o Israeli commando attack Beirut 12/68
6447	4B	18/03/61	BEA	03/61	G-ARDI	lsd Olympic SX-DAO 03/61-11/69, BEA G-ARDI 11/69, Channel A/W 04/70, Dan-Air 04/72 and scrapped
6448	4C	05/03/61	MEA	03/61	OD-ADS	w/o Israeli commando attack Beirut 12/68
6449	4B	05/04/61	BEA	04/61	G-ARCO	cr into Mediterranean after bomb explosion 10/67
6450	4C	09/03/61	MEA	03/61	OD-ADT	Dan-Air 10/73 and wfu
6451	4B	11/04/61	BEA	04/61	G-ARCP	BEA Airtours 05/70, Dan-Air 10/73, rereg G-BBUV 12/73, wfu 10/78
6452	4B	04/05/61	BEA	05/61	G-ARJK	BEA Airtours 03/70, Dan-Air 10/73, wfu 11/76
6453	4B	27/04/61	BEA	05/61	G-ARGM	BEA Airtours 03/70, Dan-Air 11/73 and wfu
6454	4C	30/05/61	Utd Arab	06/61	SU-ALL	renamed Egyptair 10/71, wfu 10/76 and scrapped
6455	4B	19/05/61	BEA	05/61	G-ARJL	lsd Olympic 10/64-02/70, BEA Airtours 03/70, Dan-Air 11/73 and wfu
6456	4B	08/06/61	BEA	06/61	G-ARJM	cr after t-o Ankara 12/61
6457	4C	05/11/62	Sudan	11/62	ST-AAW	wfu 10/73, Dan-Air G-ASDZ 06/75, wfu 10/75
6458	4C	30/06/61	Utd Arab	07/61	SU-ALM	renamed Egyptair 10/71, Dan-Air G-BEEX 10/76 and wfu
6459	4B	21/07/61	BEA	08/61	G-ARJN	BEA Airtours 03/70, Dan-Air 02/73, wfu 12/77
6460	4C	21/08/61	AA	04/62	LV-PTS	ex G-AROV, rereg LV-AIB 05/62, Dan-Air G-AROV 10/71, wfu 11/77
6461	4C	29/03/62	Saudi Govt	06/62	SA-R-7	VIP, cr Italian Alps 03/63
6462	4C	25/03/62	Utd Arab	04/62	SU-AMV	renamed Egyptair 10/71, Dan-Air G-BEEY 10/76 and wfu
6463	4C	08/12/62	Sudan	12/62	ST-AAX	Dan-Air G-BDIF 06/75, wfu 11/79
6464	4C	03/04/62	Utd Arab	04/62	SU-AMW	cr Thailand 07/62
6465	4C	14/12/62	Kuwait	01/63	9K-ACA	lsd MEA 12/68-06/69, Dan-Air G-AYWX 03/71, wfu 05/78
6466	4C	08/12/62	Utd Arab	12/62	SU-ANC	renamed Egyptair 10/71, Dan-Air G-BEEZ 10/76 and wfu
6467	C.4	15/11/61	RAF	06/62	XR395	Dan-Air G-BDIT 08/75, wfu 10/80
6468	C.4	28/12/61	RAF	03/62	XR396	Dan-Air G-BDIU 08/75, wfu 10/80
6469	C.4	28/12/61	RAF	02/62	XR397	Dan-Air G-BDIV 08/75, wfu 11/79
6470	C.4	13/02/62	RAF	03/62	XR398	Dan-Air G-BDIW 08/75, wfu 11/80
6471	C.4	26/04/62	RAF	04/62	XR399	Dan-Air G-BDIX 08/75, wfu 10/80, Royal Museum of Scotland
6472	4	12/03/62	EAA	04/62	VP-KRL	rereg 5Y-AAA 04/64, Dan-Air 02/71 and wfu
6473	4C	26/09/63	A&AEE	12/63	XS235	
6474	4C	17/12/63	Kuwait	02/64	9K-ACE	lsd MEA 12/68-07/69, Dan-Air G-AYVS 03/71, wfu 01/77
6475	4C	04/02/64	Utd Arab	02/64	SU-ANI	cr Adis Ababa 01/70
6476	4C	25/10/65	–	–	–	cvtd HS.801 Nimrod prototype XV147 ff 31/07/67
6477	4C	23/05/67	–	–	–	cvtd HS.801 Nimrod prototype XV148 Spey engines

BAC-AEROSPATIALE
CONCORDE

Prehistoric monster or modern technical marvel? The long camera lens and heat haze exaggerates Concorde's 'droop snoot' and complex wing leading edge profile as it prepares to take off. (BA)

PRELIMINARIES

As these words were written in early 1996, the world's only operational supersonic transport – Concorde – had just achieved the significant milestone of two decades in service. Twenty years of routinely performing what many considered to be impossible – sustained cruising at twice the speed of sound while carrying over 100 passengers in comfort and safety. This is the real achievement of Concorde, Its ability to perform the role for which it was designed with a minimum of fuss. Routine but extraordinary.

Twenty years on, Concorde has become a familiar sight and sound around the world but nevertheless still attracts considerable attention wherever it goes. Twenty years on, Concorde remains one of only two SSTs to take to the air. Twenty years on, Concorde remains the only SST to enter regular, routine service.

The achievement of Concorde's British and French designers and builders is quite remarkable. Developed during the 1960s they had to rely on the technology of that era and expand upon it, inventing many new processes, materials and design philosophies along the way. A multitude of technical problems had to be overcome in order to make the aircraft's operation reliable, safe and routine. It was one thing to design and build an aircraft which could fly at twice the speed of sound and quite another to produce one which would be suitable for airline service.

Apart from the technical issues which had to be overcome, Concorde also had to survive political, financial, commercial and environmental issues before and after it entered service. Environmentally, it is certainly noisy and thirsty and the period immediately prior to its introduction to service coincided with the rise of the environmental movement around the world and the 'fuel crisis' scares of the early 1970s. Politically, there were several attempts (especially by the British) to cancel the aircraft and political pressure was also forthcoming from the other side of the Atlantic. Financially, by the time Concorde entered service in early 1976 it had cost about seven times as much as the original £150-170m estimates. Commercially, it was a flop with total production amounting to just 20 aircraft including prototypes and pre-production aircraft and only the state owned national carriers of the sponsoring nations – BOAC/British Airways and Air France – ordering it.

Despite all this, Concorde survives and plans are in place which could see it remain in service for up to 40 years. There have been numerous studies for a second generation SST from both sides of the Atlantic and these continue through the 1990s, but by 1996 there was still no definite sign that a Concorde successor would be developed. Even if the go ahead for a new SST was announced before the ink on this page is dry it would be doubtful that such an air-

craft could be in service before 2010, by which time Concorde would be celebrating the 41st anniversary of the prototype's maiden flight and 34 years in service.

British Origins

The British road which eventually led to the Concorde started on 5 November 1956 with the establishment by the British government of the Supersonic Transport Advisory Committee (STAC), a body comprising representatives from all of Britain's major airframe and engine manufacturers, the airlines, the appropriate government ministries and the Royal Aircraft Establishment (RAE) at Farnborough, the body responsible for the bulk of the nation's supersonic research work up to that point.

Chaired by M B (later Sir Morien) Morgan, the STAC was established at a time when the increasing number of supersonic military aircraft had prompted many in the industry to begin applying the "what if" train of thought to the possibility of a supersonic commercial aircraft.

At that point, Britain had only two aircraft capable of achieving supersonic speeds in level flight, the English Electric P.1 (which was developed into the Lightning fighter) and the Fairey Delta Two. Both had resulted from Ministry of Supply Specification ER.103 for supersonic research aircraft and were of differing configuration. The P.1 featured two afterburning

Concorde 210 G-BOAD, delivered to British Airways in December 1976. (Philip J Birtles)

The Fairey Delta Two set a new world's air speed record in 1956 and would go on to have direct influence on the thinking which created Concorde.

Rolls-Royce Avon turbojets mounted on top of each in the fuselage and a highly swept wing of unconventional planform, while the FD.2 was a tailless Delta powered by a single afterburning Avon. The prototypes of these aircraft first flew in August and October 1954, respectively.

While the P.1 eventually went into series production in highly modified form as the Lightning, FD.2 production was limited to just two aircraft. Nevertheless, the first of them (WG774) established a new world's air speed record of 1,132.136mph (1,821.946 km/h) or Mach 1.71 in March 1956 in the hands of Fairey's chief test pilot, Peter Twiss. This speed bettered the previous mark (set by a North American F-100 Super Sabre) by a whopping 310mph (499km/h) or 38 per cent, the largest increase in the history of the record.

The FD.2 played an indirect part in the evolution of the Concorde design due to its influence on French thinking, while the record breaking aircraft would later have a significant direct role in proving an important part of the Concorde's concept, its wing design.

After more than two years of meetings and research into the various aspects of supersonic transport design, the STAC was able to present a report on its findings in March 1959. Its broad recommendation was to examine the potential in developing two designs: one to carry 100 passengers over 1,500 miles (2,400km) at Mach 1.2 and the other offering a speed of Mach 1.8 over trans-Atlantic ranges of up to 3,500 miles (5,630km) while carrying 150 passengers.

From there, the concept evolved in favour of the longer range aircraft while wind tunnel and other research into the best configuration for such an aircraft quickly revealed that a slender delta wing had several advantages over other layouts. It was found that the delta wing provided better aerodynamic efficiency up to about Mach 2.2, resulting in the decision to work towards an aircraft capable of cruising at twice the speed of sound.

Design Concepts

In late 1959, Hawker Siddeley and Bristol Aircraft (the latter becoming part of the British Aircraft Corporation – BAC – the following year) were awarded contracts by the Ministry of Aviation (MoA) to carry out further studies and to prepare proposals for a delta winged supersonic transport.

The two manufacturers approached the problem in different ways, Hawker Siddeley coming up with a kind of flying wing concept in that the fuselage was integrated with a wing of deep cross section; while Bristol's concept emerged as combining a 'discrete' fuselage with a thin wing. This was considered to be the preferred path and in 1961 the Bristol (or BAC) Type 198 design was mooted. A 130 seater, it featured six Bristol Siddeley (now Rolls-Royce) Olympus turbojets mounted under the wings and a maximum takeoff weight of 380,000lb (172,370kg). The Olympus had already been developed for the Avro Vulcan bomber and in afterburning form was selected for the BAC TSR.2 strike aircraft.

Concerns about the aircraft's weight, the economical aspects of six

Drawing directly from knowledge gained with the Fairy Delta Two, France's Dassault developed the successful Mirage delta winged fighter series. This is an RAAF Mirage IIIO.

Sud-Aviation flew the first Caravelle in 1955 and although its then radical rear engined configuration caused some raised eyebrows at first, it was quickly adopted by most other airliner manufacturers. A total of 282 was built.

engines and design problems with the engine intakes resulted in the Bristol 198 being scaled down to a 100 seater with a maximum weight of 250,000lb (113,400kg) and four Olympus engines. As the Type 223, this concept formed the basis of the British side of the discussions and design features which would shortly lead to the formation of the Anglo-French team behind the Concorde.

Of interest is the fact that Bristol's contract with the MoA for further development of its SST ideas specifically included investigating collaboration with French, German or American companies as it was realised that should the project go ahead there would be very heavy demands on finances, research and development and other resources. Germany's industry was not yet ready to attempt such a challenging project and the USA showed little enthusiasm for collaboration (it had its own plans for a Mach 3 SST), but France had been doing its own SST research work and was more than interested.

French Concepts

France's positive response to the idea of collaboration on a supersonic transport came at a time when its industry was healthy but it had much to gain through co-operation as at the time, Britain was ahead in its research. Dassault had achieved considerable success during the 1950s with the Ouragan and Mystère families of military aircraft and the delta winged Mirage III series of fighters was in the early stages of a highly successful and profitable career. On the civil side, Sud-Aviation was achieving success with its revolutionary Caravelle short-medium range jet airliner.

Considered an oddity at first with its rear engined configuration, the Caravelle's layout was soon copied by British, Soviet and American manufacturers.

Dassault's success with the delta wing owed a considerable amount to Britain's Fairey Delta Two. At the time of the FD.2's speed record in 1956, it appeared that Britain held the lead in not only high speed but also delta wing design and Dassault was quick to organise a co-operative arrangement for the benefit of both. As it turned out, Dassault (and French industry generally) derived by far the greatest benefits, mainly due to the British Government's decision to abandon delta wings in favour of highly swept ones such as those fitted to the English Electric P.1/Lightning.

As a result, the French company got the benefit of extensive structural and aerodynamic information from Fairey and put it to very good use in what would become the Mirage III.

This knowledge also contributed greatly to French industry's early studies for a supersonic transport. In 1957 the French Government invited aerospace companies to submit concepts for such an aircraft, the team working in conjunction with Air France. Sud-Aviation, Dassault and

Nord responded, Sud's ideas revolving around a delta wing 70 seater powered by four turbojets and capable of cruising at Mach 2.2 over a range of 2,000 miles (3,200km).

This medium range aircraft contrasted with Britain's preference for longer, trans-Atlantic range capability. Sud and Dassault combined their efforts in 1959 and came up with the 'Super Caravelle' which by mid 1960 was a 76 seater with a range of 2,500 miles (4,000km), still insufficient for nonstop trans-Atlantic operations. When the time came for co-operation between Britain and France on the SST project, the matter of range remained an item of contention for a time with Britain adamant (quite correctly as it turned out) that it was only on longer sectors that the advantages of supersonic speeds could be fully exploited. Additionally, BOAC saw the London-New York route as being the prime one for an SST and to achieve that a range capability similar to that which Bristol was proposing with its Type 223 was required.

Towards Collaboration

The first Anglo-French discussions on the subject of jointly developing a supersonic transport took place in June and July 1961. With support from both governments, BAC and Sud set about establishing some common ground which could see them go ahead with the most advanced civil aircraft programme in history. Both sides initially stuck to their guns on the subject of the aircraft's range, Britain continuing to state the case of the longer range aircraft while France pushed for the medium range option with a view to increasing it later on.

The BAC view was that apart from any operational

The big moment – British Minister of Aviation Julian Amery (left) and the French Ambassador in London, Geoffroy de Courcel, sign the Concorde agreement on 29 November 1962.

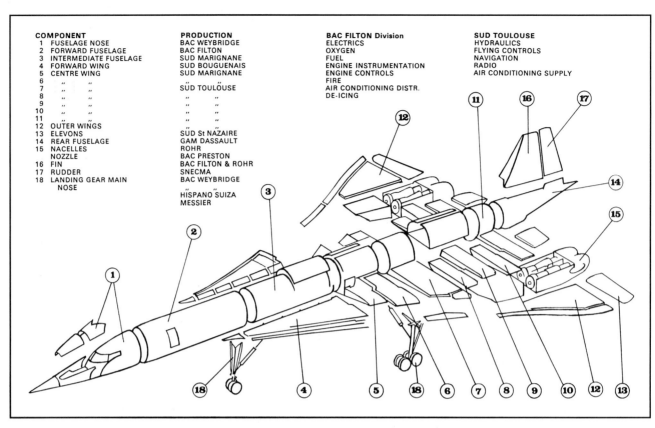

COMPONENT
1 FUSELAGE NOSE
2 FORWARD FUSELAGE
3 INTERMEDIATE FUSELAGE
4 FORWARD WING
5 CENTRE WING
6 „ „
7 „ „
8 „ „
9 „ „
10 „ „
11 „ „
12 OUTER WINGS
13 ELEVONS
14 REAR FUSELAGE
15 NACELLES
   NOZZLE
16 FIN
17 RUDDER
18 LANDING GEAR MAIN
      NOSE

PRODUCTION
BAC WEYBRIDGE
BAC FILTON
SUD MARIGNANE
SUD BOUGUENAIS
SUD MARIGNANE

SUD TOULOUSE
   „   „
   „   „
   „   „
   „   „
   „   „

SUD St NAZAIRE
GAM DASSAULT
ROHR
BAC PRESTON
BAC FILTON & ROHR
SNECMA
BAC WEYBRIDGE

HISPANO SUIZA
MESSIER

BAC FILTON Division
ELECTRICS
OXYGEN
FUEL
ENGINE INSTRUMENTATION
ENGINE CONTROLS
FIRE
AIR CONDITIONING DISTR.
DE-ICING

SUD TOULOUSE
HYDRAULICS
FLYING CONTROLS
NAVIGATION
RADIO
AIR CONDITIONING SUPPLY

The breakdown of who built what on the Concorde, as per the 1962 agreement. (BAe)

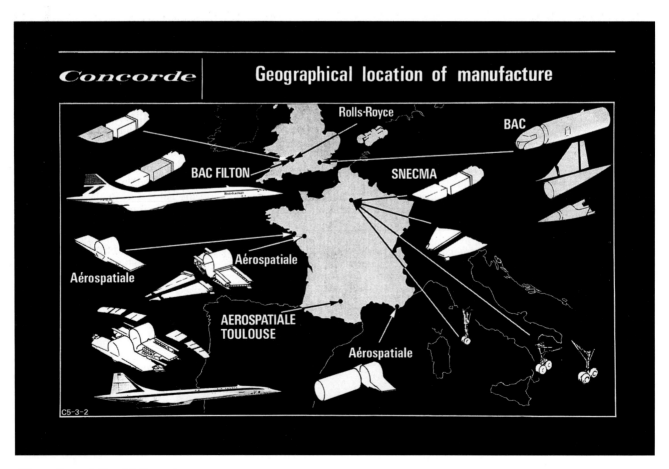

advantages the longer range aircraft might have, it would be able to circumvent a potential problem which it could foresee, that of being forced to fly supersonically only over water where the sonic boom would not be a problem. France's proposal called for an SST which would operate over land.

Some encouragement from both governments helped bridge the conceptual gaps which persisted between the two manufacturers. It was a slow and tedious process and by April 1962 – when a decision on co-operation was thought to be imminent – two versions of the Super Caravelle (as the aircraft was generally known) were still being touted: the British 80 seater with trans-Atlantic range and the French 100 seater with a shorter, 2,400 miles (3,860km) range. At least by this stage the overall design of the aircraft was basically established with the British variant trading payload for more fuel. In July 1962 Sud's president, M Georges Hereil, announced that the Super Caravelle would fly in 1965 and enter service four years later.

By the time of the Farnborough Air Show in September 1962, the basic specification of the aircraft had been established. A model was displayed on the BAC stand at the show and there was considerable speculation that a co-production agreement would be announced at the time.

Agreement

The Anglo-French supersonic transport programme became a formal entity on 29 November 1962 at a ceremony at Lancaster House in London when the British Minister of Supply Julian Amery and France's Ambassador to Britain, Geoffroy de Courcel, signed an agreement whereby the two governments would undertake to finance the development and manufacture of a supersonic airliner. Significantly, the agreement contained no 'escape clause' for either party, something which would later cause a couple of British Labour governments some anguish!

Equally significant was the fact that this was the first time an international collaborative agreement had been established in the aerospace industry – the first of Concorde's many 'firsts'.

The basic agreement provided for the development of a 100 seat delta winged SST capable of cruising at Mach 2.2 (later reduced to Mach 2.0 for structural reasons) with all costs met equally by the British and French governments and all work shared on a 50/50 basis between the aerospace industries of the two countries.

There were four major contractors: BAC and Sud-Aviation (airframe) and Bristol Siddeley and SNECMA (powerplants) as well as a multitude of sub contractors from both countries. The airframe workshare was split 60/40 in favour of France while the powerplant work was divided 65/35 in Britain's favour as the chosen engine, the Olympus 593, was a Bristol Siddeley product which was already well along the road to development at the time of the agreement.

The airframe sub assembly work was divided among several BAC and Sud facilities: Weybridge, Hurn, Filton, Preston, St Martin, Toulouse, Bouguenais, St Nazaire and Bourges. While this work was not duplicated, final assembly was, with lines established in Britain at Filton (Bristol's main facility) and in France at Toulouse, Sud's headquarters. This duplication was considered necessary not only for nationalistic reasons but also because it was thought that the potential market for the aircraft was 300-400 examples and that considerable production capacity would be needed.

Structural design responsibility was also shared, BAC looking after the front fuselage/flight deck, engine nacelles, air intakes, engine mountings, rear fuselage and fin and rudder while Sud designed the centre fuselage system, wings and control surfaces and undercarriage. The design of the aircraft's complex systems was divided thus: electrics, oxygen, fuel, engine instrumentation, engine controls, fire extinguishers, air conditioning distribution and de-icing to BAC and hydraulics, flying control, avionics and air conditioning supply to Sud-Aviation.

At the time of the agreement's signing the cost of the project was estimated at £150-170m, first flight was planned for 1966 (with service entry in 1970) and the basic shape of the aircraft was already very close to what would finally emerge – a tailless delta with a thin fuselage. One of the characteristics of the final design was already present, the distinctive 'droop snoot' nose with retractable visor allowing aerodynamic efficiency at supersonic speeds and adequate visibility at other times, especially on the landing approach when one of the characteristics of the delta wing – a high angle of attack at low speeds – was most evident.

At the time the agreement was signed the new airliner was officially without a name, but the appellation 'Concord' (in Britain) and 'Concorde' (in France) was already being used by many of those involved. Ironically in view of the meaning of the word, there would be some bickering about how the name should be spelt after it was officially adopted a short time later. For a while the British long range variant was 'Concord' without the 'e' and the French medium range version was 'Concorde' with it!

The first 'official' use of the name occurred in January 1963 when France's President de Gaulle made mention of it in public ... presumably with the 'e' added on the end.

This was the occasion of his infamous "non" speech on the question of Britain joining the European Common Market. The irony was that Britain thought that joining France on an SST project might help its ambitions in that area.

THE DEVELOPMENT PHASE

With the signing of the Anglo-French Supersonic Aircraft Agreement in November 1962 came the formal go-ahead for the most ambitious civil aviation project ever undertaken and completed. The task ahead was massive, not only from the technical point of view but also from that of administration, because without effective management there could be mayhem.

The agreement had clearly defined who would be doing what, where, and how as far as the major elements of the project were concerned, but there was considerable room for confusion simply due to the logistics of the exercise. There was the language barrier to overcome, although the higher ranked French seemed to generally have better English than the English had French; there were nationalistic jealousies, mostly in the early days and mostly quickly ironed out; and there was the question of weights and measures. The French were unfamiliar with the Imperial system and the British with metric – therefore two sets of drawings were issued for everything, one in each system.

These and other problems were overcome thanks largely to the strong leadership provided by Andre Puget, Sud-Aviation's president and the chairman of BAC, Sir George Edwards. The two men held the chairmanship and vice-chairmanship of the Aircraft Committee of Directors in rotation but at an early stage they decided to share the decision making between them. This level of co-operation considerably helped the programme run as smoothly as was possible and also set the example for everyone else involved.

There were certainly large numbers of 'everyone else' connected with the Concorde development programme. Including those working for the many subcontractors and suppliers, the number peaked at around 50,000.

Programme Evolution

With detailed, co-ordinated work able to start once the agreement had been signed, Concorde's design evolution was also able to begin. Heading the design effort were BAC's Sir Archibald Russell and Dr William Strang, working in 'concord/e' with Sud-Aviation's Lucien Sevanty and Pierre Satre. At the time of the agreement, two versions were still proposed, the longer range model favoured by the British and France's medium range variant. The overall configuration had already been set-

Overhead view of Concorde 202 G-BBDG (the second production aircraft) clearly shows the aircraft's ovigal wing planform and the windscreen visor retracted. (via Philip J Birtles)

tled – a slender delta wing, four afterburning Olympus turbojets, a long, thin fuselage capable of carrying about 100 passengers four abreast, and a speed of Mach 2.2.

A preliminary design was presented to the airlines in January 1963 and a year later the medium range variant was abandoned, all effort now concentrating on the version capable of flying the North Atlantic nonstop.

By late 1964 most of the design's major features had been settled including the use of the ogival wing planform with its subtle curves and constant camber. At around the same time a 15 per cent enlargement of the wing was incorporated to take advantage of increased thrust promised by the Olympus 593. This allowed greater fuel capacity and improved takeoff and landing characteristics as well as permitting the moving of some fuel originally intended for fuselage tanks to the wings. This in turn freed up space for freight capacity, allowing the designers to allocate some of the space previously earmarked for this purpose to be used for more passenger seats.

At this point Concorde could accommodate up to 126 passengers with seats at 34 inch (86cm) pitch. It had a maximum takeoff weight of 326,000lb (147,873kg), an overall length of 184ft 4.5in (56.19m), a wing span of 83ft 10in (25.55m) and a cruising speed of Mach 2.2 or 1,263 knots (2,338km/h) above 36,000 feet. Each Olympus 593 engine was then rated at an estimated 32,450lb (145kN) thrust for takeoff with afterburning at the time of service entry, increasing to 35,000lb (157kN) thrust afterwards.

The decision was then taken to reduce the cruising speed to a shade over Mach 2 in the interests of increased airframe life. This amounted to a reduction in speed of about 100 knots (185km/h), increasing the trans-Atlantic flight time by only a few minutes (while halving the subsonic time from seven to three-and-a-half hours anyway) and at the same time saving some wear and tear on the structure.

Politics and Marketing

1964 saw the first of what would be several attempts to stop the Concorde programme. This one was courtesy the newly elected Labour Government in Britain under Prime Minister Harold Wilson. This government is well remembered for the damage it did to the British aerospace industry during its tenure of office between 1964 and 1970, cancelling projects right, left and centre.

Concorde came under close scrutiny as a result of the government

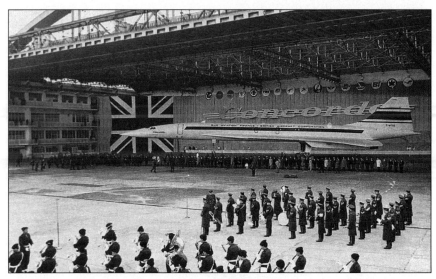

Military bands and dignitaries at the rollout of Concorde 001 at Toulouse in December 1967. It would be another 15 months before the aircraft flew.

Concorde wind tunnel model showing the intricate patterns of airflow around the fuselage and over the wings. (via Philip J Birtles)

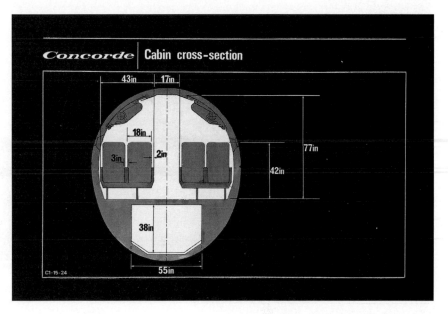

Closeup of the retractable 'bumper' wheel in Concorde's lower rear fuselage, just in case of over-rotation. (Julian Green)

Kennedy launched his country's own supersonic transport programme ... more of which later.

Options were gradually taken by other operators over the next few years and by June 1965 the total had reached 47: Air France 8, BOAC 8, American Airlines 6, Air India 2, Continental Air Lines 3, Middle East Airlines 2, Pan American Airways 6, Qantas 4, Sabena 2 and TWA 6. Other options were placed in 1966 including Eastern Airlines (4), Braniff (3) and Air Canada (4). It's important to note that none of these were firm orders but the airlines decided they couldn't afford not to have delivery positions reserved, because if Concorde proved to be a winner with the travelling public, those without it could be severely disadvantaged.

Hopes were high among the BAC and Sud sales staff. At the time the project was formally launched in late 1962 the estimated market was put at 300 to 400 aircraft and in January 1967 one BAC executive predicted sales would reach 200 by 1973 and 400 by 1980. At that time there was no reason to suspect that Concorde would be anything less than commercially successful and that the "100 Concordes, or perhaps a few more" that needed to be sold in order to achieve a reasonable return on costs would be delivered.

Towards First Flight

Meanwhile, the nuts and bolts were beginning to come together, although the inevitable delays resulted in scheduled dates for first flight and entry into service coming and going. The original first flight and in service dates were 1966 and 1970, respec-

wishing to reduce spending on what it called 'prestige projects'. Minister of Aviation Roy Jenkins visited Paris in October 1964 to discuss the cancellation of the project with his French counterpart but was quickly reminded of the lack of an escape clause in the agreement between the two nations. The agreement specifically forbade either side from unilaterally withdrawing, a touch ironic as it had been included at the insistence of the previous British (Conservative) government!

That, in combination with the possibility that the French might sue and union pressure at home gave the British Government no choice but to

continue, Jenkins announcing that fact in early 1965 "despite some doubts about the financial and economic aspects". As it turned out, those doubts would be well founded, but at the time it appeared Concorde was attracting sufficient interest from customers to make it commercially viable.

The first airline to formally indicate an interest was Pan American, which placed options on six aircraft on 3 June 1963. BOAC and Air France took options on eight each at about the same time, while of great significance was the fact that within 48 hours of the Pan American order being announced, US President John

Head on view of Concorde reveals some interesting detail including the quite widely spaced engine nacelles, the complex curves in the wing leading edges, the undercarriage geometry and the retractable visor. (BA)

tively but these gradually slipped back until in reality they became March 1969 and January 1976.

The Olympus 593D engine for Concorde recorded its first bench test run in July 1964, first metal was cut for the two prototypes in April 1965, final assembly of the first prototype (001) began at Toulouse exactly a year later and in August 1966 assembly of the second prototype (002 – the first British aircraft) started at Filton.

In December 1966 a fuselage section was delivered to the Royal Aircraft Establishment at Farnborough for fatigue testing and the design for the pre production and production standard Concorde (with new nose/visor design and longer fuselage) was finalised in early 1967.

The world got its first glimpse of a supersonic transport on 11 December 1967 with the rollout of Concorde 001 F-WTSS (*transport supersonique*) at Toulouse. Accompanied by the appropriate amount of fanfare, the appropriate number of politicians and the appropriate representatives of the airlines which had placed options, the occasion was significant not only for what it represented, but also because it settled once and for all the issue of how the aircraft's name should be spelt.

In his speech, British Minister of Technology, Antony Wedgewood Benn, specifically stated that all Concordes – including those built in Britain – would have the troublesome 'e' at the end of the name, symbolic, he said, of excellence, England, Europe and *entente*. According to Mr Benn, this was the only disagreement between Britain and France during the five years of co-operation on the project!

It wasn't realised at the time, but it would be another 15 months before Concorde 001 would fly for the first time, a gap which would allow the Soviet Tupolev Tu-144 supersonic transport to get into the air first, on the last day of 1968. Meanwhile, the British prototype (002/G-BSST) was rolled out at Filton in September 1968 in preparation for its first flight seven months later.

Concorde's Technology

Concorde's mission – flying 100 or so passengers over long distances at twice the speed of sound – required a design which was radical in many ways. Systems, powerplants, aerodynamics and structure would all be subject to forces and influences far different from any previous commercial aircraft and therefore in many cases required new solutions.

One area which did remain within the boundaries of current knowledge

Concorde 202 photographed from below, well illustrating the aerodynamic cleanliness of the underside and some of the subtle shapes incorporated. (BAC)

was the material from which the aircraft would be built – aluminium alloy. The early decision to utilise this material by necessity restricted the aircraft's speed to a maximum of around Mach 2.2 (later reduced to Mach 2) due to the effects of kinetic heating on the structure. To go faster would have required the use of either stainless steel or extremely expensive titanium alloys, the cost/benefit ratio turning out to be strongly in favour of the aluminium, particularly in view of the risks involved in pushing the limits of knowledge even further than they were anyway. Additionally, this would have added considerably to the cost of the aircraft and to its development time, all for the saving of about 15 minutes flying between London and New York.

At Mach 2, the friction caused by the air passing over the aircraft causes its structure's temperature to rise to about 120degC, hotter than the boiling point of water and a marked contrast to the temperature

even at Mach 1, which remains slightly below zero. Had Concorde been designed for three times the speed of sound (as the Americans were keen to achieve when they first looked at an SST), the structure would have needed to cope with temperatures of 300degC, just below the melting point of lead.

Even at Mach 2 Concorde's structure expands measurably due to the effects of heat and not just any aluminium alloy will do the job. Many thousands of specimens were tested for fatigue strength, corrosion resistance and mechanical properties before the copper based RR58 (AU2GN in France) was chosen as it could satisfactorily handle the three main effects of kinetic heating: deterioration of material properties; stresses induced by different expansion rates due to temperature gradients; and the phenomenon known as 'creep', the deformation of metal caused by the interaction between mechanical loadings and high temperatures.

Vulcan B.1A XA903 with Olympus 593 engine and nacelle slung underneath. This aircraft tested Concorde's powerplant for nearly five years from September 1966. (via Philip J Birtles)

The Wing

A delta wing was judged to provide the best solution to meeting the supersonic transport's needs by both the British and French teams even before they joined forces in 1962. Concorde's ogival delta wing planform looks and is complex with its balance of constant and precisely calculated camber and taper across its structure and a combination of droop and twist along the leading edges. The idea was to find a wing section which would not only allow the aircraft to fly at its designed speed but also provide acceptable handling qualities at lower speeds, especially on the landing approach.

There are no leading edge or high lift devices, and apart from the rudder, all control is performed by three elevons on the trailing edge of each wing. Of aluminium alloy honeycomb construction, each elevon is operated by a tandem jack, with each half sup-

plied by an independent hydraulic source and controlled by a separate electric system. This was the first installation of a fly-by-wire control system on a production aircraft and operates in conjunction with auto-stabilisation and hydraulic artificial feel systems. The fly-by-wire system is analogue with mechanical backup.

The wing is of cantilever construction with a thickness/chord ration of 3 per cent at the root and 2.15 per cent outboard. It has slight anhedral and its structural heart is a multi spar torsion box design.

Fuselage and Cabin

Concorde's fuselage is of conventional aluminium alloy semi monocoque construction with unpressurised tail and nose cone areas. The cabin is 6ft 5in (1.95m) high and 8ft 7.5in (2.63m) wide, allowing four abreast seating. Up to 128 passengers can be carried with a seat pitch of 34 inches (86cm)

although there is provision for a maximum of 144 passengers in a tight, 31 inch (81cm) seat pitch arrangement. British Airways and Air France have most often operated their Concordes in more spacious 100 seat layouts.

The cockpit provides accommodation for two pilots and a flight engineer. There is also a supernumerary seat behind the captain. Concorde's pressurisation and environmental control system is by necessity very powerful as its operating altitude of up to 60,000 feet (18,288m) is considerably higher than any other commercial aircraft.

The maximum cabin pressure differential is 10.7lb sq/in which provides a cabin altitude of just 6,000 feet (1,830m) when the aircraft is at its maximum height. By comparison, a Boeing 747's maximum pressure differential is a relatively modest 8.9lb sq/in.

The cabin air conditioning system has to cope with extremely low outside air temperatures at high altitude (-94degC at 55,000 feet) as well as the high structural temperatures generated at Mach 2. It comprises four independent subsystems, each with a heat exchanger. In each subsystem the air passes through a primary ram air heat exchanger to an air cycle cold air unit, and then through secondary air/air and air/fuel heat exchanger units. The air is then mixed and distributed to the flight deck, cabin, baggage holds, and radar, equipment and undercarriage bays.

The distinctive 'droop snoot' nose is hydraulically lowered for better visibility and low speeds and raised for high speed flight. Including a retractable visor, the nose can placed in

Apart from Concorde, the only other application for an afterburning version of the Olympus engine was the ill fated BAC TSR.2 strike bomber.

three positions with variations in visor position: fully up with visor in place for supersonic flight; fully up and visor retracted for subsonic cruise; five degrees down (visor retracted) for lower subsonic speeds and takeoff; and 12 degrees down for the landing approach as the aircraft's angle of attack reaches 14 degrees nose up.

Concorde's main systems comprise two primary and one standby hydraulic systems of 4,000lb sq/in pressure each operated by two engine driven pumps plus an AC electrical system powered by four engine driven alternators and producing 200/115 volts. A 28 volt DC supply is also provided.

The hydraulic systems drive the flying controls, artificial feel units, landing gear, wheel brakes, nosewheel steering, nosecone droop, windscreen visor, engine intake ramps and fuel pumps.

Powerplants

The four Rolls-Royce (originally Bristol Siddeley) Olympus 593 Mk.610 turbojet engines as fitted to production Concordes each produce 38,050lb (170kN) thrust with 17 per cent afterburning. They are also fitted with thrust reversers.

A twin spool axial flow turbojet, the Olympus has its origins in the late 1940s when it was developed to power a proposed Bristol bomber intended to meet the specification which would eventually be filled by the Avro Vulcan. At that stage the Bristol organisation comprised the Aeroplane Company and Aero Engines divisions, the latter becoming Bristol Siddeley Engines in 1959 when it merged with the Armstrong Siddeley company, and finally part of Rolls-Royce in 1966.

When the Olympus was first run on the bench it produced 9,140lb (41kN) thrust but as is usually the case, performance gradually improved and by the time the Olympus 101 entered service on the Vulcan power was up to 11,000lb (49kN) thrust. Further development resulted in the most powerful of the non afterburning Olympus variants, the Mk.301 as fitted to the Vulcan B.2 and rated at 20,000lb (90kN) thrust.

The Olympus has also been used outside aviation, finding widespread marine and industrial applications powering numerous warships including the *Invincible* class 'through deck cruisers' (Harrier Carriers!) for the Royal Navy. In maritime form, the Olympus produces up to 30,000 shaft horsepower (22,380kW). Other applications include industrial power generation. Many power stations use the engine to generate electrical power as do offshore oil rigs.

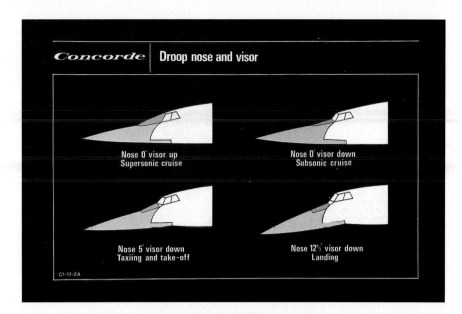

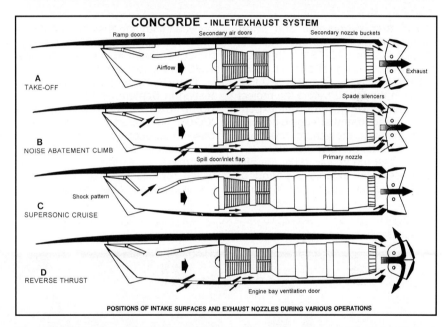

Concorde's complex engine intake system with the position of the ramps and spill doors shown at various phases of the flight. (BAC)

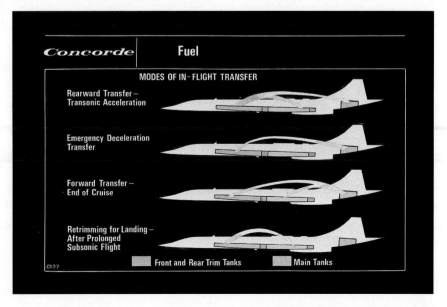

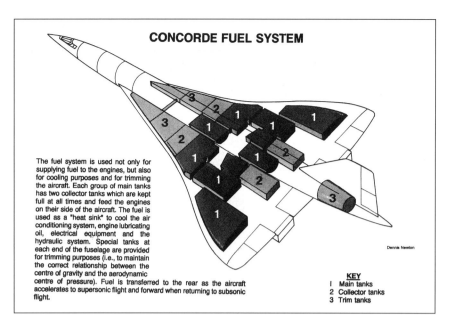

CONCORDE FUEL SYSTEM

The fuel system is used not only for supplying fuel to the engines, but also for cooling purposes and for trimming the aircraft. Each group of main tanks has two collector tanks which are kept full at all times and feed the engines on their side of the aircraft. The fuel is used as a "heat sink" to cool the air conditioning system, engine lubricating oil, electrical equipment and the hydraulic system. Special tanks at each end of the fuselage are provided for trimming purposes (i.e., to maintain the correct relationship between the centre of gravity and the aerodynamic centre of pressure). Fuel is transferred to the rear as the aircraft accelerates to supersonic flight and forward when returning to subsonic flight.

Dennis Newton

KEY
1 Main tanks
2 Collector tanks
3 Trim tanks

The first supersonic and afterburning Olympus variant was the Mk.320 for the BAC TSR.2 strike aircraft. Producing about 31,000lb (139kN) thrust, the Olympus 320 flew briefly in the TSR.2 before the project was cancelled in 1965, but experience gained from that engine contributed greatly to the variant developed for Concorde, the Olympus 593.

First test run in July 1964, the 593 underwent an extensive period of ground testing, logging 5,000 hours between then and the end of 1968. In the meantime, 35,190lb (158Kn) thrust had been achieved in October 1966 on the test bench.

The Olympus 593 began flight testing In September 1966 under the bomb bay of Avro Vulcan B.1A XA903, an aircraft which had previously been used for trails of the Blue Steel standoff bomb in the UK and at Woomera in Australia. A nacelle which represented half a Concorde installation was fitted to the Vulcan while the bomb bay had fuel and water tanks plus instrumentation installed in it. It took more than two years to convert the Vulcan to its new configuration which allowed the Olympus 593's subsonic flight envelope to be studied in detail.

All manner of tests were carried out on a variety of Olympus 593 variants ranging from the earliest test standards to a specification close to the production engine. Anti-icing trials were also conducted. XA903 recorded 219 flights and logged 420 hours as an Olympus testbed, the last of them in July 1971. This Vulcan continued its engine testbed career, subsequently having the RB199 powerplant for the Panavia Tornado installed. It was finally retired in February 1979 as the last airworthy Vulcan B.1 and consigned to the fire dump at Farnborough.

The Olympus variant fitted to the prototype Concordes was the 593B rated at 34,370lb (154Kn) thrust, although more than 40,000lb (179Kn) thrust had been achieved for limited times during test runs. These engines were extremely smoky and criticism arising from this resulted in considerable development work by Rolls-Royce from 1969. The solution was found in the adaptation of an annular combustion chamber design which had previously been used in the Viper, Sapphire and Pegasus engines

The BAC 221 was a highly modified testbed conversion of the former world's air speed record holding Fairey Delta Two incorporating a wing planform similar to Concorde's. (via Philip J Birtles)

and in combination with a new vaporising fuel injection system, resulted in a virtually smoke free exhaust for production Concordes.

Variable Intakes

One of Concorde's most interesting technical features is its variable geometry engine air intakes comprising a complex system of hydraulically controlled ramps and spill doors linked to a series of computers and sensors. Their function is to ensure the Olympus engines get the right amount of air moving at the correct speed through a wide variety of airspeeds.

Receiving an even flow of air is vital to the engines' proper functioning, and the desirable speed at which the air is delivered is between Mach 0.4 and 0.5. When the aircraft is travelling at Mach 2 it is obvious that the air has to be slowed down considerably before it enters the engines while at low speeds (such as on the approach) the amount of air flowing into the engines has to be maximised.

As can be seen from the accompanying diagram, Concorde's intake geometry is varied by the use of two moving ramps on the roof of the intake and a spill door/inlet flap on the intake floor. At takeoff, during the climb and when landing the ramps are fully open and the spill door closed. The door gradually closes as (subsonic) speed increases but the ramps remain open until about Mach 1.3 when they automatically partially lower to a point at which they slow the incoming air down to Mach 0.5 before it enters the engine.

Fuel Management

One of the phenomenon affecting any aircraft travelling at supersonic speeds is a rearward shift in the centre of aerodynamic lift when moving from subsonic to supersonic flight conditions. This causes a nose down situation which can be corrected by control surfaces but with the penalty of increased drag as these surfaces must remain deflected slightly at supersonic speeds.

The condition can be corrected to some extent by aerodynamic design in the areas of wing camber and twist but these can also cause lift/drag penalties. In Concorde, the problem is tackled by a combination of aerodynamic and fuel transfer means, the latter moving the aircraft's centre of gravity to the optimum point for the prevailing flight conditions.

Production Concordes have a total useable fuel capacity of 26,350imp gal (119,787 litres) housed in integral tanks in two groups. The main group comprises five tanks in each wing and four in the fuselage, these maintaining centre of gravity automatically

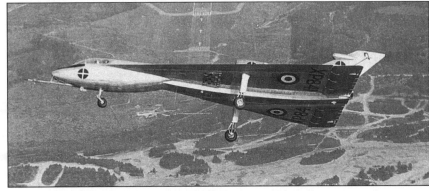

The Handley Page HP.115, used for testing the low speed handling characteristics of the delta wing.

in the cruise. The trim tank group consists of three tanks, two at the front and another in the rear fuselage.

These maintain the correct relationship between the centre of gravity and the centre of aerodynamic lift by transferring fuel to the rear during acceleration and supersonic flight and forward during the return to subsonic flight. During this operation, Concorde's centre of gravity moves by about 4 feet (1.2m) with the correct attitude maintained by the autopilot in supersonic cruise and the elevons stationary at their most efficient position.

Concept Proving

Apart from the Avro Vulcan which was used to test the Olympus engine, two other testbed aircraft played a vital role in the development of the Concorde.

The first was the Handley Page HP.115, a one-off single seat jet aircraft intended for research into the low speed handling characteristics of delta wings. Built as a result of the Supersonic Transport Aircraft Committee's leanings towards a delta wing for an SST, the HP.115 was powered by a single Bristol Siddeley Viper 9 turbojet of 1,900lb (8.5kN) thrust mounted at the rear of the fuselage. The fin and rudder was fitted above the engine and the aircraft had a long delta wing of 74deg 42min sweep at the leading edge. The undercarriage was fixed.

The sole HP.115 (XP841) was first flown in August 1961 and spent the next few years involved in low speed handling trials during which a mass of data were collected which could be applied to Concorde. Further, the HP.115 dispelled doubts about the delta wing's handling characteristics at low speeds. XP841 remained in the air until 1974 when it reached its design life of 500 hours and was retired.

The other testbed aircraft associated with the Concorde programme explored the other end of the delta wing's speed range. The BAC 221 was another one-off, but this time it was based on an existing aircraft, the Fairey Delta Two WG774 which in 1956 had set a new world's air speed record of 1,132mph (1,822km/h).

For its second life as the BAC 221, WG774 was extensively modified, being fitted with an ogival delta wing (the original was a straight delta), new control surfaces, redesigned engine air intakes, a fuselage lengthened by six feet (1.83m) to cater for the new wing planform and to house more fuel, and a longer nosewheel leg. The

Artist's impression of the Boeing 2707-200 supersonic transport as originally proposed with swing wings. Designed to carry about 300 passengers at Mach 2.7, over 120 options had been placed by most of the world's major international airlines when the project was cancelled in 1971. By then, the 2707 had evolved into a delta wing design. (PanAm)

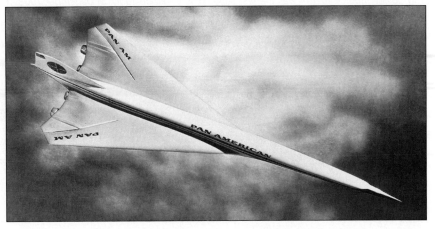

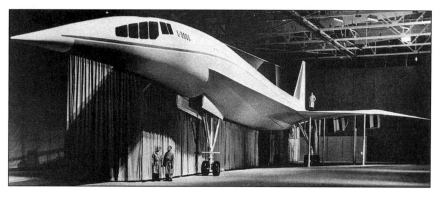

Full scale mockup of Lockheed's SST proposal, the delta wing L-2000.

original Fairey designed 'droop snoot' was retained as was the afterburning Rolls-Royce Avon RA.28R of 14,000lb (63kN) thrust.

Also incorporated was an auto-stabilisation system, including automatic throttle control, which had provision to simulate changes in certain stability characteristics.

The 221 (the last aircraft to carry a Bristol Type number in its designation, incidentally) was flown from Filton for the first time in May 1964. Two years' development flying followed during which some further modifications were added – including a fin of increased height – and in May 1966 it was delivered to the RAE at Bedford where it joined the HP.115.

The 221 was used for both high and low speed research, but concentrated mainly on the high subsonic, transonic and supersonic areas. Maximum speed was around Mach 1.6 at altitude. Flying of the BAC continued until June 1973 when it was retired, like the HP.115, to a museum.

Politics and Competition

The Concorde programme is by its very nature a highly political one, but not all of the politics which have influenced it has been from the two governments directly involved.

Even before the Concorde project had formally got underway, it appears the Americans had tried to scuttle it, fearful that Europe would steal a

march on its own industry. A gentleman called Eugene Black, a former chairman of the World Bank, was behind early attempts to thwart the project before it began.

Black – who had friends in high places in Washington – became a very vocal critic of the whole concept of a supersonic transport but as time went on it appeared his real intention was to stop only a European SST so an American one could go ahead.

One American who was publicly very much in favour of a US SST was Najeeb Halaby, the head of the Federal Aviation Administration. Halaby had been lobbying hard to get a project underway and told the British that President Kennedy would shortly be establishing a committee investigating the development of a supersonic transport and the head of that committee would be none other than Eugene Black. Sensing they were being set up, the British and French developed a new determination to go ahead. Despite this, behind the scenes lobbying by the Americans continued for a time, until it was realised that nothing could be done.

The USA wavered on the idea of developing its own SST despite strong lobbying. President Kennedy had informed the interested parties he was going to make a decision in early June 1963 but actions by Pan American boss Juan Trippe forced his hand. On 3 June, Trippe reserved six

Concorde delivery positions for his airline; on 5 June, Kennedy announced the USA would develop its own supersonic transport.

Trippe's ploy was quite deliberate as he knew full well that Kennedy would have to decide in favour of an American SST or look as if he was surrendering the USA's lead in aviation technology to Europe. On 15 August 1963 the USA's manufacturers were invited to submit plans for an SST which would be "superior to the European Concorde".

To achieve this end, Boeing and Lockheed came up with advanced designs which were much larger and faster than Concorde, capable of carrying about 280 people over a range of 4,600 miles (7,400km) at a speed of Mach 2.7 or 1,550 knots (2,900km/h). That speed made construction from titanium alloys necessary, creating an aircraft which would cost many times more than Concorde to develop. Boeing's submission, the Model 733, subsequently referred to as the 2707-200, featured variable geometry wings, canard foreplanes (later) and a large 'tailplane' under which the engines were mounted. When the wings were fully swept, they merged with the tailplane to form a delta layout. Lockheed's L.2000 had a fixed delta wing arrangement.

In December 1966 the Boeing design was selected as the one most likely to succeed and $US1.6bn was allocated to the project the following year. On paper, the Boeing SST was an extraordinary aeroplane. Quite apart from its planned performance capabilities it was very large with an overall length of 306 feet (93.3m), some 30 feet (9.1m) longer than the Antonov An-225 heavy transport (the world's largest aircraft from 1988) and no less than 75 feet (23m) longer than the Boeing 747. Power was to be provided by four huge General Electric GE4 turbojets each producing nearly 70,000lb (314kN) thrust with afterburner and maximum takeoff weight was set at initially 675,000lb

The Soviet Tupolev Tu-144 was the first supersonic transport to fly, in December 1968. It is shown here in its later form with lengthened fuselage, retractable foreplanes and other modifications. (via Philip J Birtles)

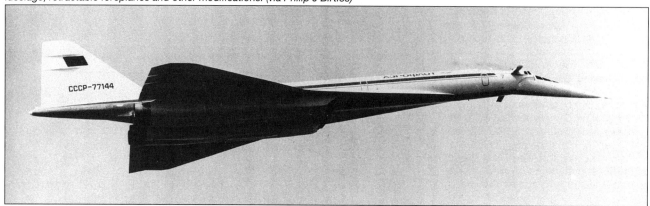

(306,180kg) with growth potential of 750,000lb (340,200kg).

The Boeing SST project was in trouble almost as soon as it started, with slippages making the planned first flight date of September 1970 impossible to achieve. It was quickly discovered that the weight and complexity of the variable geometry wings were such that the performance penalties were unacceptable and the technical risks too great. The design was therefore revised in 1968 to incorporate a fixed delta wing incorporating high lift flaps. A conventional tailplane was also added to the design and the engines were now mounted under the trailing edges of the wing.

Boeing submitted its new proposals in early 1969 and in September of that year President Nixon approved the finance to build two prototypes, the first of which was scheduled to fly in 1972. As the 2707-300, development of this design continued with considerably more promise than the original but political opposition mounted, mainly due to the increasing influence of the environmental movement within and outside the government.

By early 1971 the 2707-300 was proceeding on time and within budget. About 15 per cent of the first airframe had been completed and 122 delivery positions had been reserved by most of the world's leading international carriers including BOAC and Air France.

Finally, in March 1971 and after an often bitter battle, the environmentalists had their way and both houses of the US Government voted to stop funding the Boeing SST, and the project was cancelled. Many Boeing workers lost their jobs as a result and Concorde became the next target of the environmental movement. Although the environmentalists claimed the 'credit' (if that is the right word) for stopping the American SST, their vocal and very public point of view more likely gave courage to those within the US Government who opposed the project on very different grounds, mainly that of cost. These unlikely allies found a common cause, and the politicians were in the main happy to let the public think the environmentalists were largely responsible for the cancellation of the programme.

Soviet Supersonics

One nation which didn't have to worry about the opinion of environmentalists or any other pressure group was the Soviet Union, whose own supersonic transport at least flew and entered limited service.

The Tupolev Tu-144 is a historical inconvenience in the Concorde story in that it stole the Anglo-French aircraft's thunder in achieving of some important milestones. Recording its first flight on 31 December 1968 it beat Concorde into the air by two months; it went supersonic for the first time in June 1969 (four months before Concorde) and achieved Mach 2 in May 1970, six months ahead of Concorde. It also entered service – of sorts – first, in December 1975 but unlike Concorde cannot be regarded as successful despite these 'firsts'. Perhaps the Soviets' desire to gain political and nationalistic mileage from being first caused the programme to be rushed and corners to be cut, with unfortunate results.

Due to its overall similarity to Concorde the Tu-144 was quickly dubbed 'Concordski' by the Western press, but there were several significant differences. In its original form the Tu-144 was shorter than Concorde but featured a wider but shorter cabin seating a similar number of passengers in a five abreast arrangement.

Power was provided by four Kuznetsov NK-144 turbofan engines each rated at a claimed 38,580lb (173kN) thrust with afterburner. The engines were mounted very close to the centreline in a single large nacelle arrangement with individual intakes and compartments for each. The use of turbofan engines automatically compromised the aircraft in the eyes of Concorde's designers as they are inherently less efficient at supersonic speeds. Despite this, the Tu-144 was intended to cruise at Mach 2.35, or about 180 knots (328km/h) faster than Concorde.

The wing, although superficially similar to Concorde's was more of a double delta which lacked the sophistication (and presumably efficiency) of the European aircraft's with the subtle camber, droop and twist missing. Like Concorde, the Tu-144 featured a 'droop snoot' nose design for improved visibility at low speeds.

A heavily redesigned Tu-144 appeared at the 1973 Paris Air Show. It was now some 35 feet (10.7m) longer than before, the wing span was increased and some Concorde-like features including more widely spaced pairs of engines in separated nacelles and a fully cambered delta wing had been incorporated. The most obvious change was the addition of a pair of retractable canard foreplanes just behind the cockpit windows, these intended to enhance takeoff and landing performance. The NK-144 engines were now rated at over 44,000lb (197kN) maximum thrust. Tragically, the aircraft which appeared at the Paris show crashed during one of its display flights.

It is apparent the Tu-144 never achieved its design goals, much of the problem stemming from the need to have the engines running with at least partial afterburner in order to sustain a supersonic cruise. This had obvious effects on fuel consumption and therefore range. It is also known that at least one other Tu-144 was lost in testing.

The Tu-144 entered limited service in December 1975 between Moscow and Alma Ata in Kazakstan, carrying mail and freight over the 1,800nm (3,330km) route. It was withdrawn in June 1978 and little is known of its subsequent service history except that passenger services over the same route began in November 1977 and that by 1984 the whole project had been abandoned. It is likely that service had actually ended well before that.

Curiously, the Tu-144 appears to have gained a reprieve in the mid 1990s with the announcement that the USA's National Aeronautics and Space Administration (NASA) is planning to operate one as a testbed.

An early Tu-144. The curved wing shape was similar to Concorde's in planform but without the more complex droop and camber profiles. Note how the four engines are very close together, a marked contrast to Concorde's configuration. (via Philip J Birtles)

Power and grace as a British Airways Concorde departs on another supersonic journey.

Two views of British Airways Concorde 206 G-BOAA displaying some of its salient features such as the undercarriage, 'droop snoot' nose, engines installation and complex wing shape.

Concorde has brought safe, reliable and comfortable travel for more than 20 years thanks to British Airways and Air France. Plans are in hand for it to remain in service for up to another 20 years, and by the mid 1990s, no replacement aircraft had progressed past the project stage. (Paul Merritt/Julian Green)

British Airways Concordes fly about 50 per cent more hours than do Air France's. F-BTSD (now F-BYSD) is the 13th production Concorde, first flown in June 1978. (BA/Julian Green)

FLIGHT TESTING and PRODUCTION

Into The Air

There seemed to be an interminable wait between the rollout of Concorde 001 in December 1967 and first flight 15 months later. There were numerous reasons for the delay, all of them associated with the complexity of the aircraft, the need to have everything 'just right' and the fact that at the time of rollout, 001 was lacking a considerable amount of internal equipment.

By the time the great occasion arrived in early March 1969 the air of excitement and anticipation had reached momentous proportions. More than six years' work by the partners was about to reach its first climax and although neither of the two prototypes were by any means truly representative of the planned production model, the success or otherwise of the concept would quickly be proven.

The general world situation as it applied to supersonic transports also added to the tension. When the decision to go ahead with Concorde was taken in late 1962 it was the only aircraft of its type on the drawing board. By early 1969 that situation had changed. Concorde now had two competitors, the Boeing 2707 was under development and the Tupolev Tu-144 had already flown the previous December. All this made the occasion of 001's first flight even more significant.

Concorde 001 had been cleared for flight on 28 February 1969. The flight had originally been planned for the next day – 1 March – but a heavy mist prevented it. On 2 March the big event finally took place with the aircraft under the command of Andre Turcat, Sud-Aviation's chief test pilot. With him were Jacques Guignard, Henri Perrier and Michael Retif.

Present at Toulouse to witness the flight were airline guests, representatives of the manufacturers and subcontractors and a large number of the world's press. The event was televised live to the UK by the BBC with commentary by former RAF fighter pilot and BBC personality Raymond Baxter, well known among aviation enthusiasts as the 'voice of Farnborough' on telecasts of that famous air show.

Baxter's commentary tells the story: "She rolls ... 45 knots ... lots of dust showing on the runway ... 90 knots ... 135 ... rotate any second ... nose gear well up now ... smooth rotation continuing ... nose comes up to 20 degrees ... she's airborne ... in 26 seconds. She flies! Concorde flies at last!"

Turcat kept 001 aloft for less than 40 minutes, flying a long left hand extended circuit and reaching a height of 10,000 feet (3,050m) and a speed of 250 knots (463km/h). The undercarriage remained down during the flight as did the drooping nose.

After the excitement of the first takeoff came the tension of the first landing which was successfully completed to the accompaniment of swirling dust and smoke vortices spreading out from under the wing and curling inwards around the tips. "The big bird flies", said Andre Turcat in both French and English.

Concorde 001 was joined in the air just over a month later by the first British assembled aircraft, 002 (registered G-BSST). On 9 April, this aircraft lifted off from Filton under the command of BAC's chief test pilot, Brian Trubshaw, with John Cochrane acting as copilot and Brian Watts as flight engineer. Also on board were three observers.

This 25 minute flight was preceded by much the same anticipation as had been 001's just over a month earlier and was also performed without incident. This time, the Concorde didn't return to its point of departure, Trubshaw instead taking 002 to RAF Fairford, about 50 miles (80km) away, from where flight testing would be carried out. Part of the reason for this was the fact that Fairford had a longer runway than Filton's 9,000 feet (2,740m), that length being considered marginal for test flying of the aircraft.

Now the Concorde team could get on with the job of proving their aircraft. Certification was planned for June 1973, but events would see Concorde's testing phase take over six years to complete.

Testing, Testing

By the time it entered service in early 1976, Concorde was by far the most thoroughly tested airliner ever built, both on the ground and in the air. The programme involved the use of ten Concordes (two prototypes, two pre production and six production aircraft) between them logging 5,540 flight hours (of which 1,900 were supersonic) in the course of 2,480 flights. The Olympus 593 engine had logged 52,000 hours of running on the bench and in the air by late 1975.

The test programme started long before first flight, one of the first tasks undertaken being the selection and proving of the materials used in Concorde's structure. As mentioned in the previous chapter, the aluminium alloy RR58 was chosen due to its properties after thousands of samples had been examined. Testing them involved chemistry as well as metallurgy while other materials also needed thorough examination: the resins used for bonding, the tank sealants, the paints, the hydraulic oils and lubricants.

Aerodynamic research took up more than 4,000 hours of testing in subsonic, transonic and supersonic

Concorde 001 F-WTSS, the first prototype, flown on 2 March 1969 from Toulouse. (via Philip J Birtles)

Concorde 002 G-BSST, the first British assembled aircraft first flew on 9 April 1969. (Philip J Birtles)

wind tunnels as the designers looked for the best wing shape for Concorde. This involved the building of several hundred scale models for use in the tunnels, while some were dropped from helicopters and allowed to free fall so their characteristics could be examined.

Structural testing is of obviously vital importance, especially since Concorde would be entering new areas of stress due to its high sustained speed and the temperatures generated and the fact that its cabin pressure differential was greater than any other commercial aircraft.

Airframe assemblies of all sizes were tested for many years. They were alternatively overheated and frozen in the search for weaknesses and cracking, while structural testing on a rather larger scale was conducted at Farnborough where a complete airframe was encased in a huge metal glove and alternately cooked by hot air and cooled by nitrogen. This allowed the enormous temperature variations experienced by the airframe in flight to be simulated time and time again in a short space of time, permitting a safe life to be calculated. A second Concorde airframe joined the ground test programme in October 1969, this one being tested to destruction, its demise occurring in June 1974.

Concorde's systems and mechanical components were also subjected to tortuous testing while perhaps the most interesting was the rig built to test the aircraft's complicated fuel management system which not only had to supply fuel to the engines but also act as a heatsink and trimming mechanism by transferring fuel fore and aft.

This test rig was basically a full scale replica of Concorde's fuel tank and systems, the whole assembly controlled by computers to duplicate

Supersonic pas de duex? Concordes 001 and 002 in the air together at the 1969 Paris Air Show.

Andre Turcat, Sud-Aviation's chief test pilot and the first man to fly Concorde.

the movements and attitudes it would be subjected to in flight.

Flight testing of the prototypes was recorded by a large number of 'black boxes' installed in both aircraft. Weighing about 12 tonnes and taking up a large proportion of the cabin space, these data recording machines were connected to sensors which monitored every part of the aircrafts' structures and systems.

More than 3,000 different parameters could be measured simultaneously in flight, some of the more vital of which were transmitted direct to ground stations by telemetry while the flight was in process. The remainder were recorded on magnetic tape in the aircraft and the information downloaded to computers at the completion of the flight.

Milestones

With both prototypes flying, the test programme accelerated with just about every flight achieving some sort of milestone, however minor. Both aircraft made their public debuts in June 1969 at the Paris Air Show.

The first major milestone was recorded on 1 October 1969 when 001 exceeded the speed of sound for the first time following a six week grounding during which the engine intakes were modified. On its 41st flight, Andre Turcat took 001 to Mach 1.05 at 36,000 feet and the aircraft remained supersonic for nine minutes. Concorde 002 joined the supersonic club in March 1970.

The next major step in the gradual increasing of speeds attained was that of achieving Mach 2. 002 had originally been earmarked to perform this first, on 4 November 1970, but an engine fire warning while travelling at Mach 1.35 put an end to that. Instead, 001 achieved the magic figure later in the same day while cruising at 50,000 feet (15,240m) and maintained the speed for 53 minutes. 002 finally reached Mach 2 on 12 November.

Achieving Mach 2 left the way open to conduct one of the potentially more interesting tests which had to be performed – cutting two engines on the same side while flying at that speed so as to examine the aircraft's controllability. There were some who had predicted that doom and disaster would result, citing the previous example of the four engined (in underwing pods) Convair B-58 Hustler delta winged supersonic bomber which could not survive a single engine failure at Mach 2, let alone a double failure on the same side. Indeed, the Hustler had a habit of crashing at much lower speeds than that when engine asymmetry was involved.

In Concorde there was no such drama. The test was performed on numerous occasions with autorudder both connected and disconnected, and control was maintained without difficulty.

The French aerospace industry underwent some organisation in January 1970 with the merging of the Sud-Aviation, Nord-Aviation and SEREB companies into the state owned entity *Societe Nationale Industrielle Aerospatiale*, or most usually simply Aerospatiale. This created the largest aerospace group in Europe, producing airliners, light aircraft, helicopters, missiles and spacecraft.

Seven years later, in 1977, the British industry was reorganised again with the formation of British Aerospace which combined most of the country's aircraft manufacturers into one. The British Aircraft Corporation, Hawker Siddeley and Scottish Aviation were included in the rearrangement. BAe was government owned until 1981 when it was floated on the stock exchange and became fully privatised in 1985.

Brian Trubshaw (left) and John Cochrane, Concorde 002's pilots on its first flight.

Concorde 001 over Athens during one of the overseas flights undertaken as part of the lengthy test programme. (via Philip J Birtles)

Steady Progress

By the end of 1970 the two Concorde prototypes had accumulated 300 flying hours between them and already several pilots from some of the airlines which had optioned the aircraft had flown it. The first of these occurred as early as November 1969 when Captains James Andrew (BOAC), Maurice Bernard (Air France), Paul Roitsch (Pan Am) and Vernon Laurson (TWA) all flew 001 after a stint on the simulator at Toulouse. The pilots were permitted to take the aircraft up to a speed of Mach 1.2, the cleared limit at the time.

Concorde's horizons began to spread as 1971 dawned. The 100th supersonic flight was completed in January, 500 flight hours achieved in June and the 100th Mach 2 flight performed in August.

Concorde was taken overseas for the first time in May 1971 when 001 flew from Paris to Dakar and back again the following day to appear at the Paris Air Show. The return flight covered the 2,170nm (4,020km) distance in 2hr 52min, an average speed of 756 knots (1,400km/h) or Mach 1.32 at altitude. Just over two hours of the flight was carried out at supersonic speed.

A much longer overseas jaunt followed in September 1971 when 001 was taken on sales demonstration tour of South America. Flying from Toulouse, the aircraft visit Rio de Janeiro, Sao Paulo and Buenos Aires, making 16 flights in the space of 15 days.

The tour was significant because it gave Concorde a chance to see if it could fit in with existing air traffic control procedures (it did) and also provided some feedback from invited guests who flew as passengers. Their comments were added to those received from government, airline and press people who had been taken up on demonstration flights during the Paris Air Show four months earlier. The predominant opinion seemed to be one of amazement that the act of

'going supersonic' was very much a non event and not one involving shakes, rattles and rolls from within the cabin. This, of course, is precisely the reaction Concorde's designers were hoping for.

There were also some very distinguished guests who sampled Concorde during 1971. France's President Pompidou flew supersonically over the Bay of Biscay, while HRH The Duke of Edinburgh (a qualified pilot) took the controls of 002 while travelling at Mach 2.

Other events also coloured the Concorde story in 1971, the main one being the cancellation of the American SST programme in March. At first glance this appeared to be a stroke of good fortune for Concorde as half of the competition had been removed, but close examination revealed it to be anything but.

1971 also saw financial problems bring Rolls-Royce to its knees. For a time it looked as if the great aero engine company might disappear, but it was rescued by the British Government and a new entity – Rolls-Royce (1971) – formed.

By now, options had been placed on 74 Concordes by 16 operators: BOAC 8, Air France 8, Air Canada 4, Air India 2, American Airlines 6, Braniff International 3, Continental Airlines 3, Eastern Air Lines 6, Japan Air Lines 3, Lufthansa 3, Middle East Airlines 2, Pan American 8, Qantas 4, Sabena 2, Trans World Airlines 6 and United Air Lines 6. None of these were as yet firm orders, including those of BOAC and Air France. China was added to the list in 1972, signing a preliminary purchase agreement for three.

A view inside Concorde 002 showing part of the vast array of data recording equipment installed in the cabin and the flight test observers monitoring it. (via Philip J Birtles)

BAe/Aérospatiale
CONCORDE 001

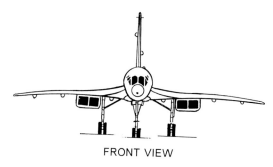

FRONT VIEW

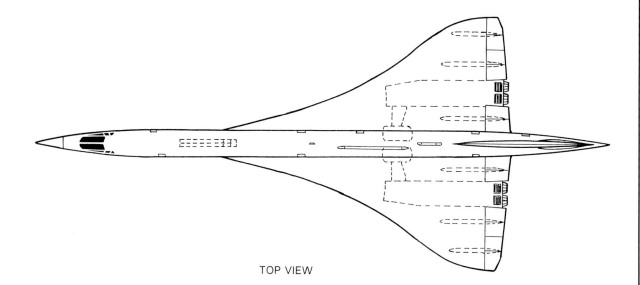

TOP VIEW

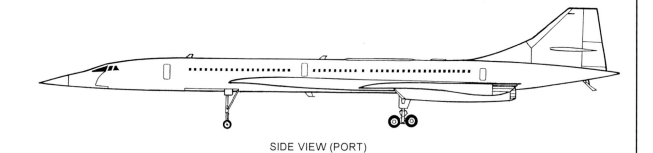

SIDE VIEW (PORT)

Concorde 001 (F-WTSS) was the French-assembled first prototype which initially flew from Aérospatiale's Toulouse factory on 2 March 1969, just over a month before the British -assembled second prototype Concorde 002, which had its maiden flight from the BAC Fulton (Bristol) factory on 9 April.

Dennis Newton

BAe/Aérospatiale
CONCORDE 02

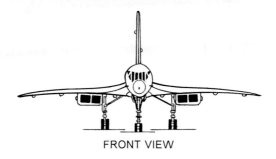

FRONT VIEW

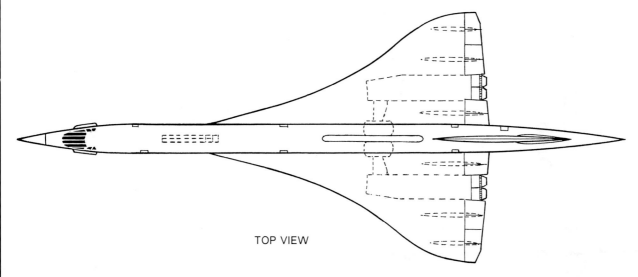

TOP VIEW

Extended low-drag rear fuselage ⎯

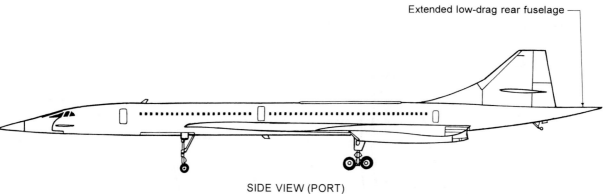

SIDE VIEW (PORT)

Concorde 02 (F-WTSA) was the second pre-production aircraft and the first be representative of the series production standard. The two significant new features were the extended low-drag rear fuselage and the engine thrust reverser/silencer.

Dennis Newton

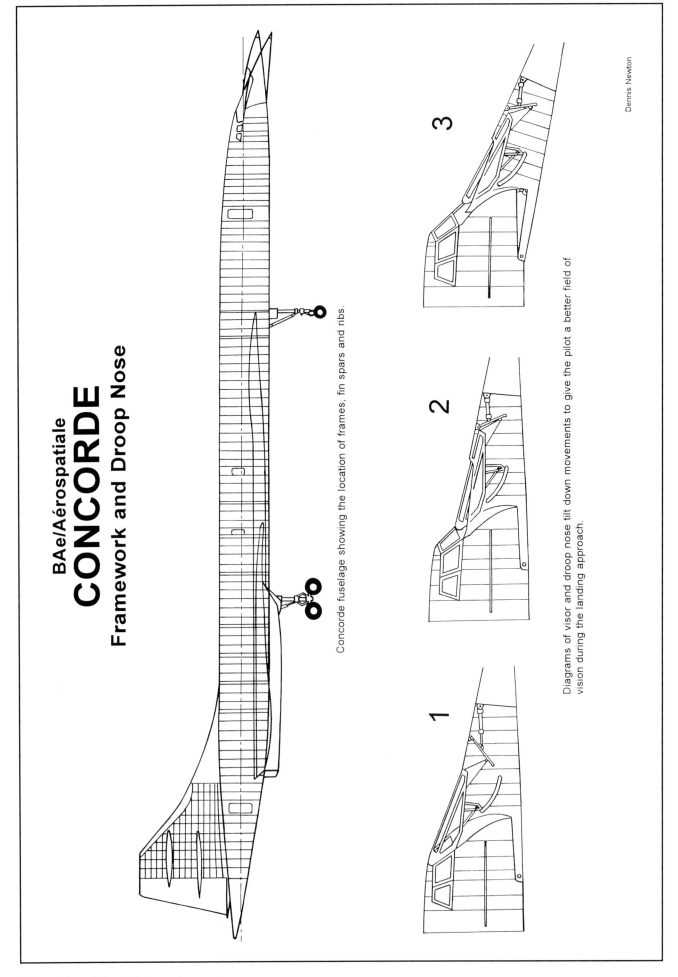

BAe/Aérospatiale
CONCORDE
Framework and Droop Nose

Dennis Newton

Concorde fuselage showing the location of frames, fin spars and ribs.

1

2

3

Diagrams of visor and droop nose tilt down movements to give the pilot a better field of vision during the landing approach.

Concorde 01 G-AXDN in flight. Compared with the prototypes, the two preproduction Concordes were longer, heavier, more powerful and had a new nose/visor design along with many other changes. (via Philip J Birtles)

Expanding The Family

The first preproduction Concorde 01 (G-AXDN) joined the flight test programme in early 1972 after having flown for the first time from Filton on 17 December 1971. This aircraft incorporated some substantial differences from the prototypes including a longer fuselage which increased overall length from 184ft 6in (56.24m) to 193ft 0.5in (58.84m), 34,730lb (154kN) thrust Olympus 593-4 engines with revised thrust reverser nozzles, a redesigned fully transparent retractable windscreen visor of the type which would installed on production aircraft, increased maximum takeoff weight and a 19ft 3.5in (5.88m) increase in the length of the pressurised cabin area.

Concorde 01 was subsequently joined by the French assembled preproduction 02 (F-WTSA) which flew for the first time on 10 January 1973. This aircraft featured further modifications, the primary one being incorporation of the production standard extended tailcone for reduced drag. This increased the overall length of the aircraft to 203ft 9in (62.10m).

The two preproduction Concordes further expanded the aircraft's horizons, 02 performing a fully automatic landing on 13 January 1973 at the end of its third flight using the SFENA/Marconi-Elliot AFCS (automatic flight control system) developed for production aircraft. In February 1973 the same aircraft demonstrated Concorde could meet its payload/range requirements by carrying 28,000lb (12,700kg) – 8,000lb (3,630kg) more than guaranteed) nonstop from Toulouse to Iceland and back, a dis-

tance of 3,255nm (6,030km). The flight was completed in 3hr 27min including 2hr 37min at supersonic speeds of which 2hr 9min was flown at Mach 2.

The flight testing programme continued: Concorde 002 completed 'hot and high' trials at Johannesburg in January and February 1973; 02 was used for cold weather trials at Fairbanks, Alaska, in February 1974; and 002 completed high altitude certification trials at Torrejon, Spain in July 1973.

Despite this progress, the in service date continued to slip and the costs kept rising. By early 1975 the British estimated the final cost would be £1,096,000m, of which £853m had been spent so far. The cost of high technology has always been great, but in this case inflation also

Concorde 01 G-AXDN, the first preproduction aircraft, departs Filton. This aircraft first flew in December 1971. (via Philip J Birtles)

The second preproduction Concorde 02 F-WTSA, first flown in January 1973. Note the longer tailcone compared with 01 and the contemporary Air France markings. (BA)

had a hand in the equation as did the cost of the Anglo-French partnership itself – as much as 30 per cent of the total according to one estimate and taking into account the inherent inefficiency of operating two assembly lines for what turned out to be a very small production run.

001 conducted an interesting sortie June 1973 when it flew a load of astronomers to Fort Lamy in Chad, allowing them to observe an eclipse of the sun *en route*. Flying at Mach 1.5 over central Africa, the astronomers were able to watch the eclipse for 80 minutes, whereas on the ground they would have been limited to just seven minutes.

The remarkable Concorde fuel system test rig, a full scale reproduction of the real thing. (via Philip J Birtles)

Around The World

Meanwhile, in June 1972, 002 had undertaken the most ambitious journey of Concorde's career thus far, a sales demonstration tour of the Middle East, Far East and Australia. The 30 day, 40,000nm (74,000km) round trip saw the second prototype visit 14 airports in 12 countries – Athens, Tehran (resulting in Iran Air optioning two aircraft), Bahrain, Bombay, Bangkok, Singapore, Tokyo, Manila, Darwin, Sydney and Melbourne. The return journey was made via Darwin, Singapore, Bangkok, Bombay, Dhahran, Beirut and back to Toulouse, the latter leg including the longest overwater stage of the tour, 2,400 miles (3,860km).

The logistics of the trip were impressive, and support was provided by an RAF Short Belfast and Vickers VC-10. This prompted some critics to comment that Concorde must be unreliable as it needed to take its own supply of spare parts with it! This completely ignored the fact that in service, the aircraft would – like any other – have substantial parts inventories at its major bases around the world.

Only two technical problems caused delays to 002's schedule, a glitch in the weather radar which delayed departure on the Singapore/Tokyo leg for 10 hours and a problem with an air conditioning valve which had to be replaced at Manila and delayed arrival at Darwin by 90 minutes.

Local demonstration flights were put on for interested dignitaries and airline executives and everywhere it went, Concorde attracted an enormous amount of attention from the public and press. This writer well remembers its arrival in Sydney on 17 June after a mainly supersonic flight from Darwin and the following day, when 002 was on display at the Kingsford Smith Airport's international terminal before departing on a demonstration flight.

It seemed that most of Sydney's 2 million or so people at the time went

The 'nose' have it! Concordes 001, 002 and 01 (centre) at the Fairford flight test centre clearly showing the different nose/visor design of the production aircraft compared with the prototypes. (via Philip J Birtles)

to Kingsford Smith Airport to see this wondrous new aircraft in the flesh. We were all truly impressed, and indicating how different attitudes were then is the fact that most of the people I spoke to loved the thunderous roar of the engines as Concorde took off! The other overriding impression was how small the aircraft looked when parked among a gaggle of Boeing 747s.

The tour was judged a success and came at a critical time in Concorde's career. The time was quickly approaching when the airlines which had optioned it had to decide whether or not to convert these options to firm orders. The American SST had

been cancelled and trans-Atlantic politics were again coming to the fore, the environmental movement was growing in size and influence and the world was about to be hit with the so-called 'oil crisis'.

Another significant Concorde tour occurred in September 1973 when 02 made the new airliner's first visit to the USA. Flying from Paris, the aircraft flew to the new Dallas-Fort Worth Airport for its opening, having been invited there especially for the occasion. Carrying dual British Airways/Air France livery, 02 travelled via Caracas in Venezuela. The Paris-Caracas leg included a refuelling stop at Las Palmas (Canary Islands) and

the elapsed time for the 4,500nm (8,350km) journey was 6hr 25min, or about five hours less than the normal subsonic time.

02 then flew to Dulles Airport in Washington DC and despite having to remain subsonic, it still covered the distance about 20 minutes faster than a subsonic airliner due to its ability to fly at a higher subsonic Mach number. The return journey from Washington to Paris-Orly set a new record of 3hr 33min, six minutes faster than the previous mark set by a Convair B-58 Hustler bomber in 1961. For the journey, 02 carried 25 passengers and test equipment, representative of a full payload.

Concorde 002 over the Sydney Harbour Bridge during its tour of the Far East, Middle East and Australia in June 1972. Only two delays due to technical problems were suffered during the 46,000 miles (74,000km) round trip from Britain. (via Philip J Birtles)

Artist's impression of a Concorde in BOAC markings at London Heathrow Airport. By the time Concorde entered service, BOAC and BEA had become British Airways. (BA)

Production Concordes

By the end of 1973 Concorde's flight test programme had progressed to the point where the detailed work which would lead to certification could be carried out, aided by the availability of several production aircraft over the next two years.

The first two production aircraft were flown from Toulouse (c/n 201 F-WSTB) and Filton (c/n 202 G-BBDG) on 6 December 1973 and 13 February 1974, respectively, both going supersonic on their maiden flights. Neither were to full production standard and remained with the manufacturers during their relatively brief service lives. In July 1974 the manufacture of a further nine production Concordes was approved, bringing the total to 16. Production Concordes carried the constructor's numbers 201-216, odd numbers assembled in France and even numbers in Britain.

201 and 202 were used for various certification and manufacturer's trials and demonstrations and were joined in early 1975 by Concordes 203 (F-WTSC initially) and 204 (G-BOAC). This pair performed the brunt of the final parts of the flight test and certification programme which included about 1,000 hours of route proving and endurance flying. 203 set an endurance record for the type in March 1975, remaining aloft for 6hr 16m and covering a distance of 3,250nm (6,020km). This flight was conducted entirely at subsonic speeds and at an altitude of 27,000 feet (8,230m).

Production Concordes 205 and 206 were in the air by November 1975 by which time the certification programme was virtually complete. A special category Certificate of Airworthiness had been awarded to 203 as early as May 1975, while 204 followed suit the next month.

On 9 October 1975, Concorde's nearly seven year flight test programme achieved its aim with the awarding of a full, unrestricted French Certificate of Airworthiness. The British equivalent was received on 19 December after a programme involving 2,480 flights and 5,540 hours in the air. Concorde could now do what it was designed for – carry fare paying passengers around the world at twice the speed of sound.

Air France took delivery of its first Concorde (c/n 205 F-BVFA) on 19 December 1975; British Airways' first (c/n 206 G-BOAA) was handed over four weeks later on 15 January 1976. Services were simultaneously launched by both airlines on 21 January. In the meantime, production continued with four Concordes flown in 1976, two in 1977, three in 1978 and the last (c/n 216) on 20 April 1979 from Filton.

BAC/AEROSPATIALE CONCORDE
Production Model

Powerplants: *Four Rolls-Royce/SNECMA Olympus 593 Mk.610 turbojets each rated at 38,050lb (170kN) thrust with 17 per cent afterburning. Fuel capacity 26,350imp gal (119,786 l) in wing and lower fuselage tanks.*

Dimensions: *Wing span 83ft 10in (25.56m); length 203ft 9in (62.17m); height 37ft 5in (11.40m); wing area 3,856sq ft (358.25m²); wing aspect ratio 1.7:1; wheel track 25ft 4in (7.72m); wheelbase 59ft 8.25in (18.19m).*

Weights: *Max takeoff 408,000lb (185,069kg); max landing 245,000lb (111,132kg); max zero fuel 203,000lb (92,080kg); operating empty 173,500lb (78,700kg); max payload 29,500lb (13,381kg); typical payload 25,000lb (11,340kg).*

Accommodation: *Normally 100 passengers but up to 128 passengers, four abreast at 34in (86cm) seat pitch. Cabin length 129ft 0in (39.32m); height 6ft 5in (1.96m); width 8ft 7.5in (2.63m); volume 8,440cu ft (239m³). Baggage/freight capacity 697cu ft (19.74m³) in underfloor and rear fuselage holds.*

Performance: *Max cruising speed Mach 2.04 or 1,176kt (2,178km/h) at 51,000ft (15,545m); takeoff speed 214kt (397km/h); landing speed 162kt (300km/h); initial climb 5,000ft (1,524m)/min; service ceiling 60,000ft (18,288m); takeoff distance to 35ft 11,200ft (3,414m); landing distance from 35ft 7,300ft (2,225m); range (max fuel, 23,700lb payload, reserves) 3,550nm (6,575km); range (max payload and reserves) 2,760nm (5,112km) at Mach 0.95 and 30,000ft.*

Concorde production: *2 prototypes, 4 preproduction, 16 production, total 20.*

Concorde 201 F-WTSB, the first production aircraft, first flew in December 1973. 201 is photographed here at Toulouse in current Air France markings long after it had been retired. Neither 201 nor 202 entered airline service.

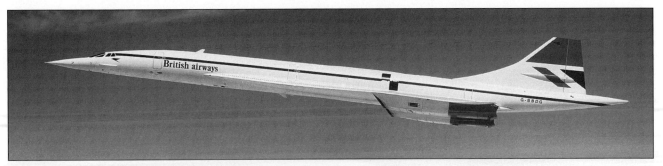

Concorde 202 G-BBDG, the second production aircraft first flown in February 1974. It was retired in 1981. (via Philip J Birtles)

Difficult Questions

The problem with Concorde was that it was just a few years too late. The world was a very different place in the first half of the 1970s than it had been just a decade and a half before when the first investigations into a supersonic transport started. Even when the Anglo-French agreement was signed in 1962, those involved could have no idea as to what was going to happen over the next ten years, how attitudes to many things would change so radically.

Concorde's critics had always latched onto the economic aspects of the vastly expensive programme. As it turned out, they were correct, but as is always the case in stories such as this, there were an awful lot of 'what ifs' involved. What if the American SST had continued? What if the massive cultural changes of the 1960s hadn't happened and much different thinking among many young (and some older) people emerged? None of this could have been foreseen in 1962.

You have to draw the line somewhere, but the fact remains that 1972 was vastly different from 1962 in so many ways, including that of attitudes towards the environment. Rightly or wrongly, people began to question whether having an aircraft which cost a huge amount of money, made a lot of noise and created a sonic boom was worth having and there was always those who considered the money could be better spent on social security or saving whales ...

One of the more persistent environmental criticisms of supersonic transports generally was the damage some claimed they would do to the ozone layer. The vast majority didn't know or didn't care, but as is often the case, a few people making a lot of noise – ironically enough – had a large influence on Concorde's chances of commercial success.

Concorde's manufacturers spent a lot of time and effort trying to refute claims that the aircraft would kill unborn babies and destroy the earth's ecology by publishing vast amounts of information dealing with takeoff and approach noise levels, the sonic boom 'corridor', fuel consumption, engine emission and smoke (the latter largely eliminated as described earlier) and the atmosphere. Even though none of these issues prevented the aircraft from entering service, they did seriously effect both its commercial and operational prospects.

In the case of the sonic boom Concorde was restricted to basically overwater supersonic flight, while the efforts of the environmental lobby prevented it from operating to two of its prime market destinations – Washington DC and New York – until some time after commercial operations began.

Commercial Realities

The 1971 cancellation of the American SST was the first tangible step in the series of events which would contribute to Concorde's commercial downfall over the next two or three years, while the environmental movement's push – largely in the USA – gained greater influence with some sections of the public and politicians as it went on.

The strong anti Concorde lobby in the USA achieved a major win when it convinced the House of Representatives to ban the aircraft from operating in the USA. A conspiracy theory has often been suggested here, particularly in view of the fact that neither the US airline or aircraft manufacturing industries offered any public support. Was this to ensure that a foreign aircraft would not be able to take the glittering prize of supersonic commercial flight while American industry could not even compete for it?

Anti Concorde sentiment gradually spread among some other nations which wanted to be seen as 'politically correct' and perhaps also wanted to keep in the USA's good books. Landing rights began to be denied as the time for Concorde to enter service approached, these severely restricting its operational options. When it entered service in January 1976, Concorde could only fly to and from London, Paris, Bahrain, Rio de Janeiro and Dakar, although other routes were able to be added within a few months. Washington was among them but New York would have to wait until the end of 1977.

Then there was the world economic slump of the early 1970s and the oil crisis of 1973 which saw fuel prices skyrocket. For a relatively

Concorde 203 F-WTSC, the first of the 14 production Concordes which went into airline service. It was first flown in January 1975 and handed over to Air France the following December as F-BTSC. (via Philip J Birtles)

Concorde 206 G-BOAA, the first example delivered to British Airways in January 1976. (BA)

thirsty aircraft (on a fuel burn per passenger basis), this was a killer for Concorde.

The real crunch came during 1972 when it was time for the airlines to start converting their options into real orders. In July 1972 BOAC placed a firm order for five Concordes and Air France for four. These were later increased to seven each and remained the only orders for the aircraft.

The key was Pan American, now no longer controlled by the bold and adventurous Juan Trippe. As negotiations with the airline continued through 1972, it became clear that PanAm's enthusiasm for Concorde was not what it had been. Heavy lobbying by Britain and France failed, and on 31 January 1973 Pan American cancelled its options, stating "studies indicate the airplane will be capable of scheduled supersonic services but since it has significantly less range, less payload and higher operating costs than are provided by the current and prospective wide bodied jets, it will require substantially higher fares than today's. Concorde does not appear to be an

airliner that satisfies PanAm's future objectives and future requirements as the company now sees them".

This was probably the telling blow, with the *coup de grace* delivered by the circumstances of the time. At the same time, TWA also decided not to take up its options and within a few months all but a couple of airlines had also cancelled their options. Finally, none remained, leaving Britain and France to go it alone.

Britain made one more attempt to bail out of Concorde. Another Labour government was elected in 1974 and

Concordes undergoing assembly inside the 'Brabazon Hangar' at Filton. (via Philip J Birtles)

immediately starting examining its options for cancelling the programme. But as the previous Labour government had discovered a decade earlier, this was not possible and the manufacture of more aircraft up to a total of 16 production models was authorised.

In Britain, public support was still strong. An independent survey conducted by the *London Daily Mail* newspaper in March 1974 (the time the new government came to power) showed that Britons were in favour of the programme by 2 to 1. A 1974 French poll also showed good results. Another poll had been conducted by London Weekend television in January 1973, immediately after Pan American and TWA had cancelled their Concorde options. This showed 71 per cent support for the aircraft.

To add to the programme's woes at the time, British Airways' purchase contract reflected the airlines' opinion that it would not be possible to make money from Concorde operations. Still state owned at that stage, BA insisted that the government guarantee to subsidise any operating losses incurred. This demand was met.

Concorde 216 G-BFKX, the last Concorde built. Devoid of livery, it is photographed here on the occasion of its maiden flight from Filton on 20 April 1979. (BA)

CONCORDE PRODUCTION

Concorde 001
Prototype, ff 02/03/69 at Toulouse as F-WTSS; to *Musee de l'Air*, Le Bourget 10/73; flying time 870hrs (254hrs supersonic).

Concorde 002
Second prototype, ff 09/04/69 at Filton; Ministry of Technology, Ministry of Aviation Supply; to Science Museum 07/76, preserved Yeovilton.

Concorde 01
Pre-production, ff 17/12/71 at Filton as G-AXDN; Ministry of Technology, Ministry of Aviation Supply; to Duxford Aviation Museum 08/75.

Concorde 02
Pre-production, ff 10/01/73 at Toulouse as F-WTSA; Aerospatiale; preserved Paris-Orly Airport.

Concorde 201
First production, ff 06/12/73 as F-WTSB; retained by Aerospatiale; stored at Toulouse.

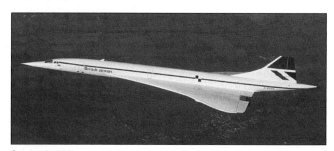

Concorde 202
ff 13/02/74 at Filton as G-BBDG for BAC/BAe; retired 12/81 and stored at Filton.

Concorde 203
ff 31/01/75 at Toulouse as F-WTSC for Aerospatiale; rereg F-BTSC 05/75; leased to Air France 01-12/76 and 06/79; purchased by Air France 10/80.

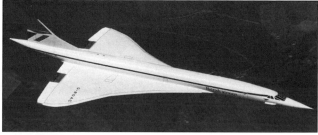

Concorde 204
ff 27/02/75 at Filton as G-BOAC; delivered British Airways 13/02/76; rereg G-N81AC/N81AC for BA/Braniff 01/79; rereg G-BOAC for BA 08/80.

Concorde 205
ff 27/10/75 at Toulouse as F-BVFA; delivered Air France 19/12/75; rereg N94FA for Air France/Braniff 01/79; rereg F-BVFA for Air France 06/80.

Concorde 206
ff 05/11/75 at Filton as G-BOAA; delivered British Airways 14/01/76; rereg G-N94AA/N94AA for BA/Braniff 01/79; rereg B-BOAA for BA 07/80.

Concorde 207
ff 06/03/76 at Toulouse as F-BVFB; delivered Air France 08/04/76; rereg N94FB for Air France/Braniff 01/79; rereg F-BVFB for Air France 06/80.

Concorde 208
ff 18/05/76 at Filton as G-BOAB; delivered British Airways 30/09/76; rereg G-N94AB/N94AB for BA/Braniff 01/79; rereg G-BOAB for BA 09/80.

Concorde 209
ff 09/07/76 at Toulouse as F-BVFC; delivered Air France 03/08/76; rereg N94FC for Air France/Braniff 01/79; rereg F-BVFC for Air France 06/80.

Concorde 210
ff 25/08/76 at Filton as G-BOAD; delivered British Airways 06/12/76; rereg G-N94AD/N94AD for BA/Braniff 01/79; rereg G-BOAD for BA 06/80.

Concorde 211
ff 10/02/77 at Toulouse as F-BVFD; delivered Air France 26/03/77; rereg N94FD for Air France/Braniff 01/79; rereg F-BVFD for Air France 06/80; retired 27/05/82, total flying time 5816hrs; stored as source of parts, scrapped early 1995.

Concorde 212
ff 17/03/77 at Filton as G-BOAE; delivered British Airways 20/07/77; rereg G-N94AE/N94AE for BA/Braniff 01/79; rereg G-BOAE for BA 07/80.

Concorde 213
ff 26/06/78 at Toulouse as F-WJAM for Aerospatiale; rereg F-BTSD 09/78; leased Air France 09/78; rereg N94SD for Air France/Braniff 01/79; rereg F-BYSD for Aerospatiale 03/79; leased Air France 05/80; purchased by Air France 10/80.

Concorde 214
ff 21/04/78 at Filton as G-BFKW for BAe; delivered British Airways 06/02/80; rereg G-BOAG 02/81.

Concorde 215
ff 26/12/78 at Toulouse as F-WJAN for Aerospatiale; delivered Air France 23/10/80 as F-BVFF.

Concorde 216
Last built, ff 20/04/79 at Filton as G-BFKX for BAe; rereg G-N94AF/G-BOAF for BA/Braniff 12/79; delivered British Airways 09/06/80 rereg as G-BOAF.

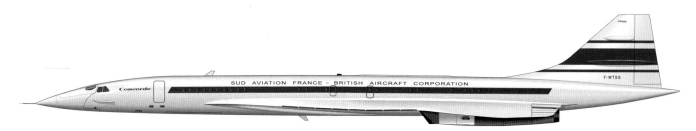

Concorde 001 F-WTSS first prototype, maiden flight 2 March 1969.

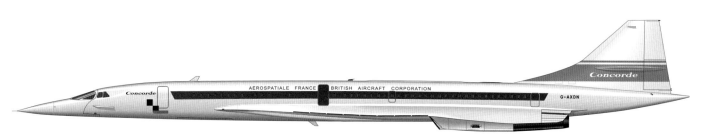

Concorde 01 G-AXDN first pre production, maiden flight 17 December 1971.

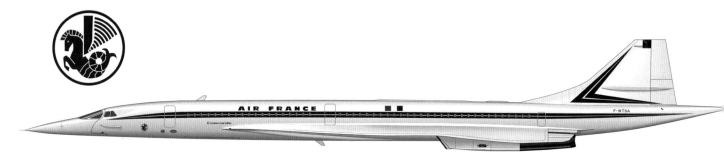

Concorde 02 F-WTSA second pre production in contemporary Air France markings at time of first flight January 1973.

Concorde 204 G-BOAC, British Airways early markings.

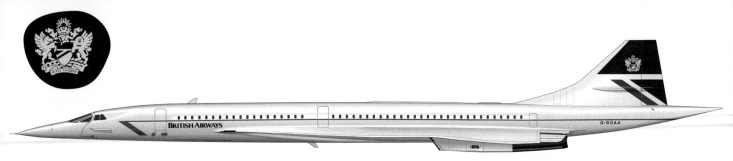

Concorde 206 G-BOAA, British Airways later markings.

Concorde 210 G-BOAD, Singapore Airways marking on port side for Singapore services January 1979 to November 1980.

Concorde 201 F-WTSB in 20th anniversary of first flight colour scheme, Toulouse March 1989.

Concorde 213 F-BTSD Air France, 'The Coors Light Silver Bullet'; eastbound around the world speed record flight from New York 15-16 August 1995.

SUPERSONIC SERVICES

By early 1976, most things were in place to allow Concorde commercial services to begin. Both British Airways and Air France had opened Concorde reservations the previous October, the aircraft was certificated, the airlines' operational infrastructure was largely in place and despite the strong anti Concorde sentiment being expressed by some, most people remained fascinated with the aircraft and followed its every move with interest. Concorde fares were established with the agreement of the International Air Transport Association (IATA) at the first class rate on a given route plus 20 per cent.

A major stumbling block which inhibited early operations was the barring of Concorde from operating to US airports. Services across the North Atlantic were obviously intended as Concorde's jewel in the crown, the route for which the aircraft had been primarily designed. Apart from the economic aspects of these potentially lucrative UK/Europe/USA services, the route was ideal for a supersonic transport as the vast majority of it was over water and the problem of sonic boom noise did not arise.

Put simply, without approval to fly to the USA, Concorde was as good as a dead duck, and considerable effort was put into winning the right to fly there. The battle was eventually won, but for the moment alternative routes had to be found for Concorde's inaugural services.

Air France decided on Paris to Rio de Janeiro via Dakar, which although having lower traffic density than services to New York, proved to be sufficiently busy in the early days of operations to justify it. Also, it was operationally a good route and the elapsed time between the two cities was about seven hours – four hours less than subsonic.

British Airways opened Concorde operations with the less satisfactory London to Bahrain service, the first leg of the 'Kangaroo Route' to Australia. This was a difficult segment for Concorde as it involved a subsonic leg over Europe, a curved track over the eastern Mediterranean and the need for absolutely precise navigation through the narrow corridor over the unstable Middle East. Despite this, Concorde still managed to complete the route in four hours compared with 6.5 hours in a subsonic airliner.

The great moment occurred at 11.35am on 21 January 1976 when British Airways Concorde 206 G-BOAA departed London Heathrow and Air France Concorde 205 F-BVFA departed Paris-Charles de Gaulle, bound for Bahrain and Rio, respectively. The BA aircraft had 30 paying passengers and 70 guests aboard; Air France made rather more money from its inaugural flight with 93 real passengers and just seven guests flying to Rio on that historic day.

Block times for the two services were 3hr 38min London-Bahrain (nonstop) and 6hr 14min Paris-Rio, including a stop at Dakar.

The Battle For America

The right to fly Concorde to the USA wasn't just desirable for BA and Air France, it was essential. Behind the scenes, intensive lobbying and legal argument had been carried out by both sides. All the early victories went to the environment movement and those within the US Government who were anti Concorde not just because of environmental issues but also because it was 'not invented here'.

It is true that Concorde was noisy – although under some circumstances actually quieter than a Boeing 707 or Douglas DC-8 on takeoff and approach – but noise abatement procedures were being developed to minimise the problem. Something which annoyed Concorde's supporters to a very large extent was the fact that in the case of New York, the aircraft was banned without ever having been there so proper noise measurements could be taken.

The door opened slightly in February 1976 when William Coleman, the US Secretary of Transportation, gave approval for BA and Air France to each operate one Concorde service per day to Washington and two per day to New York on a 16 month trial basis. Despite this approval, New York would have to wait for a further 18 months as Kennedy Airport's owner, the Port of New York Author-

The first commercial departure. British Airways Concorde 206 G-BOAA departs London Heathrow bound for Bahrain on 21 January 1976. At the same time, Air France's F-BVFA departed Paris for Rio via Dakar. (via Philip J Birtles)

ity, refused landing rights despite the Transportation Secretary's ruling. This delay was probably the final act in the campaign to sell more Concordes, because even as late as early 1976 there was still the slight possibility that a couple of operators – notably Iran Air and China's CAAC – might buy.

In the meantime, the business of flying into Washington had to be organised and the inaugural services were flown on 24 May 1976 – the world's first commercial supersonic services across the North Atlantic.

This great occasion demanded something special and it was provided by the nicely stage-managed joint arrival of the BA Concorde from London and Air France's flight from Paris. The 16 month trial period was successfully completed and permanent approval given. Nearly 19 years later, on 8 November 1994, Concorde services to Washington ended when British Airways withdrew its flights to and from Heathrow due to declining profits. From then, Concorde passengers from Washington had to travel on a USAir commuter flight to New York's JFK where they could catch a Concorde to Europe.

New York At Last

The battle to earn the right to fly into New York continued throughout 1976 and most of 1977 and was finally resolved in favour of Concorde.

Regular services were preceded by a proving flight by the first production aircraft (201) on 19 October 1977. A joint crew from British Aerospace and Aerospatiale operated the flight which was very much a test as the aircraft was subject to intense

The flight crew of G-BOAA on the first commercial supersonic service in January 1976: Captain Norman Todd (front left), Captain Brian Calvert (front right) and Senior Engineer Officer John Lidiard. (BA)

noise monitoring and measuring. By using a carefully planned noise abatement procedure on takeoff, the Concorde was able to keep its perceived noise down to a level which satisfied all but the most ardent of the many protesters present.

Regular services to New York began on 22 November 1977, and both BA and Air France have continuously maintained schedules on the route ever since. In fact in 1995, Paris-New York was the only scheduled service on which Air France operated Concorde.

Annual Report

Concorde's first 12 months of operations were carefully analysed by many when they were completed if only because of the nature of the aircraft. Any new airliner's first year of service is not typical of what will follow but in Concorde's case this was probably exaggerated because there were so few aircraft involved – only eight between the two operators.

Despite these unusual circumstances, Concorde's first year report card might have read something like

British Airways and Air France Concordes meet at Washington-Dulles Airport on 24 May 1976 after having the made the first supersonic commercial crossings of the North Atlantic. (via Philip J Birtles)

"quite good and shows potential for improvement". Some of the vital statistics were: 45,000 passengers carried, average overall load factor 64.5 per cent, 3.5 million miles (5.6 million kilometres) flown, dispatch reliability 93 per cent.

Air France's Paris-Rio service returned a 65 per cent load factor which was considered healthy. Of interest was the fact that Concorde operations did not adversely effect the airline's subsonic services on the same route and if anything, helped it because of the associated publicity.

Load factors were much higher westbound (72 per cent) than they were in the opposite direction, which managed around 53 per cent. Of note is the fact that all Concorde operations in the first year showed higher westbound load factors than the reverse, possibly indicating that passengers were spending the extra money on just one leg of a return journey so as to experience supersonic flight and then reverting to subsonic for the flight home.

BA's London-Bahrain service achieved an average load factor of 47 per cent which was considered to be mildly encouraging as this was only the first leg of an onward journey to Australia. In fact, had any more Concorde seats been sold, BA would have had trouble accommodating them in the first class section of the Boeing 747 which completed the trip!

Air France launched a Paris-Caracas service via Santa Maria in the Azores during April 1976 and

achieved load factors of only about 36 per cent. An interesting theory was put forward as to what Air France's benefits were on this route. There was just sufficient traffic to cover the service's direct costs, indicating the airline worked out it would lose less money flying to Caracas than it would if the aircraft was sitting idle.

The services to Washington were undoubtedly the most successful with an average load factor of 90 per cent achieved despite a relatively small potential market and the fact that the lion's share of it – US government passengers – was not available to Concorde. A feature of this service was the number of passengers whose ultimate destinations weren't London or Washington at all, but other cities on either side of the Atlantic. Two-thirds of BA's passengers were transferring to other flights at either Washington or London and one-third transferred at both ends. It was also discovered that 15 per cent of passengers were using Concorde to fly from London to New York, via a connecting flight at Washington.

Utilisation of the Concordes in the first year was much lower than ideal, Air France reaching only about 1,200 hours per annum per aircraft, less than half the target of 2,750 hours once a full route network was in place. BA achieved even lower utilisation thanks to route availability problems (notably New York) and a crew shortage.

Concorde's dispatch reliability of

93 per cent during its first year was an area which needed improvement and was very much better soon afterwards as experience grew. The aircraft's low utilisation contributed to the relatively low figure, BA's Concorde Director of the time, Gordon Davison, likening it to a car that's been sitting in the garage for too long ... the battery and tyres go flat (figuratively speaking, in the case of Concorde, of course) and as is the case with all machines, things tend to stop working if they're not used regularly.

Revised procedures such as starting the checklists three hours before scheduled departure rather than one hour gave more time to rectify problems which were detected and thus improved the chances of departing on time. An on time departure, incidentally, is defined as leaving within 15 minutes of the scheduled time, excluding technical delays.

Commercial Partnerships

Two interesting commercial alliances involving Concorde were established in the late 1970s, one with Singapore Airlines (SAL) and the other with American operator Braniff International.

The Singapore connection came about as a result of British Airways wishing to extend the supersonic option on the 'Kangaroo Route' to Australia as far as Singapore. This would result in the aircraft being available on the original London-Bahrain sector and also between Bahrain and Singapore.

BA had always planned to operate

After having to wait for 18 months, services to New York's John F Kennedy Airport began on 22 November 1977. Air France flew its Concorde from Paris and British Airways' aircraft arrived from London. (via Philip J Birtles)

An interesting angle on a British Airways Concorde in one of the livery variations used over the years. Note the single word 'British' on the aircraft's flanks. (BA)

Concorde services all the way to Australia (to Melbourne), and a supersonic flight corridor was established down the length of Australia to cater for some proving flights in the second half of 1975. In May 1976, Australian government approval was given for thrice weekly London-Melbourne flights to start in January 1977 but these never came to fruition for various operational and political reasons. Later, when BA in particular began operating worldwide Concorde charters, Australia would see the aircraft on a fairly regular basis. The first of these was operated in February 1985 and set a new London-Sydney record of 17hr 03min in the process.

In December 1977, joint BA/SAL Airlines services between Bahrain and Singapore began with Concorde 210 G-BOAD painted in BA livery on one side and SAL colours on the other. 210 remains the only operational Concorde to have appeared in livery other than that of British Airways or Air France. The flight crews were British while the cabin crews came from both airlines.

After much fanfare, the number of Bahrain-Singapore flights conducted in December 1977 amounted to just three, following which the Malaysian Government withdrew permission for Concorde to fly over the Straits of Malacca. The service was therefore suspended for over a year until Malaysia restored the overflying rights in January 1979 after much negotiation.

The thrice weekly service resumed (again with G-BOAD), continuing until November 1980 when poor load factors (down to 40 per cent) which could be largely blamed on a worldwide recession forced BA to withdraw from the route.

This service was of importance to the Concorde programme generally as it provided a possible opportunity to move one of the five unsold Concordes which remained on the manufacturers' books at the time. At that stage BA and Air France had placed firm orders for five and four, respectively, while production approval had been given to manufacture 16 production Concordes including the first pair which were never intended to enter airline service.

This left two British and three French assembled Concordes available for customers of which it was thought Singapore Airlines might purchase at least one. This came to nought, as did other sales prospects and the spare Concordes ended up in service with their sponsoring nations' airlines.

The second alliance was between BA, Air France and Braniff International, an arrangement which allowed passengers coming into Washington from London and Paris to fly on to Dallas-Fort Worth. American crews flew the aircraft on the Washington-Dallas sector at subsonic speeds and the aircraft remained in their original liveries – despite there having been

some retouched publicity photographs of Concordes in Braniff markings issued at the time.

One external change which was applied was that of hybrid registration markings on the aircraft flown on what was in effect a US domestic service. A listing of these can be found in the Concorde production table elsewhere in this book, but examples include G-N94AA and N94FD, the last two letters reflecting the final letters of the original British or French registration.

The Braniff services between Washington and Dallas began in January 1979 and lasted until June 1980 when recession and US airline deregulation contributed to load factors becoming too small to sustain economic operation.

Services Come and Go

Throughout its career Concorde has come and gone on several scheduled routes in addition to those mentioned above. Air France ended its original Paris-Rio service in March 1982 and its Washington flights seven months later. At the same time, the Washington-Mexico City extension of this service (which had started in December 1978) also naturally ended, these cancellations resulting from French Government attempts to reduce its Concorde deficit. This left the once daily Paris-New York flight as Air France's only Concorde scheduled service, at the time operating on

Air France's Concorde 205 F-BVFA on the ground. (via Philip J Birtles)

a 50-60 per cent load factor which the French Government considered satisfactory.

British Airways began a thrice weekly service to Miami via Washington in March 1984 which lasted until March 1991, while a twice weekly London-Dallas service was introduced in June 1988, operating only for two months each year during the northern hemisphere summer.

Another seasonal service began in December 1987 between London and Barbados. This service still operates at least once per week during the northern winter and usually flies via Lisbon outbund and nonstop on the return journey with the help of the prevailing tailwind. As mentioned earlier, Washington services ended in late 1994 leaving New York (twice daily) as BA's only major scheduled route, although Toronto is also served during the summer months.

Charters have become a significant part of BA's Concorde operations over the last decade and Air France's to a lesser extent. Originally introduced to help fill seats when worldwide traffic was slumping, they have seen the aircraft add more than 200 destinations to its log of places

visited on all the continents except Antarctica.

These charter flights have been arranged through travel groups, special interest groups and in conjunction with other travel organisations such as the Cunard shipping line. In the case of the latter, many involve around the world journeys with some of it spent aboard a luxurious ocean liner such as the *Queen Elizabeth II* and the remainder aboard Concorde. Other charters have been much less adventurous, involving a brief local flight.

More milestones were achieved as Concorde's service continued: the one millionth trans-Atlantic passenger was carried in October 1987; Richard Noble, the world's land speed record holder set another record by crossing the Atlantic three times in one day (on Concorde, of course!) in November 1987; a New York-London record of 2hr 56min was set in January 1983 (and beaten again in April 1990 at 2hr 54min); and in December 1985 Concorde 204 G-BOAC recorded the highest ground speed by the aircraft in commercial service of 1,292kt or 1,487mph (2,393km/h).

The fastest Concorde overall (in terms of true airspeed) was the preproduction 01 G-AXDN which during a test flight had achieved Mach 2.23 or about 1,280 knots (2,370km/h) some years earlier.

Some other records and milestones have been achieved in more recent times. July 1995 saw Concorde's Olympus 593 engines reach 750,000 flying hours of which 480,000 were at supersonic speeds and in August 1995 Air France's F-BTSD (213) beat Concorde's around the world record (32hr 49min in 1992) by flying from New York and back via Toulouse, Dubai, Bangkok, Guam, Honolulu and Acapulco in the elapsed time of 31hr 27min at an average speed of 969 knots (1,793km/h). On board were 48 winners of US beer manufacturer Coors' Light Memorial Day Sweepstakes who witnessed three sunsets and sunrises during the flight. The aircraft carried special livery for the flight (see colour drawing) and was named *The Silver Bullet* for the occasion.

Another New York-London mark was established in February 1996 when BA's G-BOAD (210) covered the distance in just under 2hr 52min,

Concorde 210 G-BOAD as used to operate a joint service between London and Singapore via Bahrain for a time from late 1977. The aircraft carried Singapore Airlines livery on its port side and British Airways on the starboard. (via Philip J Birtles)

an average speed of 1,086 knots (2,012km/h) assisted by a 150 knot (280km/h) tailwind.

Money Matters

Financial matters have always been a significant part of the Concorde story with support for the development, manufacture and operation of the aircraft coming directly from the British and French governments. This changed radically in 1984 when after a period of investigations and negotiations lasting several years, British Airways became responsible for funding its own Concorde operations. The French Government, on the other hand continued paying all depreciation and financial costs connected with Air France's aircraft, plus 90 per cent of operating losses.

The first step in Britain's financial reorganisation of the Concorde programme came in February 1979 when a review of BA's operations concluded the airline could not make a profit from the aircraft if conventional accounting methods were employed. This resulted in the Labour government of the day announcing that the £160m purchase cost of BA's then fleet of five aircraft would be written off and appear in the balance sheets as a fully depreciated asset. In return, BA had to pay the government 80 per cent of all future operating profits on Concorde operations. The government would in the meantime continue supporting the aircraft's manufacturers.

In September 1979, with no prospects for more sales on the horizon, it was decided that the remaining five unsold Concordes be placed with BA and Air France, bringing their fleets to seven aircraft each.

Political circumstances then changed in Britain with the election of Margaret Thatcher's Conservative government and the privatisation of both British Airways and British Aerospace during the course of the 1980s. This new situation prompted further investigation into Concorde's financial situation, many of the meetings held in conjunction with the French. By late 1982 it was decided there were three options: to cancel the whole project and withdraw the aircraft from service; instigate a gradual rundown; and continue indefinitely.

All sorts of factors had to be taken into account including balancing the potential profits generated under the 1979 arrangement (and the 'royalties' which would flow back to the British Government as a result) against continuing support for the aircraft in the meantime.

The decision was taken in August 1982 by the British Government that it would cease to fund Concorde's manufacturers. British Airways then agreed to examine the feasibility of funding the aircraft's support costs wholly from its own resources. It should be noted that in theory none of this had any effect on France's position, except that if the British cancelled the programme outright, the French would probably have to follow.

It was a terribly complicated business and negotiations between the British Government, BAe and British Airways continued for 18 months or so before, on 31 March 1984, it was announced that the Government's involvement in Concorde would be reduced to almost nothing and that BA would be entirely responsible for Concorde funding. The 80 per cent of

profits agreement was scrapped and BA paid £16.5m for all Concorde spares, the second production aircraft (G-BBDG) which had been retired since the end of 1981 and a large quantity of test equipment including the structural test specimen at Farnborough.

These negotiations saved Concorde as an ongoing programme, at least as far as Britain was concerned. Without a successful conclusion to them, there would have been no more in view of the government's determination to bail out.

Operational Issues

Considering the nature of its design and the operations it undertakes, Concorde has been remarkably reliable and trouble free in service. It has had no major accidents and problems which have arisen have been reasonably easy to fix.

One of the more visible problems was the failure of the upper rudder on a couple of aircraft. The first failure (resulting from delamination) occurred in April 1989 when BA's G-BOAF (216) lost part of the rudder while flying between Auckland and Sydney at supersonic speed. The aircraft was in the middle of a 38,300 miles (61,600km) circumnavigation of the world charter when the incident took place and the aircraft was landed safely at Sydney. After repairs, it was able to continue the flight.

A second upper rudder failure occurred in January 1991, prompting development of an improved design which would eliminate the problem. Nine replacement rudder sets were built at a cost of £5m, the first of them fitted in 1993.

Concorde 206 (usually G-BOAA) carrying the composite registration G-N94AA for use on a joint subsonic service with Braniff between Washington and Dallas. The service operated from January 1979 to June 1980, using both British Airways and Air France Concordes. All had to carry hybrid registrations while flying on what was in effect a US domestic flight. Despite the appearance of some retouched photographs showing Concordes in Braniff markings, no aircraft were so painted. (via Philip J Birtles)

One of several upper rudder failures suffered by Concorde since 1989. In all cases there was no problem with control and all aircraft landed without further incident.

In 1994, hairline cracks were found in the aft wing spar webbing of all British Airways Concordes. Two aircraft were immediately repaired and the remainder cleared to continue flying subject to an inspection every 10 flights. The affected part was not load bearing and the repair was simple.

An inspection of Air France's Concordes revealed no sign of the cracking, which was not unexpected as its aircraft have lower hours logged than BA's, annual utilisation of the aircraft averaging only about two-thirds of that recorded by their British counterparts.

One problem of a non structural nature which had to be overcome was that of fitting traffic alert and collision avoidance systems (TCAS) which are now mandatory for operations in the USA.

The original deadline for installation of TCAS was 31 December 1993 but for Concorde this was extended twice to the end of 1995 due to antennae problems. The original standard Collins external antenna were incapable of withstanding the physical stresses and temperatures (-60 to +135degC) to which they were subjected during routine Concorde operations. New antennae (there are two per aircraft) were developed by the Flight Refueling Group's Chelton Electrostatics subsidiary and US FAA approval for the installation was awarded in November 1995.

For a time it appeared that both British Airways and Air France Concordes would be banned from flying to the USA due to their lack of TCAS equipment but common sense prevailed and extra time was given to allow the development of the new antennae.

Concorde's Future

As Concorde celebrated its 20th anniversary of commercial operations in January 1996, plans were in place which could well see it operating for another 20 years. There is no successor on the horizon and as long as a demand for supersonic passenger flights remains (and the aircraft remains profitable) there is every incentive to keep Concorde flying.

British Airways has already invested in an interior refurbishment for its aircraft and in 1995 the Concorde Re-Life Group was established with the specific purpose of examining the aircraft's structural potential for an ongoing carer which will extend in the 21st century. The years 2005 to 2010 have been most commonly mentioned, but it is possible some Concordes could remain in service for a few more years after that.

Comprising representatives from the British CAA, French DGAC and the manufacturers, the group is looking at extending Concorde's structural life from the present 6,700 'reference flights' (a trans-Atlantic flight at a takeoff weight of 375,000lb/170 tonnes) to as many as 10,000 flights, although 8,500 is a more realistic target.

Concorde's low utilisation and the heat generated in the airframe by flying at Mach 2 (which dries any moisture which may have gathered in the structure) have combined to keep the airframes very 'young'. The aircraft are almost completely free of corrosion and their condition is equivalent to a subsonic airliner which is only three or four years old. In 1994 BA's Concorde's averaged only 984 flying hours each, or only a quarter of the time logged by the airline's Boeing 747s.

This, in combination with the stringent checks it undergoes, tends to ensure Concorde's long term future. The static test airframe has been taken to the equivalent of 21,000 flight cycles without problems and the most used of BA's aircraft had logged about 6,400 cycles logged by 1995. This means they will reach their limit in 1997-98 while others won't get to that point until later. Air France's Concordes have even fewer cycles in their logbooks.

Extension to 8,500 flights will give the aircraft an extra decade of life, while a 10,000 cycle extension could see some reach their 40th birthdays.

In 1996, British Airways had all seven of its Concordes still in service, while Air France had six. Its F-BVFD (211) was retired in 1982 after logging 5,816 hours and was used as a source of spare parts. 211 became the first Concorde to be scrapped, in early 1995, but its brethren all survive, the prototypes, preproduction and early production aircraft preserved on the ground and the remainder still flying.

If the refurbishment plans are realised, the final chapter of this remarkable aeroplane's story will not be written for many more years.

Concorde 214 G-BOAG of British Airways. If life extension plans come to fruition, this aircraft could be 40 years old by the time it retires. (BA)

FLYING CONCORDE

Cruising at twice the speed of sound, Concorde reaches New York one hour before it left London – in local time. British Airways' pilot Christopher Orlebar describes a typical Concorde passenger flight, this article reproduced with grateful thanks to *The Rolls-Royce Magazine.*

The westbound Concorde passenger travels backwards in time. Local time, that is. One does not need to be an Einstein to know that at 50° of latitude a westward velocity of 1,320mph (2125km/h) will produce this effect.

Should there be any doubters, they should take a supersonic flight on British Airways flight BA 195 between about November and March. The flight leaves London in the dark of a winter evening. Later on, if the passenger is not distracted by his dinner turning into a late lunch, he will observe the sun rising from the west. In the meantime his eastbound counterpart will have the sun setting behind him at three times its normal rate.

Mercifully Concorde's clientele do not come solely to observe astronomical phenomena. Concorde can save them not only hours, but days: indeed, one passenger, who has made more than 500 flights in Concorde, says he gains an extra four to five weeks' work a year by flying supersonically. Passengers also avoid the purgatory of overnight sectors. Concorde flies between London and the United States only during the

waking hours of Atlantic seaboard dwellers.

What is it like to pilot this aeroplane which arrives in New York one hour before its local time of departure from London?

Ninety minutes before departure the crew, consisting of captain, first officer and flight engineer, assemble in the Queen's Building at London's Heathrow airport for the flight briefing. Weather forecasts, serviceability of airfields, load and fuel requirements are studied in detail. But with an expected flight time of only 3 hours 23 minutes for the 3,565 mile (5,735km) journey, emphasis is also placed on the current weather at the destination.

The required fuel to take today's load of 78 passengers is 166,500lb (75,540kg) – nearly a ton of fuel for each passenger carried. This figure has been based on expected winds as well as the planned weight of the aeroplane. But of equal significance is the temperature which will be encountered between 50,000 and 60,000ft. Less fuel has to be carried if the forecast temperature is low. To the fuel figure is added a reserve of 33,700lb (15,300kg), plus 3,100lb (1,405kg) of taxying fuel at London, bringing the total to 203,300lb (92,160kg). With the aircraft, payload and crew of nine (including six cabin crew) the takeoff weight comes to 391,600lb (177,785kg).

After loading, the aircraft it is essential to ensure that the centre of

gravity is in the correct position for takeoff. This is done by making small adjustments to the distribution of the fuel within the aircraft.

Each of the 13 fuel tanks signals the centre of gravity computer with its fuel load. The computer is also fed with information about the weight and whereabouts of the payload and it then indicates the centre of gravity of the aeroplane.

One hour before departure the crew boards the aircraft. Concorde's slender delta shape, somewhat hidden at this stage by the ground servicing vehicles, is uncluttered with the high-lift devices (flaps and slats) that are found on subsonic aeroplanes. There is a fin, but no tailplane. All the flying controls, known as elevons, are at the rear of the delta wing. Lacking hydraulic pressure from the engines at this stage, they droop, appearing to the untutored eye like flaps in the "down" position.

It is the flight engineer's job to make the external check. He inspects, among other things, the features essential to Concorde – including the engine intakes and the rear nozzles of the four Rolls-Royce/SNECMA Olympus engines. The intakes slow and compress the air. The rear nozzles form part of a convergent/divergent system; they also act as engine silencers on takeoff and as thrust reverser buckets on landing.

The internal preflight checks reflect some of the complexity of the intakes

British Airways Concorde 214 G-BOAG. (BA)

The 'office' – captain on the left, copilot on the right and flight engineer's station behind. (via Philip J Birtles)

and nozzles. But there are other systems too, which are essential for high altitude supersonic flight.

The air conditioning system must cope with incoming air at extremes of temperature far greater than for a subsonic aeroplane. The flying controls are "fly-by-wire", which means that they are electrically signalled and that this signal is modified by the autostabilisation system in the three axes – pitch, roll and yaw. The autostabilisation system receives information from gyroscopes and from the air data computer. Thus the amount of flying control movement to give stabilisation varies with speed and height. The system provides superb control throughout the 1,000 knot (1,850km/h) speed range.

There is even a radiation meter to warn the crew to descend in order to avoid potentially hazardous radiation from a solar flare. There is also a lever for lowering the visor and nose.

Just as important are the systems which appear on any long range subsonic aeroplane: the triple inertial navigation system, the flight instruments (but with the machmeter calibrated up to Mach 2.4), the autopilot and the radios, which are used both for navigation and communication. Radio navigation aids confirm and update the information derived from the inertial navigation system.

Some controls are notable by their absence. There is no flap and slat lever and no speed brake control. The latter has been replaced by the ability to select reverse thrust on the inboard engines in flight.

Initially each crew member carries out a precise scan check of his particular cockpit area. Later they will co-ordinate their actions from a checklist.

Go ahead

During this time the passengers have been pampered in the special Concorde lounge adjacent to the aeroplane. By half an hour to go the ramp co-ordinator checks with the crew: "OK for boarding?" With everything looking good on the technical front and no air traffic control (ATC) delays, he receives the go ahead.

Should the passengers look to their left on boarding they will see the narrow "tunnel" to the flightdeck busy with ground personnel, each with some piece of vital paperwork, be it load sheet or technical log, for approval and signature. On continuing to their right into the cabin the passengers are welcomed and settled by a cabin crew ever mindful that the passengers require nothing less than superlative service during their supersonic sojourn.

At the captain's discretion, he and the first officer alternate the flying and the copiloting. With the captain flying the sector, the first officer's duties include the performance calculations for takeoff and the reading of the check list until taxying begins, when the flight engineer takes over. Contact is made with ATC, starting off with the clearance to fly the route, which is always the same – unlike subsonic tracks across the Atlantic, which are changed to benefit from the winds. The only problem ATC has is to ensure a 12 minute gap between the westbound Concordes of British Airways and Air France on entry into the supersonic route.

Pushing back from the stand with two engines running (the thrust from all four might damage the tow bar), the controls are checked in their two electrical signalling modes and one mechanical mode. Taxying is straightforward once it has been learnt that the nosewheel is 37ft (11.3m) to the rear of the pilots. Even when the engines are switched to ground idle thrust the aircraft bounds along, so the brake temperatures are carefully monitored.

With checks complete and ATC clearance to go from 28 Left (the southerly of the two west facing runways at Heathrow) the brakes are released and the throttles are opened rapidly to takeoff power. Simultaneously, the stop watches are started.

Concorde has a fully electronic engine control system which operates efficiently in all subsonic and supersonic flight conditions. Such good care do the electronic control units (known as throttle amplifiers) take of the engines that the throttles may be slammed open with impunity. As engine speed increases the preselected reheat lights up to boost the thrust. Each engine is now burning more than 44,000lb (19,975kg) of fuel per hour and giving 38,000lb (170kN) thrust.

By 100 knots (185km/h) a green light for each engine confirms satisfactory performance. Decision speed (V_1), typically around 160 knots (295km/h), is called. Up to V_1 the aircraft can stop safely in the event of an engine failure. Beyond V_1 it is committed to completing the takeoff, which it now has the speed to accomplish safely. "Rotate" (typically 195 knots/360km/h) is called and the aircraft attitude is increased to 13.5° nose up. At about 215 knots (398km/h), Concorde becomes airborne.

The delta wings form a pair of horizontal vortices which give very effective lift at low speed but at the expense of a great deal of drag. In order to reduce the drag, and so to steepen the climb gradient, the speed is allowed to build to 250 knots (463km/h), where it is held by further increasing aircraft attitude to more than 20°.

At 75 seconds from the start of the takeoff roll (the timing varies according to the weight of the aircraft and air temperature), the reheat is switched off, the thrust is reduced and the attitude brought down to 12° to maintain 250 knots (463km/h), thereby reducing noise level on the ground under the flightpath. This reduces the rate of climb from more than 4,000ft per minute to a gentler 1,250ft per minute.

The Woodley beacon, near Reading, must be crossed at or above 4,000ft. Consistent with this and ATC requirements the speed is allowed to build to V_{mo}, the maximum operating indicated air speed allowable. This is 400 knots (740km/h) at this stage,

but it varies with altitude and reaches a maximum of 530 knots (982km/h) at 44,000ft.

With the drag down and engine efficiency up (because of increased speed) the performance becomes phenomenal. By the time maximum climb power is restored at 8,000ft, rates of climb greater than 6,000ft per minute are commonplace. Above 250 knots (463km/h) the vortices go and so does the vibration they cause. Also, the nose and visor are raised, and a glorious calm settles over the flightdeck; conversation is now possible without having to use the intercom.

The subsonic cruise to the South Wales coast is flown at Mach 0.95 (95 per cent of the speed of sound) and at 28,000ft, overhauling other subsonic traffic at nearly 100mph (160km/h). The fuel has already been pumped rearwards to move the centre of gravity about two feet (61cm) back from the takeoff position, thus giving a small increase in aerodynamic efficiency. The track is maintained by using the mean position derived from the triple inertial navigation system.

Smoothly through Mach 1

At the acceleration point, full climb power is applied after ATC clearance is given. Two small nudges are felt as the reheats come on in pairs, increas-

ing the thrust by 20 per cent. Just as the captain has briefed the passengers, Concorde accelerates smoothly through Mach 1 – the speed of sound. At 28,000ft, in the cooler air, Mach 1 is 585 knots (1,085km/h); on the surface of the earth, where it is warmer, Mach 1 is about 660 knots (1,223km/h) true airspeed.

Although the autopilot is almost always used, manual control through Mach 1 is very straightforward, thanks to the delta wing and auto-stabilised controls. This is in sharp contrast to the experiences of the earliest pilots who attempted to penetrate the sound barrier. Their aircraft were plagued with control and vibration problems as the sonic shockwaves began to form around them. On Concorde there is a kick on the pressure-sensitive instruments as the formation of the shockwaves is detected by the "static" pressure sensing ports on the side of the fuselage.

Above Mach 1, rather like a boat forming waves on the water, Concorde forms shockwaves in the air. They reduce the efficiency of the wings and increase drag, thereby lowering the aircraft's lift-to-drag ratio, and they can be heard on the ground as a supersonic "boom". They also move the aircraft's centre of lift rearwards.

Concorde is designed and flown to

Just airborne, with the speed at about 215 knots (400km/h) and accelerating. (BA)

It all seems so serene, but at twice the speed of sound at 55,000 feet there's lots happening with Concorde's structure. (BA)

overcome these effects. The shock-waves are put to work in the engine intake system: they slow the air down to half the speed of sound, thereby raising the overall compression ratio and thus making the engines thermally the most efficient in the world. Indeed, the engine efficiency is more than 40 per cent at Mach 2, which is the most economical speed for Concorde in spite of the loss of aerodynamic efficiency.

Behind the intake system the engines go to work on the high pressure air supplied. The Olympus 593 turbojets succeed superlatively: at Mach 2 and 58,000ft each generates more than 8,000lb (36kN) thrust with fuel flows as low as 9,500lb (4,315kg) per hour per engine. The efflux is expelled through the convergent-divergent exhaust duct, the setting of which is continuously altered in flight to maintain maximum engine efficiency.

To overcome the effect of the sonic boom, Concorde is flown supersonically only over unpopulated areas. The boom carpet is less than 40 nautical miles (75km) wide, so any boom sensitive area is kept at least 20nm (37km) to the side of the aircraft track. When the aircraft turns this distance is increased to 30nm (56km) because of the greater effects of shockwave propagation.

The boom first reaches the ground at a point 50nm (93km) ahead of the point where the aircraft exceeded Mach 1 in the acceleration. On deceleration, Concorde must become subsonic at least 35nm (65km) before reaching a boom sensitive coast. Turns and accelerations can focus the shockwaves, forming a super-boom on the ground. Secondary or reflected booms are sometimes propagated, depending on atmospheric conditions. Aircraft flying below Concorde occasionally experience the boom.

Rearward movement of Concorde's centre of lift during supersonic acceleration is compensated for by moving the aircraft's centre of gravity backwards by a further 4ft (1.2m) through fuel redistribution. In the cruise at Mach 2 the correct aircraft attitude is maintained by the autopilot, and fuel is used to trim the aircraft so that the elevons are all precisely $1/2°$ down – their most efficient position.

Mach 1.7 is reached at 43,500ft. At this point the reheats are extinguished since the speed is now sufficient for the improved engine efficiency to be effective. Should the speed be allowed to drop, a descent would be necessary to regain it.

Mach 2 is achieved at 50,000ft. Concorde is flying at 23 miles (37km) a minute – faster than the speed of a rifle bullet. The climb now gives way to a cruise/climb. The throttle amplifiers are switched to "cruise", thus marginally reducing the thrust.

Maintaining Mach 2 in an undisturbed atmosphere, Concorde climbs very gradually from 50,000 to its ceiling of 60,000ft as fuel is consumed and its weight is reduced. Occasionally when the outside air temperature increases, the Mach number has to be reduced to prevent the fuselage, already expanded by eight inches (20cm), from overheating. At 100°C on the outside, the windows feel warm to the touch. The autopilot is programmed so that Concorde never exceeds the lowest of three limits: Mach 2.04, 530 knots (983km/h) indicated air speed or 127°C on the nose (the hottest part).

The passengers enjoy their haute-cuisine meals served in style and apparent ease by the cabin crew, who have been finely drilled to cope with the none-too-large galleys. After lunch, time permitting, the passen-

"More posh plonk, madam?" Twice the speed of sound and not a drop spilled! (via Philip J Birtles)

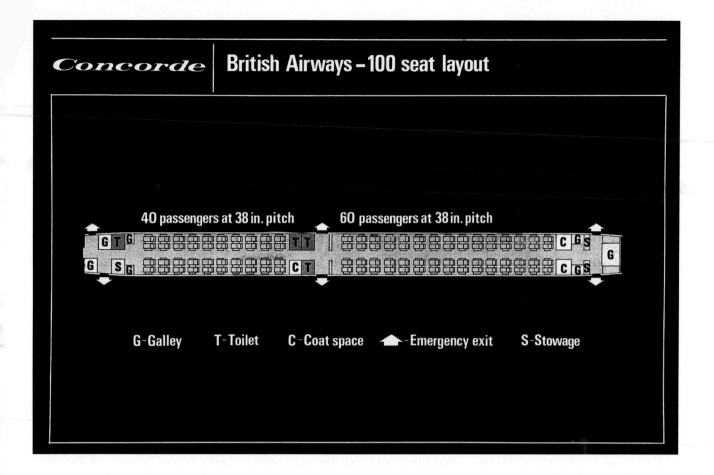

Concorde | **British Airways – 100 seat layout**

40 passengers at 38 in. pitch   60 passengers at 38 in. pitch

G-Galley   T-Toilet   C-Coat space   ▲-Emergency exit   S-Stowage

Concorde 202 on final approach with 160 knots (295km/h) on the clock and 11 degrees angle of attack on the attitude indicator. (via Philip J Birtles)

The fact that Concorde can travel at Mach 2 over extended periods as a matter of repetitive routine with no fuss is perhaps its designers' greatest achievement. (BA)

gers visit the flightdeck. Two hours into the flight on a clear day they can see much of Newfoundland to the north of track. Otherwise it is clearly visible to the pilots on the weather radar.

Here, on the threshold of space, the sky above is a dark blue and the atmospheric pressure is only a tenth of its sea level value. Careful observation of the horizon will just reveal the earth's curvature.

Descent into New York

The deceleration and descent into New York take place over the ocean. Deceleration from Mach 2 to Mach 1 covers typically 130nm (240km) and begins just past Cape Cod. The only constraints on this descent are that the aircraft must clear a military flying area, which extends to 50,000ft, by at least 2,000ft, and then be at 12,000ft or below at the point – also over the sea – where it joins the regular traffic flow bound for the airfield. At most other locations the deceleration point is determined by the need to be below Mach 1 at least 35nm (65km) before reaching a populated coast.

The achieved altitude of around 58,000ft is maintained while thrust is partially reduced; idle thrust could cause air-conditioning problems and might induce an engine surge (similar to a backfire). Once the aircraft has decelerated to 350 knots (650km/h) indicated airspeed – around Mach 1.6 at 58,000ft, the descent is commenced. Usually there is a step in the

descent at 41,000ft for the aircraft to become subsonic. Without the drag from the shockwaves the subsequent descent is less steep. As Concorde decelerates the aircraft balance has to be restored again, this time by pumping the fuel forwards from the tank in the rear.

The New York radar controller gives headings to bring the aircraft onto final approach at a comfortable distance (at least 6nm/11km) behind any preceding traffic. By 250 knots (463km/h) the nose and visor have been lowered, improving the view but increasing the noise level on the flightdeck. A fully automatic landing with manual rollout could now be carried out in visibilities down to a little over 600ft using a 15ft "decision height", ground radio aids permitting. At this height the mainwheels are 15ft (4.6m) above the runway; the pilots are 37ft (11m) higher than the mainwheels.

Usually, in good weather, Concorde is flown manually on a "reduced noise" approach. For this a slightly higher approach speed of 190 knots (352km/h) is used down to 800ft above the ground, as opposed to the "all weather" approach, where the speed is 175 knots (325km/h) to 1,500ft. Thereafter in both cases the aircraft decelerates to the threshold speed – typically 160 knots (295km/h). The reduced noise approach takes advantage both of the reduced drag (and hence thrust requirement) experienced at 190 knots (352km/h) compared with the lower speeds, and of

the reduction of thrust during the deceleration to threshold speed which takes place between 2.7nm and 1.5nm (4.9km and 2.8km) prior to touchdown. The superb autothrottles make this manoeuvre straightforward.

The engineer calls out the heights down to 15ft above the ground from the radio altimeter. At 40ft the autothrottles are switched out and at 15ft the power is smoothly reduced to idle thrust. Just prior to landing the thrust reduction and ground effect together tend to reduce the attitude of the aircraft. To achieve a smooth landing the pilot must counteract this by maintaining the 11° final approach attitude.

After touchdown reverse idle is selected; the nosewheel is lowered onto the runway and reverse thrust is selected on all four engines. Differential braking keeps the aircraft straight, and by 40 knots (75km/h) the reverse thrust is cancelled. Concorde behaves well in crosswinds with no tendency to "drop" a wing as might be found on more conventional aeroplanes.

The captain bids "au revoir" to the passengers, inevitably pointing out that their subsonic counterparts, who left at the same time from London, would still not be quite "halfway here". As one of the outstanding achievements of the twentieth century rolls to a stop, a working day in the life of a Concorde pilot comes to its end, to be repeated, in the opposite direction, on the morrow.